# Service Provision
# under Stress in East Africa

## The State, NGOs & People's Organizations
## in Kenya, Tanzania & Uganda

# Service Provision under Stress in East Africa

## The State, NGOs & People's Organizations in Kenya, Tanzania & Uganda

Edited by
JOSEPH SEMBOJA & OLE THERKILDSEN

CENTRE FOR DEVELOPMENT RESEARCH
COPENHAGEN
*IN ASSOCIATION WITH*
E.A.E.P.
NAIROBI

MKUKI NA NYOTA
DAR ES SALAAM

FOUNTAIN PUBLISHERS
KAMPALA

HEINEMANN
PORTSMOUTH (N.H.)

JAMES CURREY
LONDON

Centre for Development Research
Gammel Kongevej 5
DK-1610 Copenhagen V
Denmark

*In association with*
James Currey Ltd
54b Thornhill Square
Islington
London N1 1BE

Mkuki na Nyota Publishers
P.O. Box 4205
Dar es Salaam

East African Educational Publishers
P.O. Box 45314
Nairobi

Heinemann
A division of Reed Elsevier Inc.
361 Hanover Street
Portsmouth, New Hampshire 03801-3912

Fountain Publishers
P.O. Box 488
Kampala

1 2 3 4 5 99 98 97 96 95

ISBN 0–85255–389–7 (James Currey paper)
ISBN 0–85255–390–0 (James Currey cloth)
ISBN 0–435–08982–X (Heinemann paper)
ISBN 0–435–08980–3 (Heinemann cloth)

**British Cataloguing in Publication Data**
Service Provision under Stress in East Africa :
State, NGOs and People's Organizations
in Kenya, Tanzania and Uganda
  I. Semboja, Joseph  II. Therkildsen, Ole
  361.96

**Library of Congress Cataloging-in-Publication Data**
Service provision under stress : States & voluntary organizations in
  Kenya, Tanzania & Uganda / edited by Joseph Semboja & Ole
  Therkildsen.
        p.   cm.
    Includes bibliographical references.
    ISBN 0-435-08980-3. — ISBN 0-435-08982-X (pbk.)
    1. Social service--Africa, East.   2. Non-governmental
  organizations--Africa, East.   3. Voluntarism--Africa. East.
  I. Semboja, Joseph.   II. Therkildsen, Ole.
  HV446.S47   1995
  361.7'0967--dc20                                      95-21488
                                                              CIP

Typeset in 10.6/11pt Bembo by Long House Publishing Services, Cumbria, UK
Printed and bound in Britain
for Villiers Publications Ltd, London N3

# Contents

# Maps,
# Figure & Tables

# Preface

Structural Adjustment Programmes (SAPs) have been implemented in Kenya since 1982, in Tanzania since 1986 and in Uganda since 1987. They aim, among other things, to increase the roles of the market and the private sector and to redefine the role of the state in the provision of services such as national defence, law and order, policy formulation, regulation and other public goods. In the social sector, this implies greater roles for the voluntary and private sectors. But what has been the practice in the three East African countries with regard to social service provision? This book analyses the roles of the voluntary sector and the state and their relations in service provision in East Africa.

Work on this book started in 1991 as part of a research project on *The Performance of Local Governments in East Africa* between the Centre for Development Research (CDR), Copenhagen, and the Economic Research Bureau (ERB) of the University of Dar es Salaam. The editors are grateful to DANIDA which, through its programme for Enhancement of Research Capacity (ENRECA) in developing countries, supported both the research and the book.

Several people have contributed at various stages of the work. The editors would like to single out Samuel S. Mushi who participated in the initial stages of its editing, Andrew S.Z. Kiondo and Alan Fowler who gave useful comments and suggestions, and Edward Kirumira for his help in finalizing some of the chapters. Most of the papers appearing in this volume were presented in two seminars, one in Copenhagen and the other in Dar es Salaam, and were then revised substantially. We are grateful to the organizers and participants for their comments and suggestions. The collection and processing of data were undertaken by N.J. Kessy, D.P. Mushi, E. Ngalewa and K.R.A. Omari. The document was word processed by Ane Toubro and proof-read by Jesper Linell. We highly appreciate their efforts in making this a successful project.

Just before the manuscript of this book was sent to the publishers, two of the Ugandan authors, Dr Emmanuel Nabuguzi and Dr Fabius O. Passi, died – on the same day. We wish to express our deep sorrow at the tragic deaths of two good colleagues.

*Joseph Semboja*
*Ole Therkildsen*

# About the Authors

**Amukowa Anangwe** is a lecturer in the Department of Government, University of Nairobi. Previously he worked in the Kenyan district administration. Now he writes on Kenyan politics and administration.

**Alan Fowler** is currently a Visiting Fellow with the World Bank in Washington. He has extensive academic and practical experience of NGO affairs in East and Southern Africa.

**Goran Hyden** is Professor of Political Science at the University of Florida. He is a prominent writer on African politics.

**Abel G.M. Ishumi** is Professor of Education at the University of Dar es Salaam. He writes on education and the relationship between education and development.

**Karuti Kanyinga** is a Research Fellow at the Institute for Development Studies, University of Nairobi. He writes on politics and local development in Kenya.

**B.M. Makau** is a well-known writer and commentator on education in East Africa. Previously he was the head of the Kenyan Examination Council. He now works as a consultant.

**Gaspar K. Munishi** is Professor of Political Science and Dean of Faculty at the University of Dar es Salaam. He writes on development policies and practices.

**Jwani T. Mwaikusa** heads the Department of Public Law at the University of Dar es Salaam. He is a well-known human rights activist in Tanzania and writes regularly on these issues.

**Emmanuel Nabuguzi** was a Research Fellow at the Makerere Institute of Social Research, Kampala, writing on the informal economy of Uganda and relations between state and civil society.

**Walter O. Oyugi** is a Professor in the Department of Government, University of Nairobi. Over the last twenty years he has published extensively on service provision, public administration and democracy.

**Fabius O. Passi** was a senior lecturer at the Faculty of Education, Makerere University, Kampala. He has published several books on the subject of educational issues in Uganda.

**Joseph Semboja** is Director of the Economic Research Bureau, University of Dar es Salaam. He specializes in public finance and decentralization.

**John C. Sivalon** is a Senior Lecturer in the Department of Sociology, University of Dar es Salaam. He does research on the voluntary sector and has written extensively about the development roles of the churches in Tanzania.

**Ole Therkildsen** is a Senior Research Fellow at the Centre for Development Research, Copenhagen. He writes on service provision, decentralization and participation in East Africa.

**Per Tidemand** is now working as a participation adviser on a social service project in Tanzania. He has just completed his Ph.D. on local politics in Uganda.

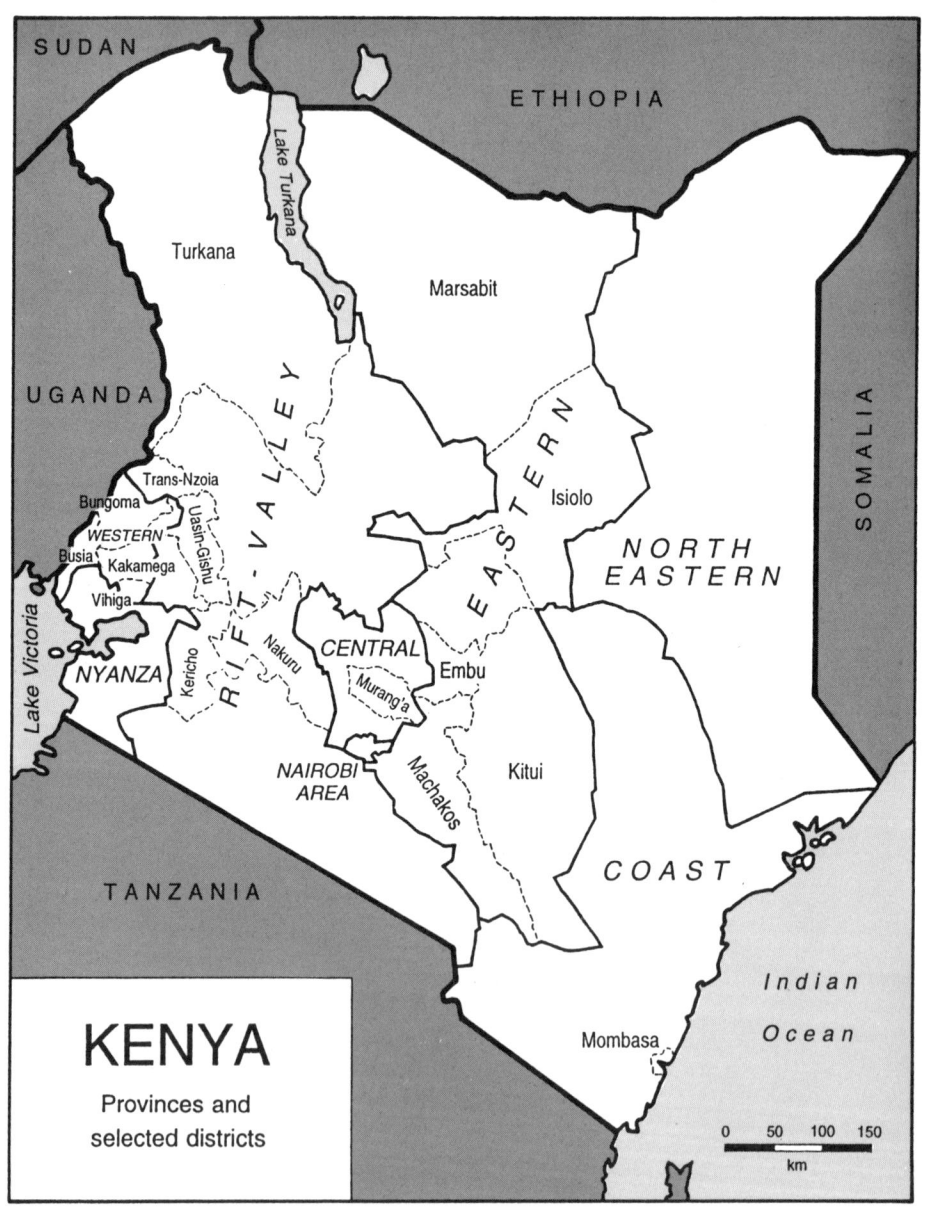

SUDAN

ETHIOPIA

*Lake Turkana*

Turkana

Marsabit

UGANDA

SOMALIA

Trans-Nzoia

Bungoma

*WESTERN*

Uasin-Gishu

Busia

Kakamega

*R I F T - V A L L E Y*

*E A S T E R N*

Isiolo

N O R T H
E A S T E R N

Vihiga

*Lake Victoria*

*NYANZA*

Kericho

Nakuru

*CENTRAL*

Embu

Murang'a

*NAIROBI
AREA*

Machakos

Kitui

C O A S T

TANZANIA

*Indian*

*Ocean*

Mombasa

# KENYA

Provinces and
selected districts

0    50    100    150
km

UGANDA

*Lake Victoria*

KENYA

Bukoba
Karagwe  x *Kanyigo*
RWANDA    *KAGERA*
Ngara
BURUNDI    Biharamulo    Geita *MWANZA*    Mwanza

*MARA*

Bariadi

*SHINYANGA*    *Shinyanga*    Mbulu    *ARUSHA*    Arumeru

*KILIMANJARO*

KIGOMA
x *Ujiji*    Urambo    Igunga    *Iramba*    Singida    Kondoa    *TANGA*

*TABORA*    *SINGIDA*    *DODOMA*    PEMBA

ZANZIBAR

*Lake Tanganyika*

x *Karema*    Mpwapwa    Bagamoyo    DAR ES SALAAM

*RUKWA*    Iringa    Morogoro    *COAST*

ZAIRE    Sumba-wanga    *MBEYA*    *IRINGA*    *MOROGORO*    *Indian Ocean*

Mufindi
*Makambako*    x
Njombe    *LINDI*

Ludewa

ZAMBIA    Songea    *MTWARA*
x *Liuli*    *RUVUMA*    Masasi

*Lake Nyasa*

MALAWI

MOZAMBIQUE

# TANZANIA

Regions and selected
districts/localities

0    100    200    300
km

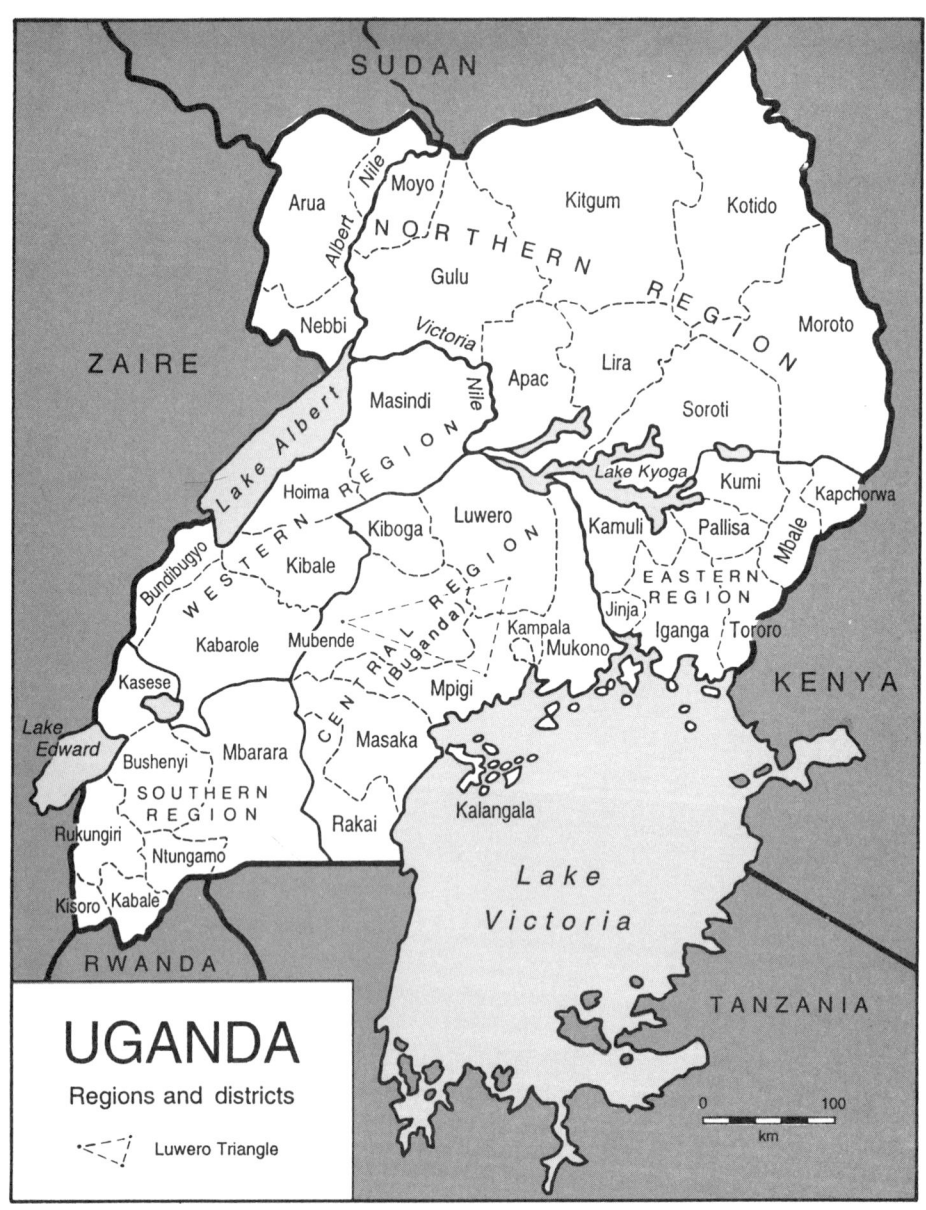

SUDAN

Arua
Moyo
Albert Nile
Kitgum
Kotido
NORTHERN
Gulu
REGION
Nebbi
Victoria
Moroto
ZAIRE
Masindi
Nile
Apac
Lira
Soroti
Lake Albert
Hoima
WESTERN
Lake Kyoga
Kumi
Kapchorwa
Bundibugyo
Kiboga
Luwero
Kamuli
Pallisa
Mbale
Kibale
REGION
EASTERN
REGION
Kabarole
Mubende
CENTRAL REGION (Buganda)
Kampala
Jinja
Iganga
Tororo
Kasese
Mpigi
Mukono
KENYA
Lake Edward
Bushenyi
Mbarara
Masaka
SOUTHERN REGION
Rakai
Kalangala
Rukungiri
Ntungamo
Lake Victoria
Kisoro
Kabale
RWANDA
TANZANIA

# UGANDA

Regions and districts

Luwero Triangle

0     100
km

# 1

## OLE THERKILDSEN & JOSEPH SEMBOJA
## A New Look at Service Provision
## in East Africa

Much of the recent debate on service provision in developing countries has focused on the need for privatization. This concept is based on the intellectual and political resurgence of market-oriented prescriptions, and is now incorporated into the structural adjustment programmes in many sub-Saharan African countries.

Unfortunately, in Kenya, Tanzania and Uganda such prescriptions pay little attention to three important features of service provision. One is that the provision of services for the majority of the population depends on collective action by the state, non-governmental organizations (NGOs) and people's organizations (POs).[1] The second is that the links between the voluntary sector and the state are becoming more – not less – important for service provision. The third feature of service provision is its growing dependence on foreign aid. Not only is foreign assistance a major reason for the growth of the voluntary sector; aid has also made it possible for the state to maintain – and recently increase – its role in service provision in East Africa.

These three important, but largely ignored, features of service provision are central themes in this book. Despite the privatization efforts and rhetoric, service provision through collective action by the state, NGOs, POs and donors remains very important for the livelihood of the majority of people. Precisely because this book focuses on service provision through these four agencies, analyses of the interfaces between them become possible. These links are normally missed by analyses that concentrate on one type of service provider only – such as the state (Hardiman and Midgley, 1989) or the market (Roth, 1987).

In addition to its specific focus on collective action, the book also provides a comparative perspective by presenting papers on similar aspects of service provision for each of the three East African countries, Kenya, Tanzania and

---

[1] For the purposes of this book the term voluntary sector includes non-governmental organizations (NGOs) and people's organizations (POs). NGOs refer to organizations formed on a voluntary basis but operating with paid staff, either for the benefit of members, or to provide services to or on behalf of others. POs refer to groups formed on the basis of locality, kinship, gender, workplace, religion, etc. As well as being small, they have no conventional bureaucracy. They engage in activities aimed at improving the livelihoods of members and are controlled by them.

Uganda. This is, in fact, the first comparative study of services in East Africa of its kind.[2]

The book deals in detail with education, health, and law and order. Households all across East Africa give high priority to the first two services, and their provision and financing are important activities for both the state and the voluntary sector. Law and order is selected because, together with defence, it is generally regarded as the state-provided service *par excellence*. That law and order is increasingly provided by non-state actors illustrates the significant changes which have taken place in service provision since independence.

The book is intended to benefit students, academics and policy-makers, but its primary purpose is not to present new policy recommendations. There is already too much general advice based on limited evidence and heavy doses of ideology floating around. Instead, the contributors to this book seek to describe and explain how relations between the state, NGOs and POs engaged in service provision have changed over time, depending on country-specific circumstances and external dependence. Their second purpose is to analyse the changing access to and quality of services provided through collective action.

This chapter provides a general introduction to the book. It highlights how the conventional concept of 'privatization' needs to be modified to be relevant to analyses of service provision in East Africa. The chapter then proceeds with a brief stock-taking of service coverage after three decades of independence. This is followed by comparisons of service agencies and financing in the three countries. Such comparative evidence forms the background for a brief analysis of the politics of service provision. Key features of service provision in East Africa are presented in the conclusions.

## Privatization and Collective Action

At first glance, the increasing role played by NGOs and POs in service provision in East Africa – as documented in this book – may be labelled 'privatization'. This concept is commonly understood as (i) the transfer of control/ownership of activities from the public to the private sector; (ii) the transfer of actual service provision to the private sector, while governments retain ultimate responsibility for the service; and (iii) the liberalization or deregulation of entry into activities previously restricted to the public sector (Cook and Kirkpatrick, 1988; Adam *et al.*, 1992). Yet what actually takes place on the ground in East Africa does not fit with these conventional uses of the term.

First, NGOs and POs are non-profit-making agencies. This distinguishes them from the profit-oriented private enterprises that are normally associated with privatization. Moreover, East African POs and NGOs do not fit the conventional view of agencies in the voluntary sector either, as most of them do not simply rely on private charity for their operations. They depend to a significant degree on external financial support from the state, foreign NGOs and bilateral or multilateral donors.

[2]  Barkan's (1984) book focuses mainly on politics and deals with Kenya and Tanzania only.

Second, 'privatization' in the East African context does not necessarily imply the reduction of the role of the state and its links to the voluntary sector. Where privatization of services in the West is typically implemented through changes in ownership, franchising, contracting-out or leasing out of public services under state supervision and control, such formal arrangements are rare in East Africa. Instead, fairly invisible adjustments of the division of labour between the state, NGOs and POs take place – often through action from below and sometimes by design from above. Local initiative may be enough to start the construction of a school, but external support is needed for completing and running it. Village groups may volunteer to pay one of their members to become a village health worker, but external assistance is needed for training, supply of basic drugs and technical supervision. Local defence groups may be able to improve safety in their locality, but not unless they have the (sometimes implicit) blessing of the state. Thus, very few NGOs and POs are autonomous and self-reliant. Most need outside approval, finance, technical advice, training or tactical accommodation. Acquisition of such support is at the heart of relations between the state, voluntary agencies and donors involved in service provision.

Third, the concept of 'privatization' implies that the demarcation between the public and the private sectors is fairly clear. In East Africa, however, this distinction is blurred. The post-independence expansion of state agencies has led to increasing 'inverse' privatization of state resources which are frequently controlled by government officials for private use. This has contributed to the involution of patronage networks (Lemarchand, 1988: 156) and to the increased embezzlement of state resources (Mukandala, 1992: 560). But the opposite also occurs and this has benefited many voluntary agencies. The Parent–Teacher Associations in Uganda, for example, have taken over the running of government-owned primary schools (see Chapter 13 of this volume). In Tanzania local governments are legally barred from running secondary schools. Instead, many set up Trust Funds and use them as fronts through which they can support private secondary schools with finance and administrative manpower.[3] This demonstrates that transfers of control, funds and personnel may not just be *from* the state *to* the voluntary sector, but *also* the reverse. Thus, the process of privatization may imply either a casting off of state activities or an invasion of state facilities by non-state actors – but rarely a disengagement, as is often argued (by, for example, Olorunsola and Muhwezi, 1988).

Finally, 'privatization' usually denotes a process based on domestic political struggles between different forces in society. In East Africa consistent and strong pressure for privatization of services in the conventional sense has come from the bilateral and multilateral donors on whose funds the East African states have

---

[3] The demarcation between the voluntary sector and the market is, of course, also difficult to make. Legal restrictions on private medical practice in Tanzania, for example, have been circumvented by the registration of private hospitals as NGOs. Many non-religious NGO hospitals in Dar es Salaam operate under this cover (Munishi, 1992; Chap. 8). Also the demarcation between the state and the market is sometimes difficult to make. In 1992 it was announced that government hospitals in Uganda would be allowed to operate private wings which could charge full cost for the services provided in government facilities.

become increasingly dependent. The ideological underpinnings of this external pressure are commercialization and marketization, but this type of privatization of services has had few domestic supporters.

Therefore, the actual provision and financing of services in East Africa do not fit common notions of 'privatization'. The term misrepresents key features of the situation. Consequently, policy prescriptions based on such notions are very problematic. As Hyden argues in Chapter 2 of this book, there is a need to bring the voluntary sector back into both the academic and the policy debate. There is also a need to focus on the interface between state, NGOs, POs and donors in service provision. The rest of this chapter provides a starting point for this task.

## The Present Situation

In East Africa some aspects of people's livelihoods have deteriorated during the 1980s, although the statistical information should be interpreted with care. For instance, life expectancy at birth no longer rises as it used to do in the 1960s and 1970s. Maternal mortality has risen significantly in Tanzania and more than doubled in Uganda between 1980 and 1988, while in Kenya there was a decline. Child mortality also rose in Tanzania and Uganda between 1985 and 1990, but not as drastically as maternal mortality. Kenya is again the positive exception. Gains in literacy during previous decades have been lost in Tanzania and Uganda, but not in Kenya (Semboja, 1992).

Improvements in these indicators may be obtained through more and better services, but the relationships are highly complex. While academics tend to discuss them *ad nauseam,* people in East Africa (including the poor) have far fewer doubts. They want better education, health care, clean water and improved roads; access to better technology and to markets; safety for their children and themselves; and protection against theft and violence (Holmquist, 1984; Rothchild and Foley, 1988: 236; Esman, 1991; Brett, 1992: 76).

Despite substantial progress in service coverage since independence, the demand appears to be growing. Past achievements have not satisfied people's present demands. On the contrary, it seems that these achievements have raised expectations about further improvements in both service quality and access. Moreover, increased social differentiation over the past decades has amplified the demand for more and better services, especially among the better-off.

State provision of services has not matched these expectations. But the growing importance of the voluntary sector in service provision does not necessarily reflect a collapse of state-provided services, as some observers argue (Wunsch and Olowu, 1990). Although this was the case in Uganda between 1975 and 1986, the state continues to play an important role in service provision in all three countries. But it has been unable to meet the rising demands and expectations of people in general and of the better-off in particular. Hence, people increasingly look to NGOs and POs to supplement state-provided services. This trend has been amplified by Western donors and NGOs who, for reasons to be discussed later, seek to switch part of their support away from state agencies. However, the end result is not a zero-sum game (Booth, 1987), but complex and conflictual co-operation and competition between the state, the voluntary sector and donors.

Four features of the present service situation are discussed below: service coverage; agencies; resource mobilization; and access and quality.

## Service Coverage

Any observer of living conditions in Kenya, Tanzania and Uganda is well aware that people's needs and priorities in terms of services have not been met. Both basic social services and the provision of law and order are cases in point.

Trends in service coverage for primary education, health services and water supply from around independence to the present are illustrated in Table 1.1. There was a fairly considerable coverage at independence and some expansion thereafter – especially in Kenya. Social service facilities in Uganda also expanded, despite the civil war. These statistics refer to installed capacity. Actual coverage may be much lower because a significant proportion of the infra-structure is out of order, is not maintained, operates at below capacity, or is not used by the intended beneiciaries. In Tanzania, for example, less than 20% of the population may actually draw water from improved supplies – less than half the published figures (Therkildsen, 1989). Official primary school enrolment figures for that country are also significantly overreported (Samoff, 1991; Tadreg, 1992). A similar situation obtains in Uganda, where the upkeep of facilities is bad (World Bank, 1991a) and the quality of services is often low (see Chapter 12). Service coverage in Kenya generally appears to be much better but with considerable variation (see Chapter 7). However, population growth often outpaces present expansions in capacity, especially in the urban areas.

Reliable statistics on the provision of law and order do not exist, but newspaper reports constantly suggest that dissatisfaction with the police and worries about crime are widespread and that crime rates are rising.

Table 1.1 Basic Service Coverage Around Independence and in 1990

|  |  | Primary education (gross enrolment ratios) | Health services (% of population with access) | Water supplies (% of population with access) |
|---|---|---|---|---|
| Kenya | 1960 | 47 | 30[b] | 17[a] |
|  | 1990 | 93 | n.a. | 31 |
| Tanzania | 1960 | 25 | 71[b] | 39[a] |
|  | 1990 | 66 | 76 | 49 |
| Uganda | 1960 | 67 | 41[b] | 18 |
|  | 1990 | 71 | 61 | 21 |

Source: UNICEF (1992, Tables 1, 3 and 4); Chazan et al. (1988: 229); World Bank (1989, 1993); de Coninck (1992, Table 1, p. 3); UNDP (1992, Table 13–10); African Development Bank (1992: 155–6).

[a] In 1970.     [b] In 1980.     n.a.: not available.

The distribution of services across localities and social strata is uneven. Only the privileged few in certain – normally urban – areas have access to services of an adequate standard. Service levels are still low for the vast majority. In Kenya, for example, the population per health facility varies from 7,900 in Rift Valley province to 22,500 in Western province. The proportion of households farther than 8 km from a facility ranges from 8% in Central province to 44% in Eastern province (World Bank, 1991b: 55). If the quality of services were taken into consideration, the inequalities would be much greater. Even in narrow physical terms, full coverage for these services is therefore still a long-distance goal. Access and quality issues are discussed in more detail by Oyugi in Chapter 7, and below.

## Agencies

Structural Adjustment Programmes (SAPs) were launched in many African countries in the 1980s. They aim at changing relations between the state and the voluntary and private sectors in order to raise their performance. The rationale is partly normative and based on views about what each type of agency *should* do, but the reforms are also based on arguments about what agencies *can do best* (see Chapter 3). Thus public-choice theorists characterize services on the basis of their technical features, such as their non-excludability and non-rivalry in consumption (for example, Wunsch, 1991). Service activities are then designated to agencies based on their specific comparative advantages. In this way the most efficient institutional framework for service provision is identified.

In practice, the importance of the state, private and voluntary sectors varies significantly among the three countries and types of services. Who provides what is socially and politically defined and constructed, and depends on past and present co-operative and conflictive relations. Furthermore, households typically use a portfolio of outlets to cover their needs for services. From a household perspective, the distinction between different types of service providers (state, voluntary and private) is likely to be less important than the cost and conditions of access to them. A later section of this chapter, and several contributions to this book, provide micro-level analyses of this issue.

Information about the relative importance of various types of service providers is scarce. Only state-provided services are (partly) included in official documents. Consequently such services are overrated compared with those provided through the private and voluntary sectors. However, the numbers involved in the latter are significant. Taking into account only NGOs recognized by NGO umbrella organizations at the end of the 1980s, there were 400 in Kenya, 200 in Tanzania, and 200–300 in Uganda. To these should be added a significant (but unknown) number of NGOs officially registered as trust funds, associations, or under other legal categories. There is even less information about the number of POs. In Kenya there are probably around 20,000 registered *harambee* groups. There are many thousands of women's groups. No figures on this type of voluntary agency exist for Tanzania and Uganda (Mushi *et al.*, 1992). Classifications of NGOs and POs by function are not available either, although Fowler (in Chapter 3) does provide some information on Kenya.

Table 1.2 is based on available information about who the main providers (as distinct from the financiers) are, and on subjective judgements about the number of people getting some sort of services on a day-to-day basis. The table should therefore be interpreted with caution.

Table 1.2  The Most Important Providers of Services in the Early 1990s

|  | Primary education | Health services | Law and order |
|---|---|---|---|
| Kenya | Central govt<br>Local govt | Private sector<br>Voluntary sect<br>Central govt | Central govt?<br>Voluntary sect? |
| Tanzania | Local govt | Private sector<br>Voluntary sect<br>Local govt<br>Central govt | Voluntary sect<br>Central govt |
| Uganda | Voluntary sect<br>Central govt | Private sector<br>Voluntary sect<br>Central govt | Voluntary sector<br>Central govt |

*Note:* most important agency is listed first.
*Sources:* see footnote 4.

Take primary education. In Kenya it is provided by central government in the rural areas and by local government in the larger towns, although some schools are run by voluntary agencies and a few are private. In Tanzania the provision of primary education has virtually been a state monopoly since 1969 (see Chapter 8), and is provided through local governments – except for a central government-run school catering for the top political elite. In Uganda things are done differently. Here primary schooling can best be described as a hybrid of the private and the public. Extremely meagre state resources for education have forced new POs, called Parent–Teacher Associations (PTAs), to take over primary schools (see Chapter 13). It was not always so. Uganda used to have a good education system (see Chapter 12) with the state playing an important role.

Health services present a different picture. The private sector is probably dominant in all three countries. Services are provided by a wide range of traditional healers, private hospitals and practitioners trained in modern medicine. Voluntary agencies, especially the churches, are important too, and have been for years. Their role may be on the increase in both Tanzania (see Chapter 11) and Uganda (see Chapter 12). In Kenya NGOs are responsible for

[4]  *Kenya*: Chapters 4 and 5 and Roth (1987) on primary education; Fowler (1992) on health; Chapter 6 on law and order. *Tanzania*: Chapter 8 and Semboja (1992) on health; Chapter 10 on law and order. *Uganda*: Chapters 12 and 13 and World Bank (1991a) on primary education; World Bank (1987) on health; Chapter 14 on law and order.

around 40% of the health services (World Bank, 1991b). This is the broad picture. It changes if specific health services are considered. In Kenya, for example, NGOs dominate in family planning activities. In Tanzania primary health care is mainly provided through local government, while half the hospital beds are owned by (mainly) church-run NGOs and the other half by the central government. In Uganda the attendance at government health units in 1988 had dropped to half the level of the mid-1970s, owing to deteriorating service quality. Moreover, some privatization of Ugandan health services has taken place. Not only have private clinics and drug stores mushroomed – also in the rural areas – but increasing numbers of government health workers provide treatment in their homes for payment (Whyte, 1991).

Yet another picture emerges with respect to law and order. As already noted, there is widespread concern about increasing crime rates. Crime does not just 'originate' from the private sector. Often the state itself, openly or covertly, breaks the law in order to favour supporters or special interest groups (and donors), or to punish opponents. In Kenya many instances of ethnic violence in the North and in the Rift Valley are suspected of having been instigated by the police and security forces. In Tanzania the grounds of primary schools in many urban areas are being encroached upon, often by or through government or party officials. Such incidents were numerous in Uganda, at least until recently. Hence the growing involvement of various POs in trying to improve members' security and property. This happens although the maintenance of law and order has many of the features that public-choice theorists assign to state-provided services.

The overall trend for all three types of services is towards privatization in a broad sense and a bigger role for voluntary agencies – resulting in a relatively declining role for the state. However, the privatization does not necessarily imply a growing independence of the voluntary agencies from the state. There are strong financial, political and personal links between the state and the voluntary sector, as shown below.

## Resources for Services

Proponents of privatization (e.g. World Bank, 1991a) often overestimate people's willingness and ability to pay directly for the services they regard as important. Unfortunately such assumptions are often made without sufficient attention to economic realities. In East Africa, as elsewhere on the continent, overall economic performance in the 1980s was significantly affected by internal policies and structural adjustment programmes, changing terms of trade, and debt-repayment problems (Helleiner, 1992). During the early 1980s gross domestic product (GDP) in constant prices[5] grew at around 0.5% per annum in Kenya and 4.9% in Uganda, but fell by 6% in Tanzania. Per capita GDP fell in both Kenya and Tanzania in this period.[6] From the mid-1980s (1987 for

[5] 1976 constant prices are used for Kenya and Tanzania; 1987 prices are used for Uganda.
[6] Prior to the introduction of SAPs in Tanzania, real per capita household incomes were almost halved between 1969 and 1982 according to Bevan et al. (1989).

Uganda) until the end of the decade, overall economic growth picked up. GDP grew by 4% per year in Kenya, 4.7% in Tanzania and 8% in Uganda, in constant prices. There are, however, signs of economic decline for Kenya, starting in 1991, suggesting that the positive trend during the second half of the 1980s may not be sustainable.

The impact of these trends on the size and distribution of household incomes is not known, although one World Bank source states that 'poverty in sub-Saharan Africa is severe and has been getting worse' (Stewart, 1991: 1851). The economic liberalization of the 1980s has probably led to increasing social differentiation in East Africa, resulting from the economic accumulation that took place within the state bureaucracy (through rent-seeking), in the parallel economy (informal economic activity, smuggling, mining, poaching) and in the formal economy (capitalist accumulation).[7]

Other important features of service financing in East Africa are also poorly understood. Resources do not just come from one or a few sources. They originate from households (with men and women having different rights and obligations), POs, NGOs, all tiers of the government, and from donors. More-over, the resources needed are not just money but also unpaid labour, people's creative energies and the status and legitimacy that they may confer on institutions supplying the services (Uphoff, 1986: 232). Unfortunately information about the multitude of such resource inputs is limited and incomplete. This should be borne in mind in the following account of resource mobilization by households, POs and NGOs, the state, and donors.

### Households

Services are generally no longer provided free (i.e. no out-of-pocket expenses for users). An increasing number of households pay *directly* for services whether the provider is the state, the voluntary or the private sector.[8] Payments take three major forms: user charges and voluntary contributions in cash (including payment for supposedly 'free' services); bribes; and self-help labour (discussed in the next section).

Both the size and extent of user fees and voluntary contributions for services provided by the state and the voluntary sector have increased in the 1980s. Some state-imposed fees are charged for services that previously were provided free. They are typically introduced as part of Structural Adjustment Programmes – often after pressure from foreign donors. Other fees for state-provided services are officially labelled 'voluntary contributions' but are *de facto* compulsory since

---

[7] Political liberalization has certainly led to much greater openness about such phenomena. Perhaps this tends to exaggerate the actual changes caused by the SAPs.

[8] Such payments are substantial. Even for state-provided and -financed services, direct household contributions often exceed the resource inputs by the state. This is, for example, the case of primary education in Kenya where parents contributed 56% of the total cost per student in 1989 (World Bank, 1991b: 94). The same pattern is found in Tanzania (Semboja and Therkildsen, 1989) and Uganda where parents pay up to 90% of the running costs of the primary schools (World Bank, 1991a: 103).

failure to pay results in exclusion.[9] Only a few state-imposed fees take into account the ability of users to pay.[10]

The voluntary sector has a long tradition of direct payment for service provision, although user fees generally do not cover the full cost of delivery.[11] In contrast to the state, many NGOs take into account the ability of users to pay when they charge fees (Mabala, 1990; Brett, 1992).

Payment of bribes for state-provided services is also increasingly common according to many reports (Whyte, 1991; Widner, 1992). But this is obviously difficult to quantify.

How such payments affect household budgets is not very well known. Structural adjustment plans are, in this respect, drawn up in the dark. Budget surveys from the early 1980s suggest that households in Kenya and Tanzania spent on average 10% of their incomes on primary education and formal health care in the early 1980s (Bevan et al., 1989).[12] Urban households spent relatively more than rural households. There are also large regional variations. The recent budget survey for Uganda suggests that some 5% of household expenditures are allocated to health and education (Republic of Uganda, 1991b: 48).

Within households the costs and benefits of different services are not necessarily allocated according to need, but may depend on the individual member's gender, age, and relationship to the household head. Cultural and socio-economic background are also important. More boys than girls are still enrolled in primary schools, for example, although the gap is rapidly narrowing in Kenya and Uganda and has closed for Tanzania. Evidence also suggests that rural women in some cases receive a relatively larger share of household resources for health services than men. According to Pitt and Levy (1992), this may reflect the crucial role that female labour plays in agriculture. However, in general not enough is known to distinguish between the bargaining and the consensus model of intra-household allocations of resources (Patton, 1993).

Depending on circumstances, husband or wife or both may be responsible for the payment of services (Nypan, 1991; Silberschmidt, 1991; Therkildsen, 1993). Members of the extended family are also often important sources of support,

---

[9] The school fee for primary education in Tanzania is an example. Introduced in 1977 as a 'voluntary' contribution, it is now common practice that primary school teachers admit pupils only if their parents pay this voluntary fee *and* equip their children with school uniforms and exercise books *and* are willing to contribute to various school funds. But also fees charged by POs – such as parents' contributions to primary schools in Uganda – are often compulsory (see Chapter 13).

[10] In some cases those who *can* afford to pay are actually exempted for political reasons. In Kenya, for example, out- and in-patient user charges were reintroduced at all state health facilities except dispensaries in April 1992 after much controversy. The following were, however, exempted from all user fees: children; the destitute and mentally handicapped in-patients; and all civil servants and the police, including spouses and dependent children under 22 years of age (World Bank, 1991b: 66; *Daily Nation*, 11 April 1992). In Uganda, many public health units at the local level have begun to charge fees after approval by their management committees.

[11] Many NGO hospitals may, however, recover most of their recurrent costs. In Uganda some 80–90% of costs are typically recovered (World Bank, 1993: 68), although it is not clear whether *all* recurrent costs (e.g. expatriate doctors' salaries; medical supplies, etc.) are included.

[12] Results of the 1991/2 government household survey for Tanzania were not yet published at the time of writing.

especially for schooling. 'Wealth' in family members may often be as significant as monetary wealth.

As noted earlier, many of the direct household contributions to social service financing are substantial – but largely unrecorded. For the majority, they have probably grown faster than household incomes during the last decade – especially for state services which were supposedly 'free'. Service provision is increasingly being commercialized. Households may respond in various ways to this situation. They may be cut off from service benefits by deliberate choice or economic compulsion, they may switch to a lower quality service, they may search for cheaper service outlets, or they may join others to provide services collectively.

### POs and NGOs

According to the conventional wisdom, POs and NGOs are often much better at mobilizing resources in cash and kind than state agencies (Cernea, 1988; Tripp, 1992). Reliable evidence is limited, however, and the variations in local circumstances and among POs and NGOs themselves are so large, that it is extremely difficult to generalize. Various examples – first on POs – demonstrate this.

In Kenya substantial resources are mobilized through *harambee* groups. Practically all the primary schools built and equipped after independence are the result of such efforts. Their contribution to the national gross capital formation has been considerable ever since independence (Ngau, 1987; Bevan et al., 1989; Hill, 1991). Until the early 1980s participation in them was widespread across social strata. Two-thirds of the rural population participated in some type of self-help project,[13] although the landless and the large landowners participated less than others. In addition to funds, rural adults also contributed on average some 15–20 days' labour per year to such projects (the landless only 5 days), while many urban households supported self-help activities in their home area with money – especially the relatively affluent, including civil servants (Barkan and Holmquist, 1989). Mbithi and Rasmusson (1977: 56–66) found that women were as active as men in *harambee* activities, although the men were the leaders in the majority of the groups. However, in recent years the character of the *harambee* movement and its relation to the state has changed dramatically, as explained later.

In Tanzania a study from the early 1980s showed that rural households spent around 30% of their working time on communal activities. Most of it was spent on the village *shamba* but around 6% (15 days a year) was used on self-help projects such as those mentioned above for Kenya. Unlike in Kenya, the poorer Tanzanian peasants contributed much more labour than the better-off – perhaps up to 30% more (Collier *et al.*, 1986: 93). Studies from the late 1980s show that communal *shamba* work has declined dramatically, although self-help on social service improvements is still substantial (Kjærby, 1989; Semboja and Therkildsen,

---

[13] In order of importance the eight types of projects were nursery schools, primary schools, secondary schools, health clinics, cattle dips, water projects, mutual assistance groups, and production groups.

1989). At present it appears that participation in law and order enforcement through *sungusungu* groups is the most prevalent communal activity, although it is sometimes compulsory (see Chapter 10).

In Uganda there is a large number of small but unregistered POs. Their activities – especially during the years of civil unrest – are poorly documented. In the past the state was active in mobilizing peasant labour under compulsion to generate contributions for various development projects (Mamdani, 1975). Today groups are voluntarily established for specific purposes, such as the running of a primary school (see Chapter 13). With the collapse of the Ugandan state for much of the past decade it is not surprising that many POs are now only marginally dependent on external funding (de Coninck, 1992: 13).

Evidence on resource mobilization by NGOs is also scattered. Little research has been done, and major service-providing NGOs, especially those run by the churches, are reluctant to disclose financial information. According to Fowler (Chapter 3) very few non-church NGOs engaged in service provision in East Africa are able to raise more than 10% of their funds locally. Church-run hospitals may be an exception (Bloom *et al.*, 1992; World Bank, 1993: 68).[14] Domestic funds come from membership contributions, but most are raised through user charges. A large proportion, however, is made up of state subsidies and foreign aid. More information on this is provided later.

Many argue that it is the failure of the state to deliver services that drives the growth of the voluntary sector (Azarya, 1988). But this is only part of the explanation. Rising expectations and rapidly growing external funding of NGOs over the last decade have perhaps contributed as much to this growth, and state financial support remains crucial to both PO and NGO activities. Typically POs and local NGOs mobilize resources for new infrastructure with the intention of securing state funds for recurrent expenditures. Without state support a large proportion of activities in the voluntary sector would come to a standstill. Matching of funds is a key feature.

*State*

It is a widespread belief that state allocations to basic services such as health and education have gone from bad to worse. Certainly there is much dissatisfaction with the quality of services and generally there is a great deal of controversy about the issue in East Africa.[15]

This is reflected in the academic debate. Many argue that the economy in general is not improving. On top of that it is believed that the Structural Adjustment Programmes imposed by Western donors have forced weak states to reduce expenditures and to slash funds for precisely those services that most benefit the poor. The issue is confused by conflicting information about state expenditures on services. Some of this information seems deliberately selected

[14]  But see footnote 11.
[15]  Funds for law and order services are not included in the analysis because of a lack of reliable information.

to reflect ideological positions, some of it is inappropriate, and some of it is simply wrong.[16]

Figure 1.1 shows state expenditures on health and education measured in constant prices per capita over time for each of the three countries. The estimates take account of inflation, population growth, and funds channelled through both central and local government.

The figure indicates that government expenditures on health and education in the early 1990s have not reached the levels achieved in the 1980s in any of the three countries. Nevertheless, expenditure patterns differ somewhat among them. In Kenya there has been a stagnating trend in expenditures at least since the mid-1970s. Tanzanians experienced drastic expenditure declines from 1979 to 1985, moderate increases between 1985 and 1990, and then declines again. In Uganda expenditures on education and health have risen consistently since 1987. The trends are remarkable considering the modest economic growth performance of East African countries in the 1980s and their growing debt burden.[17]

A closer look at expenditure trends within health and education shows the following.

In Kenya actual spending within the health sector is inconsistent with the government's stated emphasis on preventive and rural health services. Almost 90% of the health funds are spent on (curative) hospital services. Kenya National Hospital in Nairobi alone uses almost as much money (10% of the total health budget) as preventive and rural health services (13%). However, recent modest increases in real recurrent expenditures per capita have not gone just to increased wages, but have also been spent on better equipment and supplies. This follows a period from 1985 to 1988 when personnel expenditures increased by 6% per year in real terms, while non-wage operating expenditures decreased by 4% per year (World Bank, 1991b). With respect to primary education, the government only funds teachers' salaries, limited school supplies and milk for students. All other costs (most books and equipment, uniforms, etc.) are paid by the parents. State expenditures per pupil declined in real terms in the 1970s and early 1980s, but then increased steadily in the second half of the decade. Most increases have, however, been absorbed by teachers' salaries and allowances. Real expenditures on non-wage items have fallen over the years (World Bank, 1991b: Chaps 3 and 4). By 1991, teachers' salaries accounted for 85% of total expenditures and milk distribution a further 13%, leaving only 2% for all other expenditures. This

---

[16] Many authors present figures that exclude funds for services channelled through local government, thereby significantly underestimating actual resource allocations. Among the examples are Bryceson (1993), Turok (1991), Shivji (1991), Ebel (1991) and the World Bank *World Development Reports*. Other authors use budget shares to analyse trends and shifts in government expenditures, thereby ignoring changes in the size of the budget and population over time (see for example Ebel, 1991).

[17] The debt–service ratio in Kenya rose from 8% in 1970 to 34% in 1990. The trend in Tanzania has been similar (8% in 1970; 26% in 1990). Uganda had a ratio of 55% in 1990 – up from 3% in 1970. Its foreign debt grew by 50% from 1989 to 1990 according to the *World Development Reports* (World Bank, 1991 and 1992). These figures exclude domestic debts.

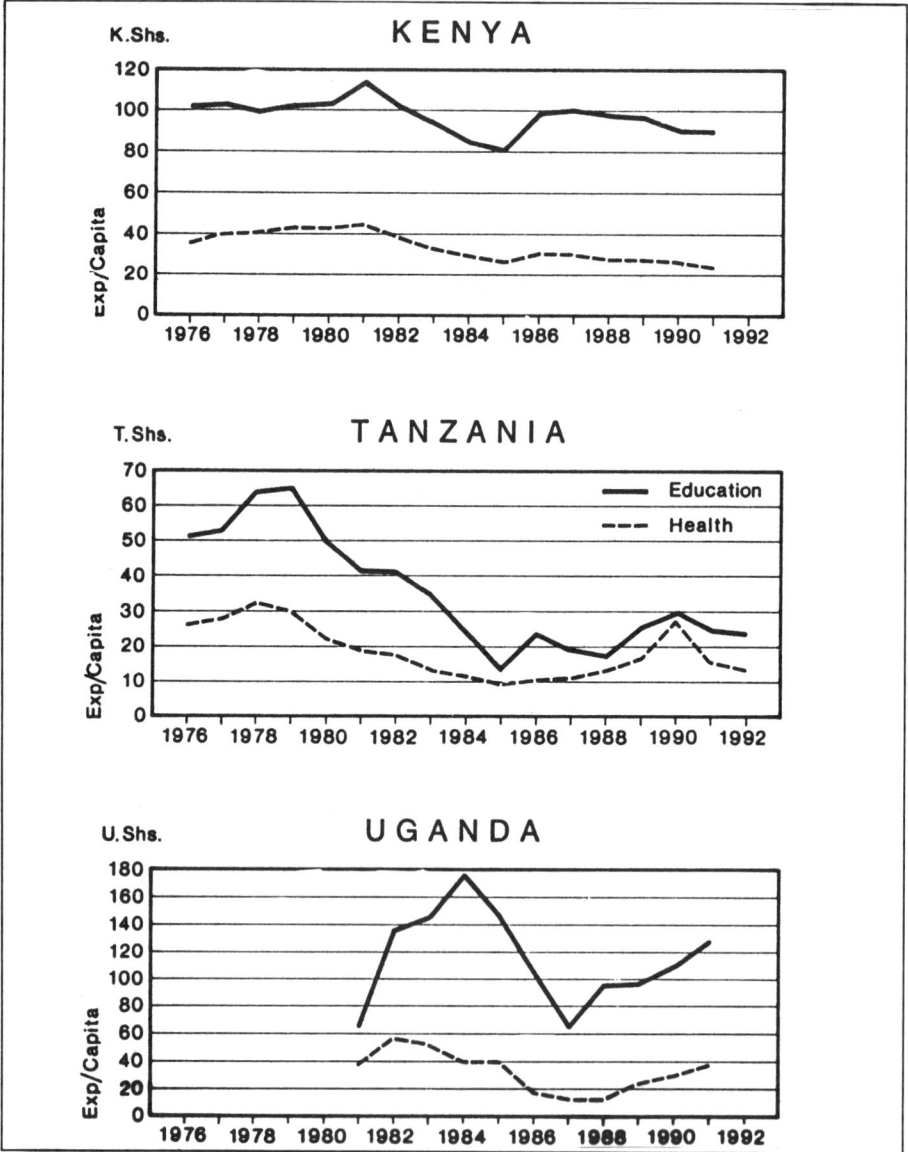

Figure 1.1. Trends in Real Government Expenditures Per Capita on Health and Education; in Constant Prices

*Note:* the figures are *not* comparable across countries.
*Sources and methods:* see footnote 18.

[18] The base year for the data series on Kenya and Tanzania is 1976; and 1987 for Uganda. Figures include investment and recurrent expenditures made through both central and local government. Expenditures from more than one ministry are included where relevant (i.e. Ministry of Education and Ministry of Higher Education). Parastatal expenditures are excluded. Expenditures funded by donors are included to the extent that they are recorded in the official government budget documents.

amounts to less than half the price of a textbook on a per student basis (ibid.: 56). Education in Kenya therefore depends on matching funds from parents.

In Tanzania real per capita expenditures on primary health care grew faster than those on curative and preventive services between 1985 and 1991 – consistent with declared government policy. However, two-thirds of all health expenditures still go to curative (hospital) services. From 1985, real per capita expenditures rose both for primary and post-primary education, but fell for higher education (Semboja, 1992). All else being equal, these trends are consistent with a poverty-oriented expenditure policy. Information about micro-level allocations are, however, needed to make more precise assessments.

In Uganda real per capita state expenditures on health did increase at the end of the 1980s – albeit from very low levels. As in Kenya and Tanzania, the funds are skewed towards hospital services. State financing of primary education declined in real terms for two decades and is only just picking up (World Bank, 1993). Without considerable contributions from parents, the system would simply collapse. State allocations to education have also been strongly biased in favour of tertiary education.

All three countries operate a local government system, in which each authority has the power to raise its own revenues. These resources are limited in Kenya (Smoke, 1993) and Tanzania (Therkildsen and Semboja, 1992) and almost non-existent in Uganda (World Bank, 1993: 35). Local government revenues are therefore not important for social service financing at present. However, especially in Tanzania, local governments receive substantial grants from central government which make them important providers of health and education services, as already discussed.

Figure 1.1 is based on local currency data which do not allow comparisons of government expenditures among the three countries. For that, health and education expenditures in local currencies must be converted to comparable units. The purchasing power parity (PPP) calculation method is one way of doing this.[19] It shows that there are significant differences among the three countries in the real levels of the economy and in real financial allocations per capita to social services. Kenya has done better than Tanzania. Uganda is clearly the worst-off.[20]

Information from all three countries also shows that during periods of

---

[19] PPP is based on the concept that nominal exchange rates, say in dollars, must be adjusted for differences in inflation rates between the local economy and the economies of its most important trading partners. The idea is that, if nominal exchange rates were adjusted to the PPP$, internal and external equilibrium of the economy would result. This PPP$ exchange rate gives a better picture of the real value (purchasing power) of the local currency, whose official value (nominal exchange rate) is to some extent politically determined.

[20] Calculated in PPP$ (1976 = 100 for Kenya and Tanzania and 1987 = 100 for Uganda) and fixing Kenya's GDP per capita in 1989 at 100, the corresponding figure for GDP per capita in Tanzania is 47 and for Uganda 40. Not surprisingly such large differences are reflected in the expenditures on services. Using Kenya's expenditure per capita on education in 1989 as the yardstick (= 100), the corresponding figure for Tanzania is 39; for Uganda it is 8. The PPP$ per capita expenditure data on health also show significant differences. Kenya (100); Tanzania (50); Uganda (5). These figures are based on statistics about the formal economy. Smaller differences would probably result if the impact of the informal economy was known.

economic stagnation or decline (as measured by real GDP) social service expenditures were reduced relatively more than other types of expenditures. On the other hand, total government expenditure expanded during periods of economic growth and benefited social services relatively more than other sectors in all three countries, especially Tanzania.

This positive correlation between economic growth and social service expenditures is based on a short time series of data, but the relationship is simple to explain. Growth allows governments to generate more domestic revenues through sales and income taxes, import duties, etc. and revenues from donor-financed import and balance-of-payment support, while the allocation of such revenues to social services is the result of deliberate policy. Whatever attempts the World Bank and the IMF made to reduce government expenditures on social services in the earlier days of the SAPs evidently did not succeed fully. This suggests that *internal* political interests have actively tried to protect social service expenditures from cutbacks. Recently such expenditures have been further boosted, especially in Tanzania and Uganda. This positive trend at the end of the 1980s would have been unlikely without substantial injections of foreign assistance. Obviously this puts a serious question mark over the financial sustainability of the positive trends that have been achieved during the last decade, and focuses attention on donors.

*Donors*

Ever since independence external resources for service provision have been important. Today both the state and the voluntary sector depend to a significant degree on them. Donor funds to the state are provided in three ways: (i) by supporting investments in new or rehabilitated infrastructure; (ii) by assistance to the running of services through recurrent financing; and (iii) by providing funds for import support of various kinds, which in turn (through cash cover) generate revenues for central government that can be used as normal budget funds.

Total Official Development Assistance (ODA) to the East African countries made up 37% of GNP in Tanzania, 15% in Uganda and 10% in Kenya, equivalent to US$30–40 per person in the early 1990s. These percentages would decrease if the informal economy could be taken into account. ODA is on the increase for Uganda, fairly stable for Tanzania and declining since 1992 for Kenya. Despite debt servicing there has been a net inflow of external funds in all three countries (UNDP, 1993). Some 20% of ODA in East Africa goes to the social sector in general. Some of this (around 50% in Tanzania and Uganda and 30% in Kenya) is allocated for human priority needs within the sector.[21]

These funds are significant compared with those generated domestically by the state and allocated for services. Unfortunately under-reporting of donor funds in recipient state budgets makes it difficult to get valid estimates. In Tanzania, for example, substantial donor inflows in 1987/8 were not reported in

---

[21] Human priority needs include basic education, primary health care, safe drinking water, adequate sanitation, family planning, and nutrition programmes (UNDP, 1992: 43).

the official documents. These may underestimate the actual figures by between 60% and 300% (Semboja and Therkildsen, 1989). There are several reasons for this under-reporting. Recipient governments are often not informed about the actual amounts of money spent on expatriate advisers and procurement of home country supplies. Furthermore, recipient governments may also want to hide their real dependence on external funds from the public and their parliaments.[22] Under-reporting of aid inflows also makes it easier to meet donor-imposed limits on budget deficits. In addition, substantial donor funds may never reach their intended uses because of corruption among both donors and recipients.

In the absence of reliable aggregate figures, a few examples will show the importance of donor funding. In Kenya the state did not intend to finance any new projects in 1992 which were not funded by donors (World Bank, 1992a: 29). In Tanzania more than 50% of the state investment budgets for health and education have been externally funded for several decades (Semboja and Therkildsen, 1994). And in Uganda donor disbursements accounted for almost three times the state expenditures in the health sector in 1991 (World Bank, 1993: ix).

Donor financing of Northern and Southern NGOs is also substantial. Globally donor funding of the voluntary sector rose from US$1.04bn to US$2.13bn between 1980 and 1988. This growth is almost five times higher than that for total ODA, and reflects a clear policy shift among donors in favour of the voluntary sector. During the same period the NGOs' own resource mobilization rose much more slowly, so that the dependence of the voluntary sector on donor funds has increased significantly in the 1980s. These figures exclude relief funding (Fowler, 1992). However, it is relevant to note that Northern NGOs still raise about two-thirds of their funds for work in the South from private contributions (UNDP, 1993: 88).

Two-thirds of NGO and donor funds to the voluntary sector are spent in the South by Northern NGOs. Only one-third is channelled through Southern NGOs, but the direct funding of Southern NGOs by Northern governments is on the increase (Fowler, 1992). Specific information on East Africa is very limited. And it is largely unknown how much of the total NGO funds is spent on social service provision. However, the general pattern is shown by the following examples.

In Kenya, NGOs command very significant resources, equivalent to one-fourth of the total government budget (i.e. US$320m per year) according to Fowler (Chapter 3) and mostly from external sources. Tanzanian NGOs are also heavily dependent on foreign funds. The German Government, for example, recently agreed to provide US$10m for church-run health and education services in Tanzania (Chapter 11). No good estimates for Uganda are available. The official figures of NGO incomes (US$10m a year) are underestimated by a very large margin (de Coninck, 1992: 14).

---

[22] Budget documents presented to the Tanzanian Parliament (in Swahili) give the lowest figures for donor assistance. Other government documents (in English) provide more realistic data. However, they all provide significantly lower figures than the donor accounts.

Despite the lack of data the trend in donor funding of NGOs is clear. There is a move away from East African governments as recipients of funds from the North, and a deliberate switch towards the voluntary sector in support of the economic and political reforms that Western countries seek to promote (see later). Fowler (Chapter 3) argues that it is the push by Western countries to reduce the role of African states – rather than NGO performance – that may be the basis for this trend. It is this larger political concern that lies behind the ability of NGOs to raise foreign resources and which constitutes their real competitive advantage. In East Africa the provision of services is not simply a domestic affair.

## Access and Quality

Most services provided through collective action depend on local resource mobilization through community self-help, as described above. These local resources are often a condition for obtaining matching funds from the state, donors or Northern NGOs. However, the willingness and ability to mobilize resources locally (political support, funds, leadership, and labour) vary widely across regions and district. Access to services is therefore influenced by the overlap between ethno-regional politics and differences in local capabilities to mobilize resources. Consequently, as Oyugi argues in Chapter 7, people have unequal access to services depending on where they live, how much money they can afford to pay, and how extensive and powerful a social network they belong to. This explains some of the inequalities in service access described above.

Oyugi's analysis applies both to the state and the voluntary sector. He is therefore in disagreement with the growing literature on the voluntary sector which maintains that NGOs are more poverty-oriented than the state (Cernea, 1988; de Coninck, 1992: 107). The implication of his argument is that the (necessary) reliance of NGOs and POs on local resource mobilization restricts their ability to provide services for the poor and marginalized. Unfortunately the mainstream NGO literature is highly normative and rarely supported by evidence. Several of the studies in this book – particularly Chapters 5, 9 and 13 – show that the poverty orientation of the voluntary sector in East Africa cannot be taken for granted.

One of the few serious attempts at assessing the poverty impact of NGOs (Riddell and Robinson, 1992) concluded that most of the NGO projects evaluated had a positive impact on poverty alleviation. Unfortunately, this result cannot be extrapolated more widely because of the biased selection of cases and the absence of service delivery projects in the sample. Much more research is therefore needed in order to assess the poverty impact of service-providing NGOs. In view of the importance of the churches and their dependence on user fees to generate funds for services, an assessment of church-provided services seems particularly relevant.

Lack of evidence about the poverty impact of donor assistance – even at the project level – is also considerable. In part, this arises because only a fraction of all aid – perhaps as little as 15% – has ever been evaluated (Riddell, 1990: 5). In part, it arises because such evaluations are difficult to do. But the most important reason is probably the lack of interest among donors for this type of research. It is in direct conflict with the proclaimed poverty orientation of most donors (Mosley, 1987).

The quality of services is also influenced by geographical location, social stratification, and the services themselves. In certain situations they combine so that 'disservice' would be a more appropriate term to use. Many reported instances of unhealthy school buildings, dangerous health equipment, polluted water from the taps and police brutality testify to this. And, although financial inputs are necessary for improved service quality, the process of converting them and other inputs into actual services depends on many factors. Wuyts (1992: 27) argues that state spending only improves people's welfare where 'people can use the state resources provided, where public pressure ensures that state expenditure schemes recognize and respond to the real need of the deprived rather than being diverted into the hands of the better off'. A combination of factors therefore influence service quality.

One is fairly technical. The social service infrastructure in Tanzania and Uganda has been run down for years, starting in the 1970s. Substantial, but not unrealistically high, expenditures are required to bring the capacity of the infrastructure into operation (e.g. Therkildsen and Semboja, 1992, on Tanzania). Despite the recent marginal additions to service financing by the state in these two countries, service quality is therefore unlikely to improve much in the near future. Throughout the 1980s, as shown earlier, state-run services in Kenya have been financed at a relatively much higher level than in Tanzania and Uganda. Additional funding of social services in Kenya may therefore have larger marginal effects.

Secondly, the quality of services for the majority may change little if additional service resources are allocated to benefit the bureaucracy providing the services, or specific groups or areas. Evidence of this was presented earlier. Some observers on East Africa argue that the political economy of equity is focused on areas (i.e. often ethnic groups) as much as on economic class (Barkan, 1992; Healey and Robinson, 1992). But the latter *is* important, as illustrated by the fact that increased funding has often gone to civil servants' salaries, employment and perks rather than to equipment and supplies.

Thirdly, quality and access to services depend on the institutions that provide them: not only the resources they control, but also the values that drive them. Injections of funds into corrupt and inefficient state bureaucracies operating with grossly underpaid staff may simply fuel embezzlement and theft – not the quality of services. In contrast, church staff may (sometimes) be motivated by altruism – religious conviction that leads to a public service ethic – and by their accountability to national or international agencies that subject them to continuous supervision (Brett, 1992: 83). Hence church-provided services may often be better than comparable state services, although church staff are not paid on the basis of performance and tend to receive lower salaries than comparable state employees, who are also frequently better trained (Brett, 1992; Munishi, 1992).

A fourth reason for the perceived fall in the quality of services may be related to rising expectations. What is regarded as acceptable is socially defined. As class formation and social differentiation in East Africa proceed, the better-off are less likely to accept standards that were satisfactory a decade or two ago. Their perceptions of declining quality are strong and they press for better services. At least in Kenya, this may have had some effect. Thus Makau (Chapter 5) argues that the quality of education for the rich in Kenya has not declined.

Whatever the case, both the unequal access to services and the wide disparities in service quality have political implications, as shown in the next section.

## The Politics of Service Provision

Two major trends have been identified in the preceding sections: (i) an increasing privatization (in a broad sense) of service delivery and financing; and (ii) a growing importance – especially in the 1980s – of NGOs and POs in service provision, linked much more to the financial role of the state and external donors than to local resource mobilization by the voluntary sector itself.

Many political scientists and historians pay little attention to these and other changes in service provision because they assume that production relations – rather than issues of service provision – are central to political struggles. The analyses by Kitching (1980) and Leys (1975) on Kenya; Shivji (1976) on Tanzania; and Mamdani (1975) on Uganda are typical examples of this view. However, struggles for improved services have played an important political role in all three East African countries, although circumstances have changed significantly over time and place. A historical perspective on this issue is therefore instructive. It starts with an analysis of the domestic actors, and then proceeds with an analysis of the role of donors.

### State Legitimacy and Service Provision

During the earlier stages of colonialism the churches were instrumental in the provision of services – especially in primary schooling and health care. This had profound and lasting consequences for class formation and for access to services by various ethnic groups. But, confronted with growing nationalism, the colonial powers needed legitimation of their rule and their monopoly on maintaining law and order (Young, 1988). Gradually the terminal colonial regimes became active providers of schools, clinics, wells, roads, etc. Service coverage at independence was therefore not insignificant, as Table 1.1 illustrates, although it was racially discriminatory.

When the nationalist movements emerged, their mass mobilization depended crucially upon the promise of a better life,[23] involving struggles against colonial

---

[23]  Social services (especially education) also figured prominently in the early manifestos of the nationalist movements, although access to land was the most burning issue in Kenya. See Mabala (1989) on the Kenya African Union, KANU, and KADU; Iliffe (1979: 512) on the Tanganyika African Association, later TANU; and de Coninck (1992: 11) on Uganda.

regimes that provided services along racial lines, catering separately and unequally for Africans, Asians and Whites. This forged a 'social contract' between nationalist movements and Africans, based on a promise of free services to all under a democratic indigenous government. People were promised amenities in return for political support. This fed popular expectations about free social services as 'the fruits of independence' (Ayoade, 1988). It confronted the post-colonial regimes with two serious problems: on the one hand, how to allocate very scarce state resources to meet widespread expectations about service improvements, and, on the other hand, how to strengthen the political base for regime support in religiously and ethnically mixed societies with large socio-economic differences. At first the political processes evolved rather differently in the three countries, although there are recent signs of convergence.

## Kenya

In Kenya the political conflicts of the colonial period continued after independence.[24] The Kenyatta regime had to deal with a growing and aggressive group of kulaks, chiefs eager to preserve the powers they had acquired from the colonial regime, settlers determined to preserve their privileges, and demands from various ethnic groups. It also faced the armed remains of the Mau Mau resistance groups.

As part of the strategy to build a broad coalition of support for the new regime, Kenyatta and his ethno-regional ruling cartel encouraged people to form self-help groups (*harambee*) to build the social infrastructure. Many such efforts – especially those involving larger projects – depended on state-provided funds to match locally mobilized resources. The success of local politicians in elections depended on their ability to mobilize people in their areas for self-help projects, without which they could not secure support from the state to provide matching funds. Local leaders who were unable to mobilize the people in their areas were not supported. In this way the access to political power was influenced from below; the fortunes of the larger *harambee* projects and local leaders were linked.

This system slowly changed in the later years of Kenyatta's regime and under Moi. The state simply did not have the resources to run all the projects started by *harambee* groups. The ability of POs to launch new projects on their own was therefore severely curtailed, as reflected in the tightening of district-level planning procedures after 1983 (see Chapter 4; Cohen and Hook, 1987).

The system also changed for another reason in the 1980s (Barkan and Chege, 1989). The matching principle benefited the core areas more than the periphery, where the economic base for local resource mobilization is small and from where the political support of the new Moi regime tended to come; the periphery therefore suffered doubly. These poorer areas benefited when state allocations no longer depended on local resource mobilization. But the change also switched control of community projects away from *harambee* groups, and

---

[24]   The following is based on Ngau (1987); Widner (1992); Barkan and Chege (1989); Barkan and Holmquist (1989); Chapters 4 and 7 of this book.

decreased the accountability of local leaders to their communities, since their ability to lead local communities was no longer as important as their loyalty to the regime. Grass-roots participation in the provision of state-assisted services has therefore been reduced significantly under Moi's regime.

*Tanzania*

A very different political process of service provision developed in Tanzania in the immediate post-independence period.[25] Here the threats to central rule were much less pronounced than in Kenya and Uganda. Nyerere's *ujamaa* philosophy of 1967 had tremendous influence at home and abroad, but the gap between principles and practice soon began to undermine its initial support. One by one the commanding heights of organizations in civil society (labour unions, co-operatives, development associations) were brought under state and party control (Kiondo, 1993). Even collective action at the grass-roots level outside party auspices was suppressed. Church- and NGO-run services in health and education were nationalized.[26]

Also elected bodies — such as local governments — were deliberately dismantled or allowed to die. State–party controls were even extended to the village level. Access to political power depended as much on loyalty to the party as on support from below. And access to state funds for social services depended decreasingly on local leadership and resource mobilization. Instead, people were promised schools, clinics and water supplies if they would move into designated villages. At first this was an offer, but the response was slow. From the early 1970s villagization was forced. Since then the party and government have at times applied considerable pressure to get communities to take part in 'self-help' activities, but overt coercion has not been consistently and constantly applied.

Under Mwinyi's rule since 1985, and following the previous regime's bruising conflicts with the IMF and the World Bank over economic policy, the ruling CCM (*Chama Cha Mapinduzi*) has backed away from the *ujamaa* principles. Faced with its first multi-party election in 1995, the CCM seems increasingly pragmatic and populist, and formal state control of NGOs and POs has been loosened considerably. Their involvement in service provision is now actively encouraged as Chapter 11 exemplifies, and at present there are few (and rather technical) restrictions on their registration.

As in Kenya, policy-making and domestic funding of voluntary sector activities are becoming more personalized. Prominent politicians frequently act as 'patrons' and fundraisers.[27] Complex networks of personal contacts between the state and the voluntary agencies are growing everywhere. Membership in

---

[25] This section is based on van Donge and Liviga (1986); Havnevik (1993); Semboja and Therkildsen (1994); Holmquist (1984); and Chapter 8 of this volume.

[26] But as Chapter 11 shows for the Catholic Church, the nationalization did not change its close links to the regime.

[27] 'Patron' is used in the legal documents required to register NGOs under the Trustees' Incorporation Ordinance. Patrons are also a prominent feature of the Ugandan scene (Brett, 1992: 69).

registered NGOs, development associations, trust funds, and betterment societies is filled with party and state officials (Fowler, 1991). But the CCM's past ideological leadership has changed significantly and none of the many new parties have yet presented coherent alternatives or specific social service policies.

### Uganda

In Uganda the very existence of the state was threatened right from independence.[28] Considerable socio-economic differences between groups and areas had been created or amplified by colonial rule and were reflected in the first Constitution of 1962, which devolved substantial power to the kingdoms in the South (especially Buganda) and left the central state relatively weak. The kingdoms had their own powers to tax, their own budgets and substantial autonomy in service provision; self-help was mainly mobilized through the system of chiefs. In the rest of Uganda state services were provided through district councils, but they received only limited funds from the centre. These areas remained deprived compared with the South, despite general service improvements up to the early 1970s. The imbalance was amplified by the historic concentration of church-based services in the South.

The post-colonial semi-federal arrangement of the state was short-lived. Ethnic and class conflicts tore it apart and the immediate post-independence political alliances collapsed. From 1967 Obote's regime ruled a unitary state with military backing but with decreasing popular support. A dictatorial state gradually suppressed all local-level institutions that could give form to local initiatives. This suppression was continued during Amin's regime, but was eased somewhat when Obote returned to power.

NGOs were important providers of services during the first decade of independence, although their role was gradually changed and eventually curtailed. On the one hand, the Obote regime deliberately enlarged the capacity of the state in service provision. Mission schools, for example, came under direct state control. On the other hand, NGOs were allowed to operate 'traditional' services such as health, and were generally given more room to operate in the remoter areas. In any case, the regime regarded the role of NGOs as transitional, pending takeover by the state when resources became available.

However, the political impetus for state-provided services declined at the end of Obote's first regime. A few years after Amin's seizure of power in 1971, service provision by the state disintegrated, the economy stagnated, institutions in civil society were further suppressed, and most donors and foreign NGOs withdrew. The churches remained the only major providers of services. By 1980 the vital social infrastructure had deteriorated substantially.

From 1980 onwards there has been a significant increase in the number of POs and NGOs involved in service provision. Unlike in Kenya and Tanzania,

---

[28] This section is based on Chapter 12 of this book; Brett (1992); Mudoola (1985); Republic of Uganda (1987); Hansen and Twaddle (1991); and de Coninck (1992).

their activities have been largely based on local resource mobilization without much support from the state. Only since 1986, when the National Resistance Council took power and the civil war died out, has the state begun to take an active role in service provision again, as discussed in detail in Chapter 12.

## Political Implications

As we have seen, a key feature of service provision in East Africa is the growing importance of the voluntary sector. What are the likely political implications of this? Obviously there are no clear-cut answers, but it is possible to give certain indications.

From a formal point of view, it is important to note that the political activities of registered NGOs and POs were banned in Kenya and Tanzania until the introduction of multi-partyism, and this is still the case in the non-party state of Uganda. Such restrictions on the political activities of voluntary organizations are certainly likely to continue under the multi-partyism that has now been introduced in Kenya and Tanzania. This is in line with the experience of other countries (Robinson, 1993). States everywhere insist that voluntary organizations should be both non-profit-making and non-political, although the legislation on the voluntary sector may be written in terms like 'the need for co-ordination', the need to 'protect NGOs from donor misuse', the need to 'prevent abuse of NGO status' and 'security reasons' (Fowler, 1991: 65). Perhaps the general feature of the voluntary sector legislation on these issues in East Africa is that decisions are left *de facto* to the discretion of the regulating agencies.[29]

While such legal aspects of voluntary sector regulation do reflect state intentions, actual practice may differ. Rules are broken and voluntary sector agencies may pursue political goals in various indirect and circumscribed ways. The extent to which this actually happens is obviously difficult to ascertain, although various examples are presented in this book. And the relevant theoretical literature is divided on this issue, as are the contributors to this book.

The optimistic view is that the overall growth in the voluntary sector contributes significantly to the democratization of society. The theoretical arguments are very general and not specifically focused on service provision – or indeed on empirical research. Diamond (1988: 26) is a good example of this. He argues that NGOs are 'small-scale settings for meaningful political participation' that contribute to the 'cumulative processes of decision-making'. Bratton (1989: 585) is more guarded. He argues that NGOs have an important political role to play in Africa, provided that they 'can offer ordinary people an opportunity to participate in decisions and represent local interests'. NGOs have the 'potential to assemble scattered social groups into integrated social movements' and '[b]y building independent organizations' NGOs have already helped to pluralize the institutional landscape and strengthen civil society. Moreover, NGOs reinforce

---

[29] On Kenya see Barkan (1992) and Kanyinga (1993). On Tanzania see Kiondo (1993); on Uganda see de Coninck (1992) and Mushi *et al.* (1992).

popular demands and empower members to assemble to take collective development action (Bratton, 1990).

Landell-Mills' reasons for optimism (1992: 567) are more closely related to the role of the voluntary sector in service provision. He argues that when NGOs and POs mobilize their own resources to pay for social services it weakens the central authorities. Furthermore, this resource mobilization is accompanied by 'more participatory forms of delivering essential services, as well as by the empowerment of beneficiaries and local NGOs'. This, he claims, is crucial to building a stronger civil society. 'It is such trends that lie behind the call for democracy now being witnessed across Africa.'[30]

The opposing view is based on two arguments. One is that the optimism is not supported by empirical evidence. Financial and personal links between the state and the voluntary sector have increased significantly in the 1980s, as shown in this chapter. The voluntary sector is *not* therefore becoming more independent of the state, as claimed by the optimists. Moreover, historical evidence presented above indicates that it is POs – rather than NGOs – that have so far played the most important political role. And this has perhaps tended to strengthen clientelist politics and the elite–factional grip on power, as Ngau (1987) argues. Similarly Fowler (1991: 73–4) observes that governments have so far been able to ensure that grass-roots organizations in both Kenya and Tanzania are often mobilized from above, with voluntary contributions tending to be replaced by compulsory ones. He also observes that 'few NGOs, whether indigenous or foreign, have democratic structures which enable their actions to be controlled by those they serve'. He concludes that the 'expansion of the NGO sector will strengthen the existing political economy of African states rather than restructure it'.

Linking the growth of the voluntary sector to democratization is also challenged by more theoretical arguments. Gibbon (1993a), for example, does not equate pluralism and democracy as Bratton, Diamond and Landell-Mills tend to do. Instead, he argues that some types of pluralism may in fact have a negative impact on the democratic process. When civil society in a capitalist society is made up of associations that pursue individualized or private projects rather than socio-political projects based on general interests, then the growth of the voluntary sector may actually depoliticize civil society.

It is premature to assess the merits of these various arguments. Evidence certainly challenges the optimistic view, while the pessimistic one is perhaps too static. The fact that groups organize to improve service provisions for themselves today does not exclude their interest in raising political demands in the future, as Gibbon seems to suggest. Certainly the macro-political environment is changing rapidly, and all three East African countries are in the process of developing multi-partyism. It is too early to predict how this may affect the political impact of the voluntary sector – or, indeed, whether this political transition is sustainable.

---

[30]  Chapter 4 on Kenya, in particular, and to some extent Chapter 14 on Uganda share such optimism, although their arguments are not identical to those quoted above.

## The Role of the Donors

Service provision in East Africa is no longer just a domestic affair, as was shown earlier. Many services currently provided by the state or the voluntary sector would deteriorate considerably if foreign aid was stopped. However, the character of donor involvement in state-provided services has changed significantly over the years. This has several political implications.

In the first decades after independence Western aid was driven by Cold War competition, an emphasis on industrialization, and Western interest in basic needs which fitted well with the aspirations of the new states for social service provision. Funds were mainly given to projects and typically tied to purchases in the donor country. Almost all assistance to service provision was channelled through the state bureaucracies, especially the central government. Local governments never received much donor support. There was a similar donor bias against grass-roots self-help during the early years of independence, although such activities were widespread in all three countries at that time (see Chapter 2). These biases helped to strengthen the centralization of the new regimes (Wunsch and Olowu, 1990) and undermined the voluntary sector.

As Africa has become marginalized in the global economy and in global politics, dependence on external aid has grown (Callaghy and Ravenhill, 1993). Aid conditionalities have increased in detail and in scope. Now – after the end of the Cold War – Western donors openly seek influence on a broad range of macro- and micro-level policy issues concerned with political, economic and administrative reforms.

Political reforms came to the fore from the mid-1980s. Human rights protection, civil liberties, the rule of law and multi-party democracy entered the aid negotiation agendas under the new catch phrase 'good governance' (*IDS Bulletin*, 1993). Apart from the ideological impetus for this trend, many donors now regard political reform as a precondition for aid effectiveness. Political conditionalities are backed with economic clout, as President Moi experienced when aid to Kenya was suspended in November 1991 awaiting the results of the multi-party elections in December 1992. His victory at the polls has, however, not yet brought Kenya back to the ranks of the favoured aid recipients.

Economic reform is also part of the good governance concept. The Structural Adjustment Programmes funded and often designed under heavy pressure from Western donors aim at economic liberalization, but are now modified – though not significantly changed – following pressures from both within and outside Africa. Their main concerns include fiscal balance, export-led growth, the setting up of a market economy, and privatization. They often affect social services through attempts to reduce budget deficits by improving state revenues (including cost recovery through user fees) and cost reductions, by promoting the role of the voluntary and the private sector, and by changing incentives to economic actors. However, many SAPs fail to produce quick recovery as intended. According to Helleiner (1992), a main reason is that adjusting countries, despite considerable domestic restructuring, have not received the external financial support that was a precondition for the success of the reform. And debt servicing remains a huge unsolved problem. On the other hand, it is undoubtedly the recent injections of foreign aid that have enabled the three East African states to increase allocations to the social services, as noted earlier in this chapter. Long-term economic growth is a precondition for a sustainable role on the part of the state and voluntary agencies in service provision – and the prospects for this are not good (Stewart, 1991; Mosley and Weeks, 1993).

Administrative reforms are also increasingly on the agenda of SAPs. The aim is to reduce the direct role of the state across the board (including in service provision), and to promote efficiency (especially to reduce corruption) and accountability. However, aid tends to be channelled through the recipient bureaucracies in ways that significantly affect the actual implementation of state-provided services. Assessments of the implementation and effects of such reforms are still premature, however.[31]

Although administrative reforms are often pushed by donors, they tend to be a significant part of the problem. The Kenya Government, for example, deals with about forty different donors. More than that operate in Tanzania (Mushi and Kjekshus, 1982). To this should be added a growing number of foreign-funded NGOs, whose number easily exceeds that of donor agencies. The effects on recipient administration of this multitude of donor-funded activities are frequently negative (Meyer, 1992). In some cases, regions of a country are divided among donor-funded projects. In other cases the division is done along sectoral lines (Mukandala, 1992). Large numbers of these aid projects are controlled by staff employed by the donors, who operate according to their own guidelines and bypass recipient bureaucracies in the process. Many of them are failures and have, in addition, fragmented and weakened many state agencies (Morss, 1984).

These attempts to restructure the state have direct implications for the voluntary sector. Donors tend to regard NGOs and POs as democratic, self-reliant, poverty-oriented and efficient organizations[32] in contrast to the authoritarian, donor-dependent and inefficient state organizations involved in service provision. As shown earlier, donor funds are increasingly channelled through the voluntary sector. They grow much faster than donor aid to states.

Nor is external support to NGOs and POs politically neutral. Tensions between states and NGOs are likely to heighten as donors shift resources towards the latter, for this reduces the dependence and allegiance of the NGOs to the state in which they operate (see Chapter 3). But tensions among NGOs may also increase because Western states tend to favour Christian over Muslim NGOs. Chapter 11 describes how this is causing problems in Tanzania. It should be added that, if NGOs align themselves to the emerging political parties, then donor support to NGOs will become an important and controversial factor in local politics.

---

[31] See special issue of *Public Administration and Development* (1993).
[32] Cernea (1988) is a good example. See also the list of books reviewed by Hashemi (1991).

# Conclusions

Privatization of social services in East Africa has taken place on a grand scale since independence, but not in ways that fit easily with textbook or Structural Adjustment Programme prescriptions. NGOs and POs – not primarily profit-making entrepreneurs – play an increasing role in service provision. This is certainly the case for basic services such as education and health, but the provision of law and order, a classic primary state prerogative, is also increasingly done by grass-roots organizations.

Moreover, the links between the voluntary sector and the state are becoming more, not less, important for service provision. Significant parts of educational and health services, for example, would grind to a halt if voluntary agencies did not have access to state-provided resources. In fact, much grass-roots mobilization of resources aims at attracting state support, failing which local initiatives would die or survive only where the local resource base is sufficient. Similarly, many voluntary agencies are run by or through state employees. This straddling between the public and the voluntary sector is a key feature of privatization of service provision in East Africa. Finally, donors play a growing political and financial role in service provision. State-provided services depend increasingly on donor resources, at least in Tanzania and Uganda. The voluntary sector is also driven by donor funds to a significant degree. A key feature of the privatization of service provision in East Africa is therefore not just the increasing role of the voluntary sector, but the continued centrality of the state – and donors.

It is remarkable that these trends are common to all three countries. Past differences among them in the way that services were provided are disappearing, although the civil unrest in Uganda that is now abating has reduced the role of the state and donors in service provision significantly, compared with Kenya and Tanzania. But the societal arrangements for service provision are converging under the pressure of political and economic forces that originate both from the outside (dependence on donors and global markets) and from the inside (social differentiation and political struggles).

In the short term the most certain implication of the above is that the role of the state and the donors is crucial for service provision in East Africa. Not only because state-provided services are significant in themselves, but also because, without links to state and donors, many voluntary sector services would cease to function. Experience from Uganda when the state collapsed during the civil unrest shows *both* the considerable resilience of the voluntary sector (expansions in social service infrastructure) *and* its limitations (widening inequity in access and drastically reduced quality of services).

The long-term implications of 'privatization' for service provision are much more difficult to assess. The optimistic view is that we are witnessing a mush-rooming and strengthening of civil society, leading to democratization which will make the state more accountable and efficient. Democratization and the successful implementation of Structural Adjustment Programmes will also promote economic growth. The state, in turn, will establish the enabling environment that allows the voluntary sector to flourish. Sustainability of services will be secured. The pessimistic view is that the location of NGOs and POs in civil society tells us very little about the values and constituencies that they represent, and therefore little about how they operate *vis-à-vis* the state or their members/beneficiaries. In fact, their close links to local elites and their dependence on patronage from the state and donors make their role in a democratization process ambiguous. Moreover, the long-term prospects for economic growth, which is a precondition for any domestically sustainable provision of services, are also in doubt – the short-term effects of Structural Adjustment Programmes notwithstanding. For years to come, the sustainability of many service will depend on uncertain donor support.

Both views are represented in this book, although individual authors may not subscribe to all the positions outlined above and some authors take no explicit position. The optimistic view is represented by Hyden (Chapter 2), Kanyinga (Chapter 4), Anangwe (Chapter 6), Ishumi (Chapter 9), Nabuguzi (Chapter 12) and Tidemand (Chapter 14). The cautious view is presented by Therkildsen and Semboja (Chapter 1), Fowler (Chapter 3), Makau (Chapter 5), Oyugi (Chapter 7), and Passi (Chapter 13). It is, perhaps, significant that the authors writing on Kenya and Uganda seem more optimistic than those writing on Tanzania.

Whatever the future of service provision, all attempts to improve it must come to terms with the specific character of 'privatization' in East Africa examined by this publication, among others.

# References

Adam, C., Cavendish, W. and Mistry, P.S. (1992) *Adjusting Privatization: Case Studies from Developing Countries*. London: James Currey.

African Development Bank (1992) *African Development Report 1992*. Abidjan: African Development Bank.

Ayoade, J.A.A. (1988) 'States without Citizens: An Emerging African Phenomenon' in Rothchild and Chazan.

Azarya, V. (1988) 'Reordering State–Society Relations: Incorporation and Disengagement' in Rothchild and Chazan.

Barkan, J.D. (ed.) (1984) *Politics and Public Policy in Kenya and Tanzania*. Revised edition. Nairobi: Heinemann Kenya.

Barkan, J.D. (1992) 'The Rise and Fall of a Governance Realm in Kenya' in Hyden and Bratton.

Barkan, J.D. with Chege, M. (1989) 'Decentralising the State: District Focus and the Politics of Reallocation', *Journal of Modern African Studies* 27 (3): 431–54.

Barkan, J.D. and Holmquist, F. (1989) 'Peasant–State Relations and the Social Base of Self-help in Kenya', *World Politics* XLI (3): 359–80.

Bevan, D., Collier, P. and Gunning, J.W. (1989) *Peasants and Governments: An Economic Analysis*. Oxford: Clarendon Press.

Bloom, G., Singleton, G. and Toye, J. (1992) 'Public Expenditure in the Tanzanian

Health Sector During Structural Adjustment'. Report, June. Brussels: European Community.

Booth, D. (1987) 'Alternatives in the Restructuring of State–Society Relations: Research Issues for Tropical Africa', *IDS Bulletin* 18 (4): 23–30.

Bratton, M. (1989) 'The Politics of Government–NGO Relations in Africa', *World Development* 17 (4): 569–87.

Bratton, M. (1990) 'Non-Governmental Organizations in Africa: Can They Influence Public Policy?' *Development and Change* 21 (1): 87–118.

Brett, E.A. (1992) *Providing for the Rural Poor: Institutional Decay and Transformation in Uganda*. Research Report 23. Brighton: Institute of Development Studies, University of Sussex.

Bryceson, D.F. (1993) *Liberalizing Tanzania's Food Trade: The Public and Private Process of Urban Marketing Policy 1939–1988*. London: James Currey.

Callaghy, T.M. and Ravenhill, J. (eds) (1993) *Hemmed in: Responses to Africa's Economic Decline*. New York: Columbia University Press.

Cernea, M.M. (1988) *Nongovernmental Organizations and Local Development*. World Bank Discussion Papers No. 40. Washington, DC: World Bank.

Chazan, N., Mortimer, R., Ravenhill, J. and Rothchild, D. (1988) *Politics and Society in Contemporary Africa*. London: Macmillan.

Cohen, J.M. and Hook, R.M. (1987) 'Decentralized Planning in Kenya', *Public Administration and Development* 7 (1): 77–93.

Collier, P., Radwan, S. and Wangwe, S. (1986) *Labour and Poverty in Rural Tanzania*. Oxford: Clarendon Press.

de Coninck, J. (1992) *Evaluating the Impact of NGOs in Rural Poverty Alleviation: Uganda Country Study*. ODI Working Paper No. 51. London: Overseas Development Institute.

Cook, P. and Kirkpatrick, C. (eds) (1988) *Privatization in Lesser Developed Countries*. Brighton: Wheatsheaf.

Diamond, L. (1988) 'Roots of Failure, Seeds of Hope' in Diamond, L., Linz, J. and Lipsett, S. (eds) *Democracy in Developing Countries: Africa Vol. 2*. Boulder, CO: Lynne Rienner.

van Donge, K. and Liviga, A.J. (1986) 'Tanzanian Political Culture and the Cabinet', *Journal of Modern African Studies* 24 (4): 619–39.

Ebel, B. (1991) *Patterns of Government Expenditures in Developing Countries during the 1980s: The Impact on Social Services*. Innocenti Occasional Papers, Economic Policy Series No.18. Florence: UNICEF International Development Centre.

Esman, M.J. (1991) *Management Dimensions of Development: Perspectives and Strategies*. West Hartford, CT: Kumarian Press.

Fowler, A. (1991) 'The Role of NGOs in Changing State–Society Relations: Perspectives from Eastern and Southern Africa', *Development Policy Review* 9 (1): 53–84.

Fowler, A. (1992) 'Distant Obligations: Speculations on NGO Funding and the Global Market', *Review of African Political Economy* 55: 9–29.

Gibbon, P. (1993a) 'Civil Society and Political Change'. Paper presented at workshop on Experiences of Political Liberalization in Africa, 3–4 June. Copenhagen: Centre for Development Research.

Gibbon, P. (ed.) (1993b) *Social Change and Economic Reform in Africa*. Uppsala: Scandinavian Institute of African Studies.

Hansen, H.B. and Twaddle, M. (eds) (1991) *Changing Uganda: The Dilemma of Structural Adjustment and Revolutionary Change*. London: James Currey.

Hardiman, M. and Midgley, J. (1989) *The Social Dimensions of Development: Social Policy and Planning in the Third World*. Second edition. Aldershot: Gower.

Hashemi, S.M. (1991) 'Review Article: The NGO Participatory Development Paradigm', *Journal of International Development* 3 (4): 421–6.

Havnevik, K.J. (1993) *Tanzania: The Limits to Development from Above*. Uppsala: Scandinavian Institute of African Studies.

Healy, J. and Robinson, M. (1992) *Democracy, Governance and Economic Policy*. London: Overseas Development Institute.

Helleiner, G.K. (1992) 'The IMF, the World Bank and Africa's Adjustment and External Debt Problems: An Unofficial View', *World Development* 20 (6): 779–92.

Hill, M. (1991) *The Harambee Movement in Kenya: Self-Help, Development and Education among the Kamba of Kitui District*. London: The Athlone Press.

Holmquist, F. (1984) 'Class Structure, Peasant Participation, and Rural Self-Help' in Barkan.

Hyden, G. and Bratton, M. (eds) (1992) *Governance and Politics in Africa*. Boulder, CO: Lynne Rienner Publishers.

*IDS Bulletin* (1993) 'Good Government?' *IDS Bulletin* 24 (1).

Iliffe, J. (1979) *A Modern History of Tanganyika*. Cambridge: Cambridge University Press.

Kanyinga, K. (1993) 'The Socio-Political Context of the Growth of Non-Governmental Organizations in Kenya' in Gibbon.

Kiondo, A.S.Z. (1993) 'Structural Adjustment and Non-Governmental Organizations in Tanzania: A Case Study' in Gibbon.

Kitching, G. (1980) *Class and Economic Change in Kenya. The Making of an African Petite-Bourgeoisie*. New Haven, CT: Yale University Press.

Kjærby, F. (1989) 'Unpaid Self-help Labour in Rural Roads Construction and Maintenance in Ruvuma Region'. Report prepared for the Prime Minister's Office and ILO. Copenhagen: Centre for Development Research.

Landell-Mills, P. (1992) 'Governance, Cultural Change, and Empowerment', *Journal of Modern African Studies* 30 (4): 543–67.

Lemarchand, R. (1988) 'The State, the Parallel Economy, and the Changing Structure of Patronage Systems' in Rothchild and Chazan.

Leys, C. (1975) *Underdevelopment in Kenya. The Political Economy of Neo-Colonialism*. London: Heinemann.

Mabala, R. (1990) 'A Summary of NGOs' Financing of Health Service in Tanzania'. Dar es Salaam: University of Dar es Salaam (mimeo).

Mabala, W. (1989) 'Nationalism and Decolonialization' in Ochieng'.

Mamdani, M. (1975) 'Class Struggles in Uganda', *Review of African Political Economy* 6 (4): 26–61.

Mbithi, P.M. and Rasmusson, R. (1977) *Self Reliance in Kenya: The Case of Harambee*. Uppsala: Scandinavian Institute of African Studies.

Meyer, C.A. (1992) 'A Step Back as Donors Shift Institution Building from the Public to the "Private Sector"', *World Development* 20 (8): 1115–26.

Morss, E.R. (1984) 'Institutional Destruction Resulting from Donor and Project Proliferation in Sub-Saharan Africa', *World Development* 12 (4): 465–70.

Mosley, P. (1987) *Overseas Aid: Its Defence and Reform*. Brighton: Wheatsheaf.

Mosley, P. and Weeks, J. (1993) 'Has Recovery Begun? "Africa's Adjustment in the 1980s" Revisited', *World Development* 21 (10): 1583–606.

Mudoola, D. (1985) 'Post Colonial Politics in Uganda: An Interpretation', *Mawazo* 6 (2): 19–29.

Mukandala, R.S. (1992) 'To Be or Not to Be: The Paradoxes of African Bureaucracies in the 1990s', *International Review of Administrative Sciences* 58 (4): 555–76.

Munishi, G.K. (1992) 'Health Services Delivery in Tanzania: Some Qualitative Differences between Government and Non-Government Primary Health Care Units'. Paper presented at Seminar on State vs. NGOs in Provision of Services in Eastern Africa, 22–24 July. Dar es Salaam: Economic Research Bureau, University of Dar es Salaam.

Mushi, S.S. and Kjekshus, H. (eds) (1982) *Aid and Development. Some Tanzanian Experiences.* Oslo: Norwegian Institute of International Affairs.

Mushi, S.S., Semboja, J. and Therkildsen, O. (1992) 'Issues of Service Provision in the 1990s in Eastern Africa'. Paper presented at Seminar on State vs. NGOs in Provision of Services in Eastern Africa, 22–24 July. Dar es Salaam: Economic Research Bureau, University of Dar es Salaam.

Ngau, P.M. (1987) 'Tensions in Empowerment: The Experience of the *Harambee* (Self-help) Movement in Kenya', *Economic Development and Cultural Change* 35 (3): 523–38.

Nypan, A. (1991) 'Women's Work and Strategies for Control of Resources: Changes in the Position of Rural Women in Tanzania', *Forum for Utviklingsstudier* 1: 79–97.

Ochieng', W.R. (ed.) (1989) *A Modern History of Kenya, 1895–1980.* Nairobi: Evans Brothers (Kenya) Ltd.

Olorunsola, U.A. and Muhwezi, D. (1988) 'State Responses to Disintegration and Withdrawal: Adjustment in the Political Economy' in Rothchild and Chazan.

Patton, J. (1993) *The Intra-Household Allocation of Resources. Is There Evidence of Gender Bias?* Development Studies Working Papers No. 58. Oxford: Queen Elizabeth House, University of Oxford.

Pitt, M. and Levy, V. (1992) 'The Intrahousehold Allocation of Medical Care in Ghana' in IFPRI *Understanding How Resources are Allocated within Households.* Washington, DC: International Food Policy Research Institute.

*Public Administration and Development* (1993) 'Reforming Public Sector Management in Centrally Planned and Transitional Economies', Special issue 13 (4).

Republic of Uganda (1987) *Report of the Commission of Inquiry into the Local Government System.* Entebbe: Government Printer.

Republic of Uganda (1991a) *Background to the Budget 1990–91.* Kampala: Ministry of Planning and Economic Development.

Republic of Uganda (1991b) *Report on the Uganda National Household Budget, 1989–90.* Statistics Department, Ministry of Planning and Economic Development, February. Entebbe: Government Printer.

Riddell, R. (1990) *Judging Success. Evaluating NGO Approaches to Alleviating Poverty in Developing Countries.* ODI Working Paper No. 37, May. London: Overseas Development Institute.

Riddell, R. and Robinson, M. (1992) *The Impact of NGO Poverty Alleviation Projects: Results of the Case Study Evaluations.* ODI Working Paper No. 68. London: Overseas Development Institute.

Robinson, M. (1993) 'Governance, Democracy and Conditionality: NGOs and the New Policy Agenda'. Intrac Workshop, Amersfoort, 4–6 June. Oxford: Intrac.

Roth, G. (1987) *The Private Provision of Public Services in Developing Countries.* Oxford: Oxford University Press.

Rothchild, D. and Chazan, N. (eds) (1988) *The Precarious Balance. State and Society in Africa.* Boulder, CO: Westview Press.

Rothchild, D. and Foley, M.W. (1988) 'African States and the Politics of Inclusive Coalitions' in Rothchild and Chazan.

Samoff, J. (1991) 'The Facade of Precision in Education Data and Statistics: A Troubling Example from Tanzania', *Journal of Modern African Studies* 29 (4): 669–89.

Semboja, J. (1992) 'The Impact of the Economic Recovery Programme (ERP) on the Provision of Social Services'. Report prepared for the World Bank, December. Dar es Salaam: World Bank.

Semboja, J. and Therkildsen, O. (1989) *Recurrent Cost Financing at District Level in Tanzania*. CDR Working Paper 89.5. Copenhagen: Centre for Development Research.

Semboja, J. and Therkildsen, O. (1994) 'Decentralization, Participation and Spatial Equity in Rural Tanzania: A Comment', *World Development* 22 (5): 807–10.

Shivji, I.G. (1976) *Class Struggles in Tanzania*. London: Heinemann.

Shivji, I.G. (1991) 'Law, Democracy and the Rights-Struggle', *UDASA Newsletter* 13 July.

Silberschmidt, M. (1991) *Women's Position in the Household and Their Use of Family Planning and Antenatal Services*. CDR Project Papers No. 91.4. Copenhagen: Centre for Development Research.

Smoke, P. (1993) 'Local Government Fiscal Reform in Developing Countries: Lessons from Kenya', *World Development* 21 (6): 901–23.

Stewart, F. (1991) 'The Many Faces of Adjustment', *World Development* 19 (12): 1847–64.

Tadreg (1992) 'Poverty Focused Primary Education Project for Tanzania Mainland: A Description and Analysis of Key Data'. Report. Dar es Salaam: Tanzania Development Research Group.

Therkildsen, O. (1989) *Watering White Elephants? Experiences from Donor-Funded Rural Water Supply Programmes in Tanzania*. Uppsala: Scandinavian Institute of African Studies.

Therkildsen, O. (1993) 'Primary Education and Local Government: Who Decides, Pays and Benefits?' Paper prepared for the workshop on 'Quality and Equity Issues in Tanzanian Education Policy and Practice: Insights from Research'. 15–16 December. Dar es Salaam: Tadreg.

Therkildsen, O. and Semboja, J. (1992) 'Short-term Resource Mobilization for Recurrent Financing of Rural Local Governments in Tanzania', *World Development* 20 (8): 1101–13.

Tripp, A.M. (1992) 'Local Organizations, Participation, and the State in Urban Tanzania' in Hyden and Bratton.

Turok, B. (ed.) (1991) *Debt and Democracy: Alternative Strategies for Africa*. London: Institute for African Alternatives.

UNDP (1992, 1993) *Human Development Report*. Oxford: Oxford University Press.

UNICEF (1992) *The State of the World's Children, 1992*. Oxford: Oxford University Press.

Uphoff, N. (1986) *Local Institutional Development: An Analytical Sourcebook with Cases*. West Hartford, CT: Kumarian Press.

Whyte, S.R. (1991) 'Medicines and Self-help: The Privatization of Health Care in Eastern Uganda' in Hansen and Twaddle.

Widner, J.A. (1992) *The Rise of the Poverty-State in Kenya. From Harambee! to Nyayo!* Berkeley, CA: University of California Press.

World Bank (1981) *Accelerated Development in Sub-Saharan Africa*. Washington, DC: World Bank.

World Bank (1987) 'Uganda Health Sector Service in Developing Contries. An Agenda for Reform'. Washington, DC: World Bank.

World Bank (1989) 'Kenya: Public Expenditure Review'. Report No. 7588-KE. 14 April. Washington, DC: World Bank.

World Bank (various years) *World Development Report*. Washington, DC: World Bank.

World Bank (1991a) 'Uganda: Public Choices for Private Initiatives'. Report No. 9203-UG, 12 February. Washington, DC: World Bank.

World Bank (1991b) 'Kenya. Human Resources: Improving Quality and Access.' Report No. 9023-KE. 7 June. Washington, DC: World Bank.

World Bank (1992a) 'Kenya. Re-investing in Stabilization and Growth through Public Sector Adjustment'. Report No. 9998-KE. 10 January. Washington, DC: World Bank.

World Bank (1992b) 'The Third Report on Adjustment Lending: Private and Public Resources for Growth'. Report, 24 March. IDA/R92-29. Washington, DC: World Bank.

World Bank (1993) 'Uganda: Social Sector Strategy'. Report No. 10765-UG. 6 April. Washington, DC: World Bank.

Wunsch, J. (1991) 'Institutional Analysis and Decentralization: Developing an Analytical Framework for Effective Third World Administrative Reform', *Public Administration and Development* 11 (5): 431–51.

Wunsch, J.S. and Olowu, D. (eds) (1990) *The Failure of the Centralized State: Institutions and Self-Governance in Africa*. Boulder, CO: Westview Press.

Wuyts, M. (1992) 'Deprivation and Public Need' in M. Wuyts, M. Mackintosh and T. Hewitt (eds) *Development Policy and Public Action*. Oxford: Oxford University Press.

Young, C. (1988) 'The African Colonial State and its Political Legacy' in Rothchild and Chazan.

# 2  GORAN HYDEN
## Bringing Voluntarism Back In

Eastern Africa
in Comparative Perspective

In recent years so much of both public and academic discourse about African development has centred on the dichotomy between the state and the market. Following the dominance of a state-directed strategy in the 1960s and 1970s, the structural adjustment policies of the 1980s have swung the pendulum full force in the direction of the market. What has been overlooked is the whole sphere between the two, which relies on neither coercive power nor profit maximization as its prime motivating force. This sphere, which depends instead on voluntarism, has become known in Africa as the NGO sector, named after its principal actors – non-governmental organizations. In many other areas it is referred to as the voluntary sector. The argument of this chapter is that it has been overlooked in Africa not only by politicians and practitioners but also by academics. There is relatively little written on NGOs in Africa which tries to conceptualize their role in the ongoing economic and political transition on the continent. Bratton's (1989a and b) contributions constitute the principal exception.

This chapter is divided into five sections. The first examines the role of voluntarism in industrial societies, drawing primarily on the observations on America made in the early part of the nineteenth century by de Tocqueville (1945). The second discusses voluntarism in Africa in the pre-independence period and relates it to the arguments of de Tocqueville. The third analyses why so much of the voluntarism that existed in Africa was discouraged in the post-independence era. The fourth examines the current challenges for strengthening voluntary action in the context of economic and political liberalization. The final section draws out some of the implications of the argumentation that are relevant for both further research and policy action.

## Voluntarism in Industrial Societies

The United States of America is usually portrayed as the best example of a country with a strong sense of voluntarism. Americans have often used such action not only to complement government services but also to hold the state at bay. The French traveller and theorist, Alexis de Tocqueville, conveyed to the rest of the world this impression of the US as the place where voluntary associations are particularly prominent.

When he visited North America in the 1830s, he was impressed by the diversity of these associations and the seriousness with which their members took them. He repeatedly referred in his writings to the role that such groups as churches, fraternal associations, community groups and civil organizations played in the lives of the American people. They did for themselves through these voluntary efforts what people in other societies expected governments and elites to do for them. When some tragedy befell them or they needed to undertake some project, they just banded together to get the job done. The result, he thought, was a much stronger and more vibrant democratic society (de Tocqueville, 1945).

But these associations were important, in de Tocqueville's view, not only because of their contribution to democracy, but also as mechanisms for express- ing and sustaining the nation's values. Because they were voluntary, they were more likely than any other type of organization in society to represent the values of the people. The nation's religious organizations provided a crucible in which spiritual convictions could be tested. By supplying assistance to the disadvantaged, voluntary organizations helped underscore the importance of such values as caring and helping. Fraternal associations, guilds and self-help groups reinforced the value of community itself. In short, these voluntary associations also con- tributed to the cultural vitality of the country.

Generations of scholars have followed in de Tocqueville's footsteps and emphasized the importance of the voluntary sector. Taking their cue from him, many, on both the political right (e.g. Carnoy, 1984; Bellah et al., 1985) and left (e.g. Poulantzas, 1978), have stressed the connection between voluntary associations and political participation and the point that needs unmet by voluntary efforts provide an excuse for government to intervene. With intervention typically comes control, and with control a top-down approach.

A long time has, of course, passed since de Tocqueville wrote his journals about America. The latter has changed. Both market and state have become more important and the voluntary sector has been reined in by their growth. It has become necessary to provide extensive pieces of legislation to identify the boundaries between the private, public and voluntary sectors. With this institutionalization of the three sectors has come an increased differentiation. The private sector is more exclusively profit-oriented and concerned with efficiency in returns on financial investments. The public sector has become increasingly 'bureaucratized' in the sense of being highly legalistic and rule- oriented. The voluntary sector has become the exclusive reservoir of civic values. This is where concern for others and a sense of community flourish. As a result, this sector is also the strongest guardian of egalitarian values in American society; it is its social and cultural backbone. Although no one can say this for sure, the voluntary sector is probably as strong today as it was in the

1830s. What is definitely different is the power of the other two sectors, which may be the reason why voluntarism is not viewed as being so prominent today as in the days of de Tocqueville.

Nevertheless, voluntarism is much more evident in the US than it is in European countries, where, by tradition, people have been more ready to turn welfare activities over to the state. While in the US the principal contradiction in people's minds has always been between the state and the individual, i.e. how much control should government exercise over the life of the individual, the equivalent in Europe has always been the conflict between classes over the control of the state. It is not the state *per se,* but which group controls it, that has been the main issue there.

These contrasts are brought out very clearly in a recent comparative study of voluntarism in industrial societies (Wuthnow, 1991). In many European countries which have grown used to effective state action to secure the welfare of citizens, voluntary action is seen as only second-best and a step in the wrong direction. That is why attempts to trim the expenses for social welfare by turning certain activities over to private or voluntary groups run into much opposition in Europe and why the ongoing structural adjustment policies there are hard to implement. There seems to be much less social elasticity in European countries than there is in the United States. The contrast between Reagan and Thatcher was telling. While Reagan's policies were widely supported in the US and both private and voluntary efforts were ready to fill the gaps left by a retreating state (though in practice it has turned out impossible to fill all of them), Thatcher could only succeed by riding roughshod over society and, by virtue of a comfortable parliamentary majority, impose legislation that reduced benefits paid to citizens. In the end, patience had run out even within her own ranks and she became the victim of a party mutiny.

In short, voluntarism in Europe has never been such a distinct entity as it has in the United States. Voluntarism has been integrated into the other sectors in the sense that, as business person or bureaucrat, everybody is expected to show concern for others. Community values permeate both state and market in ways that one does not find in the US. What is important to note for the purposes of this book, however, is how little effort has been made to extend the comparison of voluntarism to other regions of the world.

## Voluntarism in Colonial Africa

It is a not unreasonable proposition to make that, had de Tocqueville come to Africa in the 1950s, he would have been equally impressed by the evidence of voluntarism that he would have found there at the time. In fact, it may be Africa rather than North America that should be viewed as the continent where the tradition of voluntarism is most pronounced.

We know from many sources, notably Thomas Hodgkin's (1956) work, how important voluntary associations were in the struggle for independence. Because explicitly political organizations were prohibited, African nationalists had to develop their thoughts through involvement in church groups, sports and recreation clubs, community self-help associations, and trade unions. It was here that the first challenges to colonial rule emerged. One can speculate about the origins of these organizations, but there is little doubt that they built on a long self-help tradition in African society. Because African societies were either stateless or had developed only the most rudimentary elements of a state, there was no expectation that the king or the chief would provide welfare measures for the population. To be sure, much of the legitimacy of the ruler rested with his ability to provide security against external threats, but, in terms of 'day-to-day' problems, people were expected to look after themselves. Societies were typically organized to that effect, whether by clan or by age.

This principle of voluntary action at the grass-roots level was important in many parts of Africa for the purposes of building schools and sending students to universities overseas. Studies of improvement associations in eastern Nigeria (Ottenberg, 1955) and of independent schools and other efforts among the Kikuyu (Lonsdale, 1968) confirm not only the substantive benefits that followed from such action but also its political significance in terms of promoting the growth of an African elite opposed to colonial rule. The seminal study of the roots of African nationalism in Nigeria by the late James S. Coleman (1958) pulls together evidence of the full breadth of associational life among the Africans as the process of decolonization set in.

Acknowledging the importance of an indigenous self-help tradition in Africa should not make us lose sight of the fact that colonial rule triggered it into a new direction for two reasons. First, the limited scope of the colonial state left Africans with an increasing number of unmet needs, especially as modernization under colonial rule changed their habits and enhanced their expectations. Many African associations were therefore were formed to meet needs that the colonial state either explicitly ignored or to which it paid only scant attention. Secondly, the discriminatory policies of the colonial state had the effect of alienating the more educated and well-travelled segments of the population in particular, who formed associations to protect and promote their own interests *vis-à-vis* the state. Initially many of these were ethnic in composition, for example, the Bukoba Bahaya Union in Tanganyika, but later such organizations increasingly strove for a territorial membership, the Tanganyika African Association, the precursor to Tanganyika African National Union, being a case in point.[1]

One does not have to look very far, then, for evidence of the significance of associational life in African politics. It was at the very root of nationalism and it

---

[1] It is worth noting here that most of the work on these associations has been done by expatriate scholars, largely, it seems, because the historiography of the first and second generation of Tanzanian scholars has been dominated by Marxist influences in which social categories other than voluntary associations have occupied primary importance. It would not be surprising, however, if in the future a new generation of Tanzanian historians becomes much more preoccupied with tracing the rich history of how their fellow-countrymen organized themselves in various ways to challenge colonialism. The early history of TANU, and how these various groups and organizations were brought together, is only one of many topics that await a curious mind.

is probably correct to argue that it also provided the context within which democratic values were fostered. Thus, it helped to build new bonds of solidarity across ethnic lines and to foster a degree of tolerance of different viewpoints that characterized so many of these nationalist movements. If the generation of Africans who lived through these years demonstrated a higher level of commitment to democratic values than those in subsequent years after independence, it is not unreasonable to argue that it had less to do with their acceptance of the values of the British or the French than with their ability to generate new values in the context of voluntary associations.

The full breadth of voluntary associations was thus very important in Africa in the colonial period and they had a direct bearing on bringing it to an end. But unlike the United States, where voluntarism has continued to be cherished over the years, African governments turned against it after independence. Some banned outright such associations, while others just ignored them or treated them as a nuisance. The result was that, in virtually every country, the rich associational life that had been so prominent before was now being discouraged as a means of building the new nation. It becomes necessary to explore the reasons for the demise of the voluntary spirit in African countries since independence.

## The Demise of Voluntarism

The demise of voluntarism may be attributed primarily to two factors that became important in the post-independence period. The first was the drive to Africanize politics and create a new hegemonic order. The second was the influential role that foreign donors came to play in the development process of most African countries. Each will be considered in turn.

### Africanizing Politics

Independence changed the notion of state legitimacy. Whether *uhuru* was the result of a gradual and constitutional devolution of power, as in Tanganyika and Uganda, or the outcome of armed struggle, as in Kenya and the southern African states, it gave rise to new principles of accountability and state legitimacy. The colonial state owed its accountability to the metropole and its legitimacy rested on maintaining law and order. Its post-colonial successor, by contrast, was perceived as owing its accountability to the African political community and its legitimacy to the ability of the new nationalists to represent it.

Much came to be expected of the post-colonial state, one reason being that the colonial state itself had, over time, helped raise expectations, another being that the nationalists believed, and convinced their followers, that the potential of independence was virtually unlimited. Once the political kingdom had been conquered, as Nkrumah put it, everything else would be added unto them. By removing many of the restrictions that had held Africans in thrall in colonial times, the new governments redefined the relationship between rulers and ruled, between state and individual. A populist version of the state as the instrument of the 'masses' developed in the minds of many politicians and intellectuals. They, in turn, constantly conveyed this image to the people. The result was that the post-colonial state started life with infinitely more popular support than the colonial state could ever have mobilized, but it also began life with infinitely more commitments. The new leaders found themselves carrying a heavy burden of obligations but enjoyed little room for manoeuvre. In a recent volume, Patrick Chabal (1992: 68–81) discusses this transition in greater detail.

The logic of the transition implied that the state was now the true representative of the people, and so there was little need for autonomous voluntary organizations. A particularly pertinent illustration of this logic was the takeover of the Ruvuma Development Association by the party and state authorities in Tanzania in 1967. The party–state needed all the legitimacy it could get from seeing itself associated with successful efforts to meet the needs of the people. It is for this reason that nationalization of services became as important as the takeover of the means of production. The latter was aimed at providing a stronger financial base for a populist approach to politics which argued for extending benefits to everybody within as short a time span as possible. Universal primary education and plans to provide domestic water for all rural households are some of the most obvious cases in point, with respect to Tanzania.

The populist notion of the post-colonial state was taken especially far in Tanzania, but it surfaced also in Uganda and Zimbabwe (despite the rhetorical commitment of the Mugabe Government to Marxism-Leninism). Only in Kenya did the new government recognize the potential significance of self-help groups in domestic resource mobilization. Instead of taking them over, the Kenyatta Government urged local community development groups and associations into doing more and bigger things. While administrators often found themselves harassed by these organizations coming to ask for matching contributions from government, the retention and stimulation of the self-help spirit gave politics in Kenya a somewhat different flavour from that of Tanzania (Holmquist, 1970). First of all, resource mobilization was decentralized and competitive, unlike in Tanzania where the principle of central planning and direction prevailed even after the 1972 decentralization reforms. Secondly, it kept alive the notion that there is no such thing as 'a free lunch', i.e. that development comes only with the people being involved themselves. Thirdly, the vitality of self-help organizations in Kenya also helped sustain at least the rudimentary elements of civil society. Even though these entities often became absorbed into the multi-ethnic patronage system that sustained the political regime, at least in the Kenyatta days (1963–78) they made it more costly for the political rulers to ignore civil society, an experience that has hit President Moi more recently.

At the same time, Kenya and Tanzania resembled each other in terms of their preference for a single party to control the state. Politicians wanted to 'shine' without rivalry, because, to them, representing a constituency or community meant representing everybody. The effect of this was that choices among policy alternatives were deemed much less important than the choice of representative. Competitive elections within a single-party system, which developed in Tanzania, Kenya and many other African countries, was the answer. Such elections did not pose a threat to the system, yet they gave the electorate a choice that was important to them (Hyden and Leys, 1972). As René Lemarchand (1972) argued, the clientelistic politics that evolved in the context of these systems was at the time a means of achieving national integration.

Studies of Tanzania, in particular, have not recognized how real and important populism was in the first decades of independence. Most analysts chose to view things in terms of social class and to ignore or discard populism. Yet, in the heydays of the move to transform the country into a socialist state, it was the populist drive that propelled it forward. Nyerere's extraordinary ability to command this principle helped legitimize the post-colonial state to an extent that few, if any, other African leaders could match. Yet his efforts would have come to little had it not been for his ability to get the international donor community to underwrite many of his ventures.

## Donor Dependence

In a curious way, donor perceptions of the role of the state in development tallied very well with the populist aspirations of the new rulers in Africa, of whom Nyerere was the most articulate. They justified their assistance on the grounds that the post-colonial state, unlike its predecessor, was an entity representing the whole community without discrimination. They also believed, drawing on their own experience of applying the macroeconomic principles of John Maynard Keynes, that a strong public sector capable of pumping money into the local economy would be enhancing development. This perception was particularly prominent in European circles but was embraced in the 1960s and early 1970s also by US administrations. The result was that all foreign aid was concentrated on the state, and became institutionalized as a matter of transferring resources from one government to another. Donations made by Northern NGOs and churches to their 'natural partners' in East Africa were in those days only a trickle compared with the flow of official development assistance.

The problem with this approach was, of course, that the primary users of foreign aid were not individual actors or corporations, as had been the case in implementing Keynesian principles in Europe, but government departments. Donors identified only part of this problem, by suggesting that it could be solved through technical assistance and training and the education of African counterparts. The shortage of 'absorptive capacity' – the term used by the donors at the time – was perceived as a technical problem that could be solved with the appropriate complementary inputs.

While nobody wants to deny the value of these human resource development programmes, they clearly did not address the root of the problem. The way donors took for granted that the state would, in practice, function as expressed in the political rhetoric gave African leaders, especially someone like Nyerere who enjoyed their full confidence, a sense of only the sky being the limit. Social service programmes were extended to rural areas at a pace that bore little relationship to the domestic resource base. How would the state sustain these programmes on its own in the future? For some, this was not an issue, because the expectation was that foreign donors would keep on providing the money. For others, and especially among the donors, the answer was that parallel investments in strengthening the public services would yield results in terms of economic development – and hence more public revenue – as well as more reliable and effective public management.

As this account underscores, at no point, at least in Tanzania, was thought given to sharing the burden of development with voluntary organizations. Local self-help organizations were replaced by party branches and state-controlled villages. Religious organizations that had run their own schools and hospitals found themselves forced to hand them over to the government. Virtually all other organizations, with some notable exceptions, such as football clubs, were brought under the umbrella of the ruling party, including the country's once proud and strong co-operative movement.

The attitude of donors in Kenya was remarkably similar, in spite of the presence of strong self-help organizations. The latter were never considered in the context of aid negotiations and there is no evidence that Kenya earned – or tried to earn – 'bonus' support from the donors because of the important contribution to development that people made through their own efforts. It is a historical irony that when these groups finally began to earn some recognition from outsiders in the late 1970s and early 1980s, the *harambee* tradition had become so excessively compromised by patronage considerations that it had lost much of its legitimacy among the people (see Chapter 4). Unlike Tanzania, however, the vitality of civil society has not been systematically crushed.

What we have to recognize today is that the populist state, in combination with a strong dependence on almost unlimited donor funding in the 1960s and 1970s, created the legacy with which virtually all African countries are struggling today. These two phenomena promoted the unchecked expansion of the public sector at the expense of both the private and voluntary sectors. They also led to the emergence of a 'developmental dictatorship' (Sklar, 1983) rather than the developmental democracy that people had hoped for at independence. It is against this background that both economic and political liberalization appears justified.

## Voluntarism in the Context of Current Liberalization Efforts

Structural adjustment is the price that Africa is paying for the excesses of the earlier decades. If those investments had yielded returns, there would have been no need for an adjustment, at least not so far-reaching a one as the countries on the continent have had to accept in the 1980s. While Africans have reason to criticize their leaders for having brought their countries into financial bankruptcy, donors do not escape blame, as they contributed to this state of affairs by endorsing policies that were unsustainable and backing politicians who were unaccountable.

Structural adjustment, therefore, is an inevitable process in order to get African countries to take greater responsibility for their own affairs and to secure better use of domestic as opposed to external resources. As the experience with such adjustment has highlighted, however, it is not going to be easy. Above all, in economies as weakened as those of Africa, it will take a long time before results are likely to show up in such a way as to enable people to benefit. Hardship is likely to remain with most African countries for many years to come.

Structural adjustment is an ambiguous strategy. It hurts at the same time as it helps. It does give people new and more options. Those who do not seize these opportunities usually have to adopt them ultimately as a matter of necessity. In order to make ends meet, people are typically forced to earn extra income from sources outside their regular employment. Not all of this entrepreneurship is legal, and there are many who seek a short cut by earning money from bribes or theft of public property. Such cases notwithstanding, there is a widespread feeling that, after years of control, the new policies provide a sense of relief, maybe even freedom. It is this dimension that, probably more than any other, explains why structural adjustment policies have caused so few riots and demonstrations in Africa. Given what these countries have been asked to swallow, one might have expected – as African leaders did in the early 1980s – many more public manifestations of discontent.

The most problematic part of structural adjustment, at least from a social and political point of view, is that, as a 'rightist' revolution, it encourages, or at least reinforces, individualism and opportunism rather than solidarity and co-operation. It breaks up old bonds of affection and trust and, as such, increases people's sense of insecurity and fear. One can hypothesize that, if trust among people and public trust in governmental institutions are allowed to continue to decline, the new economic policies are unlikely to result in their projected benefits. More specifically, instead of freedom there might be anarchy, instead of progress there might be decay.

It is in this context that voluntary organizations and NGOs come into the picture. Individualism and opportunism (or anomie, as one sees in some countries) are not inevitable outcomes of structural adjustment, but, in situations where voluntarism has been discouraged for such a long time, the mechanisms for fully exploiting the potential benefits associated with these policies are going to be difficult to tap. Local voluntary organizations are few and weak. The strongest ones are foreign NGOs. While many of the latter do a good job in relating to local groups, they are still foreign entities and do not have the same institution-building effects as local initiatives have. If concerns about social equality are going to earn a place on the contemporary political agenda rivalling that of economic reforms, voluntary associations in Africa must be strengthened and allowed a greater voice in society.

There is a tendency both in government and in donor circles to treat NGOs instrumentally as merely another means of implementing policies decided upon by governments or donors. For example, it is well-known that donors channel more of their funding through NGOs precisely because they believe that the latter are better at getting things done than government departments are. This may or may not be the case, but such an approach is directly harmful to the efforts to get Africa back on its feet. It totally overlooks the fact that better domestic resource utilization will come about only if people are allowed to build on and organize around their own initiatives. NGOs cannot be treated just as the extended arm of the government or the donor community. They must be taken for what they potentially are: the backbone of civil society. Legislation ensuring freedom of association (and speech) is a first step in this direction, but just as important is that governments and donors treat these non-governmental organizations as equals. They have an existence in their own right; they must be allowed to grow at their own pace; they must be given the chance to make up their own minds on what to do. The impatience that undercut the public sector in the first two decades after independence must not be allowed to treat the voluntary sector in the same way.

The latter is perhaps the most important of the three sectors in the con-temporary setting, because it provides an opportunity for co-operation and collective action that helps not only individuals but also society at large. Many voluntary organizations are quite small and local in their orientation. They have difficulty in expanding because they receive little or no public attention. To make them part of the broader national development process, the most common approach has been to 'adopt' them under the umbrella of some larger and stronger NGO. This is what has happened to many women's groups, for example. While this is not always a bad approach, it carries with it the danger of choking local initiative and encouraging external dependence.

Another approach that gives more significance to the notion of local ownership and autonomy is networking among local communities with a view to building a popular movement around some shared concerns. This has been very successful in India and Sri Lanka. The Self-Employed Women's Association (SEWA), which started as a venture among the poorest of the poor women in Ahmedabad (Gujarat), has subsequently been replicated elsewhere in the country and has thus grown into a nation-wide organization. The Sarvodaya Movement in Sri Lanka, which encourages grass-roots development via the use of Buddhist principles, has also become an important actor on the national scene where it has tried to mediate in the conflict between the Singhalese majority and the Tamil minority. Popular movements built through effective networking have also become important in francophone West Africa. FONADES and SIX-S are two indigenous examples of such organizations, both of them involved in enhancing local food security through such projects as cereal banks.

East and Southern Africa has much less of this, largely because foreign NGOs have been allowed to do so much of the work. The Greenbelt Movement in Kenya, led by Professor Wangari Mathai, may be one of the few indigenous NGOs (though in this case confined to women members only) that comes close to being a popular movement in the sense of unifying members through their mutual recognition of a common cause. The once powerful co-operative and trade union movements have still to recover from the demise they suffered at the hands of post-independence patronage politics. The strongest NGOs in East Africa today are the mainstream churches (Anglican, Catholic and Presbyterian). They play an important role both as monitors of human rights violations and service providers. The Justice and Peace Commission of the Catholic Church has been very vocal on human rights issues in Zimbabwe. In both Kenya and Uganda, much of the best hospital care and education has been obtained in institutions run by the mainstream churches. In Tanzania, where hospitals and schools belonging to the churches were taken over by the government in the late 1960s, the policy is now to return them to their original owners (see Chapter 11). Even though these organizations are regaining the role they used to play, they are still viewed with suspicion by governments because, as competitors, they pose a direct threat to their legitimacy.

A third approach to stimulate voluntary action has been to encourage savings and credit programmes. Although the myth often prevails that poor people do not save, there is evidence from all over the world that savings and credit networks are particularly strong among the poorest strata of society. The Savings Development Movement in Zimbabwe was until a few years ago a successful case in point. Because of its success, however, it was 'co-opted' by the government, much as the Ruvuma Development Association was in Tanzania in the late 1960s (Fraser Taylor and Mackenzie, 1992: 250–1). Although rotating savings and credit associations are very popular in East Africa as elsewhere, the problem with this and similar rudimentary banking efforts is that they do not generate capital. Because the savings are not invested in anything, they do not yield more money. Various efforts have been made to improve on these initiatives by creating co-operative credit and savings societies that place money in interest-earning accounts. The Grameen Bank of Bangladesh is another much-heralded example of what can be done to integrate local grass-roots initiatives into the national economy without hurting them in the process. There are few successful examples of this from Africa, although co-operative credit programmes have made remarkable progress in countries like Ghana and Kenya. Perhaps the most interesting are the community banks in Nigeria which serve individuals as well as groups like 'hometown associations' engaged in community development. A particularly important feature of this programme is the matching contribution from the Federal Government so as to boost capital formation in the communities.

Returning now to Tanzania, it is probably correct to assume that the country starts from a less favourable position than that of many other African countries where civil society has been allowed to exist at least in the shadow of the state. Because the hegemony of the party–state was particularly strong in Tanzania, and is likely to take time to undo, expectations of what the voluntary sector can achieve must be modest. Measures such as returning schools and hospitals to their original owners are steps in the right direction. So is legislation which gives voluntary organizations greater autonomy and security, not the kind of legislation that was passed in Kenya in 1991 with a view to making NGOs subject to all kinds of governmental scrutiny. But, in terms of strengthening service provision and its management in the country, other measures are also necessary. One such approach is discussed below.

## Service Provision Through Competitive Funding

While the voluntary sector does require greater recognition as an actor in its own right, it is important that its status should not be overdramatized. Voluntarism is great, but there is a limit to how much can be done through popular efforts and sacrifices. Service provision in the future must be able to draw on all sectors in ways that are attuned to the needs and capacities of each country. Some activities can be quite adequately handled by private or voluntary agencies, but often government has to undertake it.

In the past, the preferred way of organizing and prioritizing activities in the social sector was through national development plans. Such plans may still have their role, but, given the limited relevance to actual practice that such plans have had in the past, it is necessary to look for other ways, particularly those that encourage the involvement of both state and civil society. One way of doing this would be through the creation of trust funds, which are independent of government and other actors but are available to support feasible project requests from any agency, whether governmental, private or voluntary.

The fund idea is not new. Most countries, at least in East and Southern Africa, have or have had a rural development fund, typically located in the President's Office, or under its direct supervision. Financed by donors, these funds have usually served as a source of patronage. The Head of State has used them to 'reward' villages or communities that have done things that he considers politically worthwhile.[2]

What is being proposed here is different. This fund model assumes a legal status that makes it totally independent of active economic and political interests. The board would be made up of individuals who are ready to sign an undertaking that they are not engaged in politics, nor do they plan to do so while serving on the board. Other qualifications may need to be introduced such as not being directly involved in any other organizations with objectives that might conflict with those of the trust fund. Individuals most likely to meet

---

[2] Tanzania's Community Development Trust Fund, originally autonomous, is slightly different in that it still enjoys a fair degree of autonomy from political considerations. Its board, however, is made up primarily of senior political leaders. Furthermore, its objective is first and foremost to support non-governmental projects.

these qualifications would be trusted public figures such as former civil servants, teachers or religious leaders. In the context of multi-party politics, it is not impossible that ex-politicians might also qualify, at least so long as they are not intent on using their position on the board to favour some and harm others for reasons relating to past political involvement. If these funds were to be financed through donor contributions, which may be necessary in the initial stages, these agencies could also be given some representation on the board, so long as it is a distinct minority.

The point about these funds is that they would be intermediaries between foreign donor agencies and local recipients, legally incorporated in the host country. As such, decisions about resource allocation would rest in the hands of trusted local individuals with a good knowledge of conditions in the country. Furthermore, financial support would be available on a competitive basis to any agency capable of producing good project proposals. This is particularly important. In the past, support for development projects has been allocated on an *ad hoc* basis either to governments or NGOs. Even though feasibility studies may have been carried out, their value has been nullified by the fact that no attempt has been made to compare it with other proposals. In the model proposed here, no agency can take its financial support for granted because it has the right political connections. Government departments will have to compete with NGOs or private contractors in order to ensure that they are sufficiently competent to deserve financial support. The same, of course, applies to NGOs and private contractors. They should not expect support merely because they are being held in high esteem by donors. With more competition for available resources comes greater effort and with that institution-building. This is what has been lacking in the past, but it is absolutely vital if Tanzania and other African countries are going to escape from their current predicament.

These trust funds should have a national mandate, as regionally based funds create envy and misunderstanding. They should typically cater for a relatively specific set of objectives, e.g. water and public sanitation measures, food security, public health care, or primary or secondary education. The mandate would be spelled out in a document that is shared with the public. The board would use it in its decisions, the professional staff would be guided by it in their evaluation of incoming proposals, and those requesting financial support would have access to it in preparing their projects.

In order to be as versatile as possible, funds may operate through separate 'windows'. One may cater for proposals where there is no immediate return on investment, such as training and education programmes. A second may address the needs of those many groups that fail to obtain credit from regular banks and credit institutions because they are too poor. Project requests from these sources may be funded on a 'soft-loan' basis so as to give them a chance of succeeding. A third window may operate with regular commercial interest loans to organizations that are capable of handling these.

The idea of trying to make these funds at least in part self-sustaining through revolving loans is important. In this respect, they would be similar to banks, but, unlike the latter, they would be more versatile and able to afford to take risks that banks cannot do. The capital base of these trust funds can be constituted in many different ways, depending on legislation and various feasibility considerations. In Tanzania, where no financial markets exist, the notion of local capital investments in these funds is out of the question, at least for the time being. The more likely immediate source of financing would be debt swaps or direct contributions by foreign donors.

This model has many advantages over existing forms of disbursing development aid. It places the responsibility for decision-making in the hands of representatives of the recipient country. It promotes local initiatives for which there is a genuine demand. It enhances capacity-building by encouraging competition among the potential users of public funds. It fosters respect for public authority by providing financial support on professional as opposed to political grounds. It makes a contribution to tolerance and pluralism by being accessible to both the public and the private and voluntary sectors.

It may still be necessary to ask why a government would want to adopt this model. Its principal advantage is that, by being an institution outside partisan politics, its resources are available to government and opposition alike. In the context of multi-party politics, when it is expected that governments will come and go, it is always a safeguard to have institutions that are not state-controlled but cater for both state and civil society. Furthermore, acceptance of institutions that are legally and politically independent potentially gives incumbent governments respect and legitimacy. For example, when this model was presented to leading representatives of the Movement for Multi-Party Democracy in Zambia, while it was still in opposition, one member commented that such independent trust funds were precisely the kind of institutions they would like to see established in order to show that they did not behave in the same way as the Kaunda Government. Some government leaders may regard the establishment of these funds as a potential loss of revenue to government. This is partly true, but it should not be exaggerated. In the first place, not all donor funds would go into these funds, only those that are typically used for medium-to small-scale projects in the fields of social and economic development. Large-scale projects, notably infrastructural ones, would fall outside the framework of the model discussed here. Secondly, government departments are not excluded from the use of resources controlled by the funds. All they need to do is to 'get their act together' and compete with private and voluntary agencies.

Donors also have good reason to consider adopting this model. In the first place, their own record of direct involvement in service provision or other projects is miserable. In the interest of sustaining public confidence in foreign aid back home, they must support 'winning horses', i.e. approaches that yield better results. Secondly, they are not going to divert all their financial resources to these funds, but, typically, only a part of their development funding. Should the model really impress them, it is, of course, possible that they might be ready to allocate a higher percentage of their budgets to these funds in the future. Thirdly, they would not hand over all control of their financial aid, since one condition would presumably be that these trust funds would continue to receive such aid only as long as they functioned according to their mandate as politically independent and professionally competent intermediaries for disbursement. Finally, if donors are serious about helping the democratization process along in African countries, this model provides a concrete way of doing so without involving them in the politics of the recipient country.

## Conclusion

Ever since independence, the voluntary sector has been the stepchild of African development. In spite of its economic and political significance during the colonial period, it has either been relegated to tertiary significance or quashed outright by the post-colonial state. As part of the continent's ongoing 'second liberation', restoring the value of voluntarism to its rightful position in society is as important as any other aspect of this process. At the same time, voluntary agencies and NGOs must not be treated differently from private and public sector actors. After all, each of them has its place in the more specific tasks of service provision as well as in the general challenges of national development. Thus, rather than placing all the eggs in one basket (e.g. the NGO sector), it is important to create the conditions under which all sectors, and individual organizations within them, can compete on an even basis and stimulate each other to greater achievements. This chapter has identified one way of doing precisely that.

## References

Bellah, R.N. *et al* (1985) *Habits of the Heart: Individualism and Commitment in American Life*. Berkeley, CA: University of California Press.

Bratton, M. (1989a) 'Beyond the State: Civil Society and Associational Life in Africa', *World Politics* 41 (3): 407–30.

Bratton, M. (1989b) 'The Politics of Government–NGO Relations in Africa', *World Development* 17 (4): 569–87.

Carnoy, M. (1984) *The State and Political Theory*. Princeton, NJ: Princeton University Press.

Chabal, P. (1992) *Power in Africa: An Essay in Political Interpretation*. New York: St. Martin's Press.

Coleman, J.S. (1958) *Nigeria: Background to Nationalism*. Los Angeles: University of California Press.

de Tocqueville, A. [1835] (1945) *Democracy in America*, 2 vols. New York: Vintage.

Fraser Taylor, D.S. and Mackenzie, F. (eds) (1992) *Development From Within: Survival in Rural Africa*. London: Routledge.

Hodgkin, T. (1956) *Nationalism in Colonial Africa*. London: Frederick Muller.

Holmquist, F. (1970) 'Implementing Rural Development Projects' in G. Hyden, R.H. Jackson and J.J Okumu (eds) *Development Administration: The Kenyan Experience*. Nairobi: Oxford University Press.

Hyden, G. and Leys, C. (1972) 'Elections and Politics in Single-Party Systems: The Case of Kenya and Tanzania', *British Journal of Political Science* 2 (October): 389–412.

Lemarchand, R. (1972) 'Clientelism and Ethnicity in Tropical Africa', *American Political Science Review* 66 (1): 68–90.

Lonsdale, J. (1968) 'Some Origins of Nationalism in East Africa', *Journal of African History* 9 (1): 119–46.

Ottenberg, S. (1955) 'Improvement Associations among the Afipko Ibo', *Africa* 25 (1): 1–23.

Poulantzas, N. (1978) *State, Power, Socialism*. London: New Left Books.

Sklar, R. (1983) 'Democracy in Africa', *African Studies Review* 26 (3–4). Also reprinted in P. Chabal (ed.) (1986) *Political Domination in Africa*. Cambridge: Cambridge University Press.

Wuthnow, R. (ed.) (1991) *Between States and Markets: The Voluntary Sector in Comparative Perspective*. Princeton, NJ: Princeton University Press.

# 3

## ALAN FOWLER
## NGOs & the Globalization
## of Social Welfare

Perspectives
from East Africa

Since the early 1980s, development politics in sub-Saharan Africa have been
dominated by measures designed to restructure national economies together
with the institutional relations through which they are expressed. Restructuring
is a means to an end, the objective being an acceleration in economic growth
within the exigencies of a market-capitalist system that is increasingly global in
reach, penetrating deeper into African economies and social relations.
Restructuring should lead to better economic performance because it is meant
to optimize the division of a nation's resources among institutional actors – the
state, the market and voluntary organizations, loosely termed NGOs – according to their perceived developmental comparative advantages.[1] Reallocating
resources to the most efficient user through adjustment should, therefore,
produce better returns on them.

Implicit in decisions about the reallocation of resources are assumptions about
which institutional type best fulfils which functions in society. One basis for
choice is normative – what each institutional actor *should* do – derived from
socio-historical and political values. Alternatively, criteria can be derived from
structural-functional considerations of what each actor *can do best,* i.e. where its
organizational comparative advantage is found to be. The normative basis of
choice is usually framed as the desired role of the state *vis-à-vis* other actors, an
issue that has occupied moral and political philosophers for millennia and
continues to do so. This chapter does not address normative questions, but
examines issues arising from assumptions within the aid system about comparative
competences in the provision of welfare services between the state and NGOs.

After clarifying terms and concepts, the first section briefly reviews the
grounds on which different types of institutions are being allocated specific
supply roles within the framework of structural adjustment. The second section
provides a further differentiation of the non–governmental, non–profit sector by
using comparisons between British and African NGOs to highlight significant
differences that are likely to influence their behaviour as service providers.

---

[1] For discussion and different perspectives on organizational comparative advantage see: Etzioni
(1968, 1971); Williamson (1981); Moe (1984); Billis (1989); and Brett (1990).

Evidence from Kenya is then used to show that the choice between state and non-state for service delivery may not be as significant as assumed. The third section draws attention to a factor that is often understated or ignored in choosing between social supplier NGOs, namely their resource base. The chapter concludes with a speculative reinterpretation of the likely scenario for the future provision of social services in East Africa. Here, the previous arguments and analyses are relocated within wider and more fundamental trends, characterized as the globalization of social welfare – a phenomenon deriving from a new motivation for international development assistance.

## Providing for Welfare: The Supply Side

Adjustment financing in East Africa is designed to reallocate socio-economic functions according to Western, market-capitalist assumptions about the distinctive competences of institutions in society.[2] The next sub-section summarizes the ideas underpinning this type of reform and clarifies what this means in terms of financing the provision of services supporting social welfare.

### Organizational Competences

The distinctive features of state, market and voluntary organizations are considered to give them particular competences in satisfying the needs of poor people in a developing society. An idealized statement of comparative institutional competences in development looks something like the following (from Brown and Korten, 1989).

State organizations can regulate and control more effectively through *legitimate* coercion; they can direct social behaviour, reallocate wealth, equalize access to services and opportunities in society, and interpret the common good in the interest of the whole. However, when a state is under the exclusive control of particular powerful political groups and consumptive elites, it may not operate for the common good but may perpetuate injustice, inequality and poverty. Given the power to command and coerce, the state does not need to be as efficient as the market or as responsive to the needs and demands of citizens. And, because maintaining the status quo is one effective way of dealing with competing demands, the state tends to be less innovative than market or non-profit-making organizations.

Commercial enterprise works on the basis of exchange by selling goods and services on the market. The need to respond to market forces promotes efficiency and innovation. Its role in society is to generate new wealth. It is most responsive to those with the ability to pay, and hence is less inclined to provide services for the poor than for the rich. And, frequently, alliances between political and economic interest groups give rise to enterprises with

---

[2] For the purposes of this chapter, institutions are defined as stable patterns of behaviour that are recognized and valued by society, while organizations are defined as purposeful, structured, role-bound social units. For further elaboration, see Fowler *et al.* (1992).

semi-monopolistic control over market sectors or operations that work against the economic betterment of the poor.

Voluntary organizations arise from a concern to promote and realize value-goals that are important to groups within society (Korten, 1990). There is no limit to what these value-goals may be, thus making the sector appear incoherent. Voluntary development organizations (NGOs) are normally united around a vision of more economically equitable, socially just and globally sustainable societies than exist at present. This shared perspective is the driving force for action that is distinct from the political agendas of governments or the imperatives of the market. Value commitment directs NGOs to social groupings that are politically marginalized and economically deprived. But, by nature of their size and social position, NGOs cannot simply command or monopolize, they must negotiate and innovate on the basis of their clients' situations, responses and needs. NGO innovation normally has to address the integrated nature of poverty (Chambers, 1983: 103-39), differentiating itself from the unit-product-based innovation usually originating from for-profit enterprise.

Further analysis suggests that in the South NGOs may possess two types of particular advantage compared with the state, when operating as agents of poverty alleviation (Fowler, 1988). First, they are able to relate to clients solely on the basis of development interests. Unlike governments, NGOs are not burdened with other functions such as security or revenue collection, which cloud relations with those to be served. This enables them to engage with people in ways that gain a greater degree of participation and local input in providing the services they need. Secondly, NGOs are in a better position than states to adapt their organizational structure, methods and processes to specific situations and population groups. They do not have to adopt the standardized bureaucratic systems that are inherent to a national civil service. If these two aspects are not called upon, one can question whether or not the institutional distinctiveness of NGOs is being fully exploited.

Ideally, the restructuring alluded to earlier should allocate to each institutional type the social development function for which it is most competent. The ability to do so in East Africa will depend on the actual nature of state, market and NGOs. It is beyond the scope of this chapter to detail the situation of the states and the commercial sector within the sub-region, which has been the subject of many studies and World Bank documents. Less well-established, however, is the nature of the NGO community, and this therefore needs some elaboration. Before going into this, the character of social services and state responsibility for them requires clarification.

## Social Services and Social Welfare: The Issue of Financing

The country studies to be found in this book focus on three types of social services, namely, health care, education, and the maintenance of law and order. These categories of service are akin to what are considered to be necessary in order to meet people's basic needs, together with the public security and social stability which are preconditions for their effective delivery. These services can be placed within a wider classification of welfare provision which would also include economic dimensions such as unemployment benefits, invalidity payments, pensions and so on.

Since the early 1950s, the state in most OECD countries has been allocated a significant and direct role in ensuring minimum standards of social and economic welfare for all its citizens. In fact, over some thirty years the state's responsibility to supply basic welfare has become a virtual orthodoxy of modern statehood. To some analysts of US social policy in the 1960s, the welfare state represented 'government protected minimum standards of income, nutrition, health, housing, and education for every citizen, assured to him as a political right, not as a charity' (quoted in Smith and Lipsky, 1993: 16). As various chapters in this volume attest, in the run-up to independence nationalist parties throughout East Africa adopted and advanced the same position. Satisfying popular expectations of the state as service provider therefore became a condition for subsequently maintaining a regime's legitimacy in the post-colonial era.

In the North, during the last decade the state's role in welfare provision has been called into question on two levels. First, there has been the functional level of comparative advantage and better cost-effectiveness noted in Chapter 1, usually framed within the context of the privatization of government functions.[3]

The second and more fundamental re-examination questions the axiom that statehood carries with it an obligation to ensure universal minimum welfare through governmental provision of services. Central to the second debate is not so much whether people have a right to expect minimum standards of well-being, but who should have the responsibility for their availability and financing. Alternative views are that the state, through general and specific taxation, should provide for individuals as citizens, or, conversely, that individuals as consumers should purchase welfare services from the market.

Obviously, conclusions reached in the second area have direct implications for decisions in the first. And both these levels of choice directly influence the role and behaviour of NGOs which, by their very nature, cannot levy tax from citizens or survive on the basis of sales to consumers. By their very purpose, developmental NGOs are unable to recover the full cost of their services from users. This means that they must rely on finance from sources other than their clients, which puts them in a distinctive, dependent, position not exhibited by government or commercial enterprise.

The results of these ongoing deliberations in the North affect public versus private choices about service provision in many of the poorer countries of the world, because they become translated into the funding policies and priorities of donor agencies. Structural adjustment lending is a case in point. The issue needing to be addressed, therefore, is what might this financing dimension mean for NGOs and state versus non-state provision of welfare services in East Africa? The following sections tackle this question.

[3] In the West, the shift in policy towards non-state supply of public services has led to an increase in voluntary organizations that function as contractors. In other words, the distinction between profit and non-profit suppliers of services is becoming increasingly vague.

# NGOs in East Africa's Development

To understand African NGOs requires a number of steps. First, there is a need to disaggregate NGOs as an organizational category within the voluntary sector. This is followed by an appraisal of the origins of African NGOs, which suggests that they cannot simply be compared with their Northern counterparts. Third, an analysis of the NGO role in Kenya's development leads to an argument that they may not possess much in the way of a comparative advantage over the state in the delivery of social welfare services.[4]

## What Are Developmental NGOs?

All writers on NGOs are faced with definitional and taxonomic problems. Originating from a United Nations Resolution of 1950, the term non-governmental organization (NGO) was a designation for non-state organizations that could be accredited to the Economic and Social Council.[5] At a time in history when colonialism was still an active force in world politics, NGOs were equated with (predominantly Christian) Western charities active in the South.

The end of colonial rule and three decades of development assistance have modified ideas on which organizations constitute the voluntary, or non-profit, development sector. Although there is still no universal agreement on the issue, a common distinction is now made between formally incorporated non-profit organizations that provide development services to, or in some other way work on behalf of, the poor and the formal and informal organizations created by poor people themselves for their own benefit.[6] In the latter case, individual material gain, rather than profit for the organization *per se,* is a strong motivation for membership of people's organizations.

For the purposes of this chapter, three types of secular organizations will be regarded as comprising the developmental NGO community. First, there are international and African non-profit organizations providing development services in or on behalf of the people of the South. For example, ActionAid supports primary and vocational education; Family Planning International provides contraceptive counselling and sterilization services, while AIDSCAP runs programmes for AIDS prevention and monitoring. The Undugu Society in Kenya runs

---

[4] Churches are treated as a distinct type of non-profit organization and are not included in this analysis. For a major study of church and development in Kenya see Chepkwony (1987).

[5] Resolution 288 (X) of 27 February 1950.

[6] Korten (1990: 96–105) identifies four types of NGOs, and goes on to make a primary distinction between 'first-party' and 'third-party' organizations, i.e. those serving members themselves and those serving others. World Bank staff identify five functional categories of NGOs along a public-private continuum, with a natural bias towards economic purposes. Their model does, however, make a distinction between organizations set up to serve those who created them and those providing service to others (Salmen and Eaves, 1989). At the local level in the South, Esman and Uphoff distinguish between three types of organization: Local Development Associations, Co-operatives and Interest Associations. They further distinguish between 'indigenous' and 'induced' and 'traditional' and 'modern' local organizations, taking into account the degree of historical rootedness in society and the stimulus for an organization's formation (Esman and Uphoff, 1984: 58–98).

health clinics in Nairobi's slums and a primary school for street children.

Second, there are community membership-based people's organizations (POs) formed by individuals in the South for their own advancement and controlled by them. Registered women's groups, traditional bodies established for mutual assistance and self-help, youth clubs and so on function as POs. Third, where membership organizations (grow to the extent that they) are staffed to provide services to members (and on occasion to others) they can be designated as member service organizations (MSOs). The National Council of Women of Kenya is one example of an MSO, as are the numerous professional associations and co-operatives in sub-Saharan Africa.

*NGOs in National Development*
Any analysis of NGOs in Africa's development must recognize the presence of two features unparalleled in the West. First, the continent's socio-political history has given rise to an NGO sector that contains both local and foreign elements. The community's behaviour is therefore likely to be conditioned in ways which are not part of Western experience. Second, NGOs in Africa contribute to the post-colonial task of nation-building. This means that NGO–state relations exist in a markedly different economic and political framework, which has consequences for any interpretation of their function.

These factors can be taken into account by using a comparative method to determine if assumptions about distinctive NGO advantages in service provision derived from Northern settings can be unreservedly applied elsewhere. Given East Africa's history and this chapter's focus on donor financing for service delivery, an appropriate comparison is between British and African NGOs.

*The British Case*
State recognition of the social value of organized voluntary action devoid of commercial intent dates back, in Britain, to the early 1600s. Informed by Christian moral obligation, the government encouraged voluntarism and personal altruism through charity laws, which defined what constituted charitable activity, regulated tax incentives for private donors and legally recognized the public benefits of philanthropic giving. Initially, charitable action could be overtly political. For example, in the nineteenth century non-profit organizations were created to lobby against the slave trade (Whitaker, 1974).

However, spurred by the industrial revolution, subsequent socio-economic developments refined ideas on what constituted charitable purposes. Charitable action became more circumscribed and limited to activity directed at the poor underclass that was a product of industrialization and expanding capitalism. The emergence of the Welfare State after World War II further shaped what were considered to be legitimate charitable purposes, refining the division of roles between state and non-state actors. Increasingly, with selective government support and regulation, the role of charities was to further welfare aims by blunting the edges and tidying up the loose ends of the expanding Welfare State, mitigating the harsher social effects of corporate capitalism. In doing so, it is argued that charities helped reduce the potential for rebellious action by the poor masses, so reinforcing and maintaining the status quo (van Rooy, 1991).

Successive revisions to the Charities Act sought to circumscribe the involvement of charitable organizations in the political realm. Today, the law in Britain (and the USA) excludes support for political action or lobbying from the list of activities that may be regarded as charitable. Inevitably, non-profit organizations dedicated to reducing global poverty and promoting social justice experience the same legal constraints as their domestically oriented brethren. The Charity Commissioners' recent (1991) censure of Oxfam (UK) for financing public campaigns for Britain's retention of sanctions against South Africa exemplifies the present state of the law, where its contemporary interpretation draws a very conservative line between legal public campaigning and illegal political lobbying (Smith, 1991). For this reason some NGOs, such as the World Development Movement, have not sought charitable status because it limits their ability to influence public policies.

*Charitable Action Towards Africa*
From the mid-sixteenth to the mid-twentieth century, Northern charitable activity directed at Africa and elsewhere accompanied and supported colonial expansion, justified as bringing civilization to colonial subjects (Lissner, 1977). It was almost exclusively missionary-led and frequently government-financed.

The post-World War II era saw a radical change in the origins and purposes of international NGOs. The experience of providing relief during the inter-war years, the provision of technical aid and organized dissent arising from concern for the effects of war on innocent civilians, all provided grounds for the creation and work of a new breed of secular internationally oriented NGOs such as CARE and Oxfam.

The three development decades that started in the 1960s have witnessed a further diversification and expansion of Northern NGOs and the developmental work they undertake.[7] From some 350 NGOs in 1900 and 1,700 in 1980, today there are an estimated 2,542 NGOs registered in OECD countries (Robinson, 1991).While firm numbers are not available, one survey suggests that a significant number of these organizations are engaged with Africa (Baldwin, 1990).

Funds available for use by NGOs demonstrate a similar growth, more than doubling in the past ten years to approximately US$5.5 billion, some 14% of total Official Development Assistance (ODA). A study of NGOs in countries of the European Union indicates that Africa received more than half of their global total of NGO aid (Stevens and van Thermaat, 1985). More recent observations and personal discussions with Northern NGOs confirm that a combination of disasters, the consequences of structural adjustment and comparatively strong economic progress in Asia and Latin America are inducing NGOs to increase the proportion of their resources allocated to sub-Saharan Africa even further.

As a result of pro-NGO policies, the proportion of their funding coming from public taxation has grown more sharply in the last decade than private donations and now amounts to 35% of the total funding. Overall, recent

[7] For an examination of the diverse origins of Northern NGOs see Fowler (1991).

NGO expansion has been resource-led with greater dependence on official aid (Robinson, 1991: 164).

## African NGOs

Although reliable, detailed figures are seldom available, recent reviews and publications indicate an uneven but usually notable post-colonial growth of indigenous NGOs and POs in every country of sub-Saharan Africa (Baldwin, 1990; Schneider, 1988). While such a change parallels, and is stimulated by, developments in the North, there are salient differences because their function in society does not arise simply from charitable or philanthropic concerns – concepts imported with colonialism (McCarthy, 1990).

Unlike their Northern contemporaries, these organizations rely heavily on external resources for the services they provide, and are likely to remain in this situation. First, while the spirit of mutual support is strong throughout sub-Saharan Africa, this is seldom expressed by people funding an intermediary organization. The lineage relationships of family, clan, tribe and ethnic group that form the roots of African society require that giving be a personalized affair, part of a valued reciprocal bond. An individual would lose the strategic benefits of mutual obligation by financing through an 'anonymous' third-party organization like an NGO. This fact, plus a very small middle class, makes it unlikely that the African NGOs described above can look to local philanthropy for much of their resource needs.

African people's or community-based organizations (POs) number hundreds of thousands. They tend to be either diverse informal groups with culturally specific traditional origins or more uniform formally registered entities induced by the development demands of the state and other agencies. The informal nature of many traditional POs makes them invisible to the aid system. This fact, coupled with past state action which denied the existence of POs because of their perceived role in perpetuating an ethnic awareness that undermines national unity, makes it very difficult to assess their developmental function and contribution. Evidence emerging from studies to be found in this volume suggests, however, that traditional POs have remained significant social organizations which, when developmentally engaged, are more likely to produce sustainable outcomes than modern, induced POs.

From a resource perspective these organizations should be able to remain functioning without external support, tailoring their level of activity to that which they themselves can afford and mobilize within the local economy. The probability of, and problems associated with, this potential for self-financing are described in this volume in Chapters 5, 9 and 13.

African member service organizations (MSOs) are argued to be a product of colonial penetration. Acting as institutions mediating between the demands of colonialism and the traditional social institutions of indigenous ethnic groups, MSOs were frequently registered as ethnic welfare associations. Their purpose was to promote and protect the interests of their respective communities, as well as providing support and linkages between urban and rural areas. Historically, African MSOs provided the organizational embryo for many of Africa's nationalist movements, trade unions and political parties (Wallerstein, 1966; Lonsdale, 1981). Formal education subsequently enabled the development of an African professional class – lawyers, journalists, doctors and so on – who formed their own membership organizations to further their interests.

In the colonial era ethnic welfare associations were initiated and financed by local people from within their economic means. They probably offered the greatest potential for evolution as endogenous non-governmental providers of services to a broad mass of the poor. However, the imperatives of regime legitimacy noted earlier, together with the post-colonial politics of East African countries, left little room for such organizations, leading to their slow or rapid dissolution. For example, after independence in Tanzania any mass organization of significant size or popularity was brought under the aegis of the party. And, in Kenya, political restructuring under President Moi required that, in 1979, all ethnic associations should be disbanded. Hence, by the 1980s, the only mass membership organizations existing outside direct state or party control were the religious ones.

Historically, the established church has functioned as the major non-governmental provider of social services. But, as other contributors to this volume show, despite its strong rooting in society, its ability to engage in service provision was and still is largely dictated by access to external finance. While acknowledging the significant, if somewhat ambivalent, role of churches in national development (Chepkwony, 1987), the concern in this chapter is to explore the dynamics of service provision associated with the rapid expansion of secular NGOs.

In sum, the evolution of the African NGO sector differs from its Northern counterpart in that it (a) is minimally rooted in the local economy, (b) has complex origins as the product of an interaction between indigenous and colonial values and socio-economic systems, and (c) has been viewed and treated by regimes as a political actor. It is against this background that NGO services have to be assessed.

Differences from the North are also to be found with POs. Here, lack of a stable economic surplus for most people, together with active curtailment of membership organizations by governments in East Africa, has restricted the growth of a system of social service provision on a mutual basis by POs or larger MSOs, such as the pension funds of trade unions.

## NGO Growth and Role in Service Provision

What is the developmental role and contribution of NGOs in East Africa? An answer to this question for Kenya can be partly derived from directories published in 1978 and 1988 (Kenya National Council of Social Services, 1978, 1988). Analysis of these and other sources, together with recent original research, provides the following picture.

Between 1950 and 1987, there has been a twenty-fold increase in the number of secular NGOs in Kenya, now numbering some 400. Moreover, the profile has changed owing to a more rapid growth of foreign versus local NGOs, the proportions altering from 33:67 to 49:51 over this period. The rate of expansion of foreign NGOs significantly exceeds that of their local counterparts (Fowler, 1993). As a product of the relative stability of the Museveni era, a significant growth of NGOs is now also being recorded in Uganda (DENIVA, 1990), while in Tanzania processes of economic and political liberalization are making more space for formally organized voluntary action, leading to the establishment, for example, of numerous community-initiated NGOs registered as Development Trusts (TANGO, 1991).

Table 3.1 summarizes trends in the reported types of development activity undertaken by secular NGOs in Kenya between 1978 and 1987.[8]

Table 3.1  Trends in Reported Development Activities of Kenya's NGOs

| | Ranking (%) | | | |
| | Local NGOs | | Foreign NGOs | |
| Sector | 1978 | 1987 | 1978 | 1987 |
| --- | --- | --- | --- | --- |
| Social development | 1  (53) | 1  (56) | 1  (58) | 1  (52) |
| Social welfare | 2  (27) | 2  (16) | 3  (6) | 3  (9) |
| Production and econ. dev. | 4  (6) | 3  (11) | 2  (17) | 2  (18) |
| Environment | 5  (3) | 4  (7) | 6  (4) | 5  (6) |
| Development services | 6  (2) | 5  (4) | 7  (3) | 6  (5) |
| Women | 3  (6) | 6  (3) | 4  (6) | 7  (3) |
| Relief | 6  (2) | 7  (3) | 5  (5) | 4  (6) |

*Source:* Fowler (1993).

Analysis indicates the predominance for local and foreign NGOs of social development activities such as community organization, health care, shelter, nutrition, legal assistance, family planning and so on. A shift of priority towards economic and productive enterprise is to be seen, however, mainly via agriculture and the provision of credit. For local NGOs, this has meant a relative reduction in emphasis on institutional welfare in homes for destitute children, schools for the blind, the disabled and so on. Environmental action is also

---

[8] The categories used by the Kenya National Council are not mutually exclusive, but comparison between two periods mitigates this shortcoming. Social welfare includes work with destitute people, orphans, the handicapped and the disabled as well as recreation. Relief incorporates famine food supplies and refugees. Social development comprises community organization, health, shelter, food and nutrition, social counselling, non-formal education and literacy, legal assistance, population and family planning, youth development and water and sanitation. Production and economic activity includes agriculture and livestock credit, non-agricultural (self-) employment and technology change. Activity dedicated to women is self-explanatory, the environmental category includes land and water conservation and protection of wildlife. Development services include management consultancy, research, information and documentation and the provision of transport.

accorded a greater significance. While the bulk of NGO action has remained the same, the marginal trends correspond to changes over ten years in the priorities of the official aid system, the increasingly important funders of NGOs.

Figures on trends in the reported activity of NGOs say little about their actual developmental contribution, which requires information on the level of finances they command. Calculations from a survey carried out in 1989/90 suggest that NGOs operating in Kenya command very significant resources – in the order of US$200m per annum – corresponding to some 31% of annual government recurrent expenditure on education, health, labour and social welfare, and 26% if capital investment is included (Fowler, 1993).

The survey also showed that both local and foreign NGOs are almost totally dependent on non-Kenyan sources for their finances. As a best case, one local NGO was able to raise about 30% of its funds locally, principally through commercial production. But the vast majority rely on foreign aid for more than 90% of their funds.

The profile of activity shown in Table 3.1 does not suggest that NGOs are involved in areas of social service provision markedly different from those of the government. In fact, with the exception of legal aid and development services such as management consultancy, the activities undertaken by NGOs essentially parallel those of the state. The history and nature of NGOs in the sub-region do not offer grounds for assuming that things would be otherwise. The division of labour between NGOs and the government in East Africa results from historical circumstance and imperatives, it is not a product of conscious choices. Overall, NGO services in the sub-region have evolved as usually welcome substitutes for limitations in state service supply.

Corresponding to their different roots and context, employment in NGOs in Africa is essentially sought as a means of livelihood; it is seldom an expression of personal philanthropic commitment such as is supposed to characterize voluntary sector employees in the North. While the concept is not simply translatable across cultures, African society offers alternative, more trusted and more valued channels for realizing what might qualify as philanthropic motivations (McCarthy, 1990). In other words, the behaviourial basis of NGO staff is essentially utilitarian rather than voluntaristic. We should not, therefore, expect significant motivational differences between the members of NGOs and other institutions. Or, put another way, NGO comparative advantage due to staff values and motivations cannot simply be assumed.[9]

Observers in East Africa already note institutional weaknesses in NGOs as service providers. For example, a survey of donor agencies in Kenya elicited the following experiences (Fowler and Bauer, 1989). NGOs were found to have limited absorptive capacity, inadequate delivery mechanisms, and a lack of technical expertise and managerial effectiveness. Resource mobilization is a wide-

[9] Conditions of service for NGO staff in Africa are frequently better than those of the civil service – apart from job security – although structural adjustment has reduced this certainty. However, staff of NGOs are far less likely to have additional jobs or to be as able to benefit from rent-seeking, which is not uncommon for public servants.

spread problem; many NGOs have no fixed assets or infrastructure, such as transport. Also, few NGOs are adept at providing the requisite financial and narrative reports to donors, thus raising concerns about their accountability. Moreover, they are not immune from problems of individual financial mis-appropriation, a fact borne out by the present writer's experience as a pro-gramme officer with the Ford Foundation in Nairobi.

Some respondents expressed concern that NGOs may replicate the corruption patterns of the public sector which the government is trying to eradicate. As one remarked, 'there are basically four ways of making money in Kenya – coffee, tea, tourism and aid – and, since the first three are spoken for, the last remains the only option'. Thus, donors worry that the sector is becoming infiltrated by NGOs whose motives are not particularly benevolent – especially NGOs created by civil servants restructured out of a job but who still retain influential contacts within ministries – a phenomenon borne out by trends in Tanzania and Uganda (Fowler, 1991).

This said, a number of factors may mitigate against endemic corruption in NGOs. First, the level of remuneration within NGOs is often greater than for the civil service, thus reducing pressures to diversify income. Further, NGOs lack statutory power, which limits the scope for rent-seeking. Third, the smaller scale of NGO operations lends itself to greater transparency and control, while the NGO value-orientation may condition more strongly against widespread misuse of organizational resources for personal gain. In other words, overall there may be less of a probability that an NGO's cost-effectiveness will be reduced by misappropriation.

In addition to doubts about NGO capabilities, a question arises from manage-ment theory as to whether the comparative organizational advantages of NGOs noted previously will be compromised, owing to the demands associated with an enlarged role in service provision – specifically, whether NGO structures and practices will become bureaucratized as is happening in Europe (Quarles van Ufford et al., 1988). In NGO circles the issue is recognized, but is usually framed as a problem associated with the scaling-up impact.[10]

What, then, of NGOs realizing and maintaining comparative advantage? One conclusion arising from the foregoing discussion is that the distinction between state and NGO provision of services must be sought not so much in what they do, as in how they do it and with whom. In other words, the issue appears to be one of method and clients reached, not the choice of service to be provided vis-à-vis the state per se.

There are few publicly available systematic studies or evaluations enabling observers to separate out rhetoric and practice in the NGO development approach and their ability to target particular disadvantaged groups. Instances can be cited, however, where state and NGOs do differ in client group and

[10]  Ways in which NGOs can increase the scale of their impact without losing their comparative advantages were the subject of an NGO conference held in January 1992 in Manchester, organized by the Save the Children Fund and the Centre for Development Policy and Management, University of Manchester (Edwards and Hulme, 1992).

method. Examples are NGOs working with the informal sector which, until recently, was treated as illegal enterprise; or NGOs providing credit to those, especially women, who do not have the collateral required by commercial or state lending institutions; or NGOs supporting community-based care for people with AIDS, issues which governments simply cannot address.

Evidence from the sub-region suggests that NGO comparative advantage is exploited most when: (i) their work is with groups considered to be 'illegal' or 'victims' and not recognizable by the state – examples would be squatters, street children and petty traders; (ii) when the services they provide require sustained community input for their maintenance; and (iii) when services need to be innovative or tailored to local circumstances.

If these factors are not in play when choosing between state and NGOs to provide social services, there is little reason to assume in East Africa that other factors will be determinant for the more efficient and effective resource use by one or the other. In fact, in the majority of cases differences in efficiency between state and NGO provision of services are likely to be marginal, especially in fields with strong professional or government regulation, such as health care and education.

An alternative perspective arising from the above analysis is that the crux of the issue of service supply between an East African state and NGOs lies not so much in their operational comparative advantages as providers as in their differential ability to mobilize resources at home and abroad. This area is now given consideration.

## The Issue of Resources

The ability of any organization to provide services to those not able to pay the full cost is determined by its access to finance from other sources. While a reduction in the quality of services can compensate for resource limitations, in the final analysis, without some form of non-client funding, a service cannot be supplied. What does this mean for governments and NGOs in East Africa?

It has been argued that NGOs are unlikely to differ significantly from the state in their operations as service providers. Where NGOs do have a potential comparative advantage over the state, however, is in their potential ability to mobilize economic resources from (a) within the communities with which they work, and (b) the international aid system.

### Community Resources

The capability of any society to provide services to its members depends on the resources at its disposal. Resource limitations constrain any state in the level of its service delivery, but this factor is particularly acute in East Africa where neither indigenous economic surplus nor government revenue can keep up with demand. Population growth rates and deteriorating internal and external economic circumstances work against maintaining, let alone expanding, the real level of resources available for social services. Increasingly, official aid is the prop supporting government service delivery, but donor reluctance to cover recurrent costs limits the extent to which this can meet people's minimal requirements in the long term.

NGOs supposedly possess one comparative advantage which offers an attractive solution to the crucial problem of recurrent finance, and hence sustainability outside of foreign aid. The advantage lies in the NGO ability to engage with communities in ways that mobilize their resources on an ongoing basis, offering a new way of maintaining supply not readily open to governments, in part because of historical popular expectations about the latter.[11] NGOs can help increase and mobilize local resources that are managed and reapplied locally and tangibly as a public good instead of their being appropriated to the political centre, as is common practice with the state. Examples of such local mobilization occurring are to be found in subsequent chapters.

For NGOs to realize their comparative advantage in local resource mobilization requires that they can and do operate differently from the government. If this is not allowed, there is little likelihood of sustained maintenance of the local services that come into being. In sum, exploiting a key potential benefit of NGO development action will depend on these organizations being free to differ from the state in what they do. This point has been forcefully made by Shaeffer (1992) in relation to education. For him, people's participation and innovation in supply are key to solving the problem of deteriorating educational provision almost everywhere in the sub-Saharan region. He argues that redressing the situation requires a new structure of collaboration between governments, NGOs and communities. If this is not achieved, there is little evidence to suggest that the choice between state and NGO as supplier of services to the poor is really very substantive.

The foregoing conclusion does, however, raise the question of equity for poorer communities which probably have little, if any, resources to be mobilized. In this situation, funding to NGOs for their work with POs will remain a foreign welfare subsidy to Africa's poor.

## NGOs and Governments: from Comparative to Competitive Advantage in Accessing International Aid

In addition to action with communities, NGOs may demonstrate a better ability than states to raise resources for welfare services from the international aid system. Two reasons can be advanced for this assertion. First, the privatization policies detailed in Chapter 1 may continue to predispose official aid agencies towards NGO funding, reinforced by public lobbying from the NGO sector

---

[11] The issue, as discussed in Chapter 1, is one of state legitimacy. Freeing African states from colonial rule relied, amongst other things, on politicians promising that citizens would obtain free of charge the services that colonialists had kept for themselves. The difficulty in Tanzania, for example, of reintroducing local development or 'poll' taxes, or in Kenya of levying user charges, stems from people's expectations that the independent state would be beneficent. No East African states have been able to mobilize local resources to meet recurrent, as opposed to capital, costs, for public services such as clinics and schools. NGOs are not burdened with expectations that their services will be free, beyond what they have themselves created through injudicious methods.

itself. The quality of this finance will, however, accelerate the growth of NGOs as non-profit contractors.[12]

Second, NGOs may also be able to access aid more easily if a regime adopts strategies that essentially use them as proxy organizations. Subject to availability of sufficient controls, it can be in the interests of an African government to promote welfare provision by NGOs where protecting or extending levels of service availability bolsters political legitimacy. This rationale is one explanation for the Tanzanian Government's decision to 'return' religiously initiated hospitals to church control, with associated commitments for German Government financing (see Chapter 11). Kenya and Uganda have been more cautious in taking over NGO-initiated services. Where they have done so, underfunding has been common, the government absorption of Village Polytechnics in Kenya in the early 1970s being one example.

If complemented by better regulatory instruments, governments have little to fear from an enlarging NGO sector also gaining greater autonomy. Recent NGO legislation in Uganda and Kenya is a sign of such considerations informing government responses to the current aid environment.

The picture emerging is one where significant dependence on foreign aid, coupled with donor privatization policies, is essentially shifting the debate on NGO versus state provision from an issue of comparative to competitive advantage. Or, put another way, the current constellation of internal forces and external conditions appears to conspire to make African governments and NGOs compete with each other in the aid marketplace.

## NGOs and the Globalization of Social Welfare

The preceding sections analysed the capacity of NGOs to raise the resources needed to provide welfare and development services to the poor. What the discussion has not addressed, however, is the financing of NGOs themselves; do they have a perspective as sustainable organizations? The answer to this question needs to be sought in an assessment of the various sources they can tap or, put differently, the economic surplus they will be able to access in the future. Such an exercise indicates that, globally, NGOs are likely to be increasingly reliant on the official aid system for their existence, African NGOs being an extreme case of such dependence (Fowler, 1992).

NGOs in Africa have always been almost totally dependent for their functional presence on the availability of external funding. As a consequence, the size of the NGO sector and the level of financial resources it applies in East African countries bear little relationship to the indigenous economic base and potential for local support. Comparing the prevailing privatization policies of international donors with the economic performance of the countries concerned suggests that the gap is likely to grow even further. Few NGOs in East Africa

---

[12] By quality is meant the conditions and expectations associated with an NGO's financial resources. Factors holding the contracting trend somewhat in check are (a) concern about the absorptive capacity of the NGO sector and (b) the inability of many NGOs actually to demonstrate what they achieve with the public and private funds they obtain.

will survive without foreign aid. If this is the case, the discussion on state versus non-state provision of services in East Africa must be broadened to include an assessment of trends in international development assistance, particularly that derived from the tax base of Northern governments. A comparative historical approach is used for such a speculative analysis.

Charitable action, the precursor of state welfarism, emerged in the North as a response to the acute distress of an underclass created by industrial capitalism in the late 1700s. Colonial expansion provided a path through which the social dysfunctions of market capitalism could slowly be exported to Southern countries. The improvement in the living and working conditions of Northern labour was made possible by government taxes and policies that effectively internally redistributed part of the surpluses flowing back to Northern economies from the colonies (Wallerstein, 1988). Within Northern states this process attenuated potentially revolutionary action by those gaining least, or suffering most, from market-led growth. The resulting stability aided capitalism, resulting in today's 'culture of contentment' amongst the Northern voting polity (Galbraith, 1992).

The present acceleration of capitalist expansion and its rapid globalization, due to the demise of the centrally planned economies, could signal a parallel process of a globalization of social welfare, with NGOs providing a channel for its realization – in other words, a move towards a selective permanent provision of welfare services to the world's underclass. Or, put differently, official aid to NGOs will provide an, albeit limited, redistribution of the global economic surpluses accruing disproportionately in the North. In doing so, aid will contribute to the security of capital investment and to the stability of the Southern regimes which maintain the environment necessary to produce returns on them.

This view of the new function of aid is supported by arguments put forward in a recent UNDP publication. The 1993 *Human Development Report* argues that East–West rivalry no longer provides the underlying justification for international development assistance. A new motivation needs to be found for aid and this lies in the realm of enlightened self-interest (UNDP, 1993: 8). The argument runs thus: if the North does not wish its own quality of life to be threatened by Southern poverty, for example through migration of poor people and their illnesses or political instability and civil strife, it is in its interest to alleviate the hardships faced by the world economy's functional underclass.

One reason against drawing such a simplistic parallel between the national evolution of state welfare in the early twentieth century and today's global scene is the lack of an effective system of global governance that functions like the sovereign states of the former era. While the UN system may indeed lack this coherence and authority, present-day communications and the 'invisible hand' steering internationally oriented economies and their perceptions of self-interest in a multi-polar world may not now require central orchestration to arrive at the welfare panorama postulated above (Rosenau, 1990). Is it not possible that the leading countries in each of the major trading blocks – the Americas, Europe and Asia – will use their dominance in aid disbursements to replicate domestic policies towards the poor within their spheres of interest and investment?

As a product of the global welfare imperative, official aid to NGOs will continue to grow, rapidly overtaking voluntary contributions from the general public. Implications for NGO autonomy and structural dependence clearly emerge. In addition, the sovereignty of poorer states, especially in Africa, may become an acknowledged fiction.[13] Some of these inorganic geo-political entities may not be economically viable as nation-states corresponding to the modern model. Their existence will therefore essentially become one of acting as local governments in the global order, able to function only on the basis of concessionary lending and grant aid.[14] Despite these conditions, if tackled strategically, their significance as service providers should enable NGOs to increase their leverage within African states by, for example, applying pro-poor practices and advocating associated government policy reforms.

The foregoing view does not imply that NGOs should discontinue efforts to build Africa's capacity to satisfy its own social service requirements. What it does suggest, however, is that the institutional development actors will need to reconsider their positions within a global dialectic of state or NGO provision of services for the world's impoverished.

NGOs must (a) reappraise their long-term strategies and role within the continent, (b) take on board the political implications of being potentially the major suppliers of social services in a country, (c) renegotiate their position with governments, lest they simply become parastatal agencies in all but name, (d) question some of the myths about their own sustainability as actors in Africa's development, and (e) recognize that in global terms their resources are negligible in relation to the forces that cause and maintain poverty. It is this latter arena that will be crucial for NGOs to increase their impact by, for example, influencing public policies and aid allocations (Edwards and Hulme, 1992).

African regimes will have to revise their ideas about their sources of legitimacy and their role and right to decide on and control social development processes. *Inter alia,* this will require the creation of mechanisms for negotiating with the NGO community and donor agencies which seldom exist at present.

Donor agencies, although unlikely to be explicit in the relations between capitalist expansion and aid as an instrument of global welfare, will have to move away from unrealistic expectations that NGOs will eventually be self-financing. Such an acceptance has critical implications for their funding commitments, strategies and contracting practices.

The current political changes afoot in the countries of East Africa, and wider afield, may provide a window of opportunity for states, NGOs and donors to look more realistically at what the poorest governments are capable of doing,

---

[13]   The issue of the sovereignty of African states is already a concern because of the conditions applied to structural adjustment loans which, it can be argued, are a new form of economic imperialism. Official funding to NGOs can be seen as part and parcel of this problem.

[14]   Here again, parallels can be drawn with dependent relations between local authorities and central governments in Northern countries. While local authorities derive authority from a separate electoral process, an ability to realize their mandates is critically dependent on conditions set by the regime in power nationally. The struggle between a Conservative central government and Labour councils in Britain is an illustration of the degree to which local sovereignty can be circumscribed.

acknowledging a needed 'complementarity-in-autonomy' of all institutions committed to the well-being of poor citizens in the new world order.

# References

Baldwin, G. (1990) 'Non-Government Organizations and African Development: An Inquiry' in World Bank, *Background Papers: Long Term Perspectives Study for Sub-Saharan Africa*, Vol. 3, Institutional and Sociopolitical Issues. Washington, DC: World Bank, June.

Billis, D. (1989) *A Theory of the Voluntary Sector: Implications for Policy and Practice*. Working Paper No. 5, Centre for Voluntary Organization. London: London School of Economics.

Brett, E. (1990) 'Competence and Accountability in the Voluntary Sector: Organization Theory, Adjustment Policy and Institutional Reform'. Brighton: Institute of Development Studies, University of Sussex (mimeo).

Brown, L.D. and Korten, D. (1989) *Understanding Voluntary Organizations: Guidelines for Donors*. Working Paper WPS 258. Washington, DC: World Bank, Country Economics Department, September.

Chambers, R. (1983) *Rural Development: Putting the Last First*. Harlow: Longman.

Chepkwony, A. (1987) 'The Role of Non-Governmental Organizations in Development: A Study of the National Christian Council of Kenya (NCCK), 1963–1978'. Doctoral Thesis, Studia Missionalia Uppsaliensia. Uppsala: University of Uppsala.

DENIVA (1990) *A Directory of Non Governmental Organizations (NGOs) in Uganda*. Kampala: Development Network of Voluntary Associations.

Edwards, M. and Hulme, D. (eds) (1992) *Making a Difference: NGOs and Development in a Changing World*. London: Earthscan.

Esman, M. and Uphoff, N. (1984) *Local Organisations: Intermediaries in Rural Development*. Ithaca, NY: Cornell University Press.

Etzioni, A. (1968) *The Active Society*. London: Collier-Macmillan.

Etzioni, A. (1971) *A Comparative Analysis of Complex Organizations: On Power, Involvement and their Correlates*. New York: The Free Press.

Fowler, A. (1988) 'Non-Governmental Organizations in Africa: Achieving Comparative Advantage in Micro-development'. Discussion Paper No. 249. Brighton: University of Sussex, Institute of Development Studies, August.

Fowler, A. (1991) 'The Role of NGOs in Changing State–Society Relations: Perspectives from Eastern and Southern Africa', *Development Policy Review* 9 (1): 53–83.

Fowler, A. (1992) 'Distant Obligations: Speculations on NGO Funding and the Global Market', *Review of African Political Economy* 55: 9–29.

Fowler, A. (1993) 'Non-Governmental Organisations and the Promotion of Democracy in Kenya'. Doctoral Thesis, Brighton: Institute of Development Studies, University of Sussex.

Fowler, A. and Bauer, G. (1989) 'A Survey of Official Aid to NGOs in Kenya'. Nairobi: The Ford Foundation (unpublished).

Fowler, A., Campbell, P. and Pratt, B. (1992) *Institutional Development and NGOs in Africa: Policy Perspectives for European Development Agencies*. NGO Management Series No. 1, October. Oxford: International NGO Training and Research Centre.

Galbraith, J. (1992) *The Culture of Contentment*. London: Sinclair-Stevenson.

KNCSS (1978) *A Directory of Non-Governmental Organisations in Kenya*. Nairobi: Kenya National Council of Social Services.

KNCSS (1988) *A Directory of (Non-Government) Voluntary Organizations in Kenya.* Nairobi: Kenya National Council of Social Services.

Korten, D. (1990) *Getting to the 21st Century: Voluntary Action and the Global Agenda.* West Hartford, CT: Kumarian Press.

Lissner, J. (1977) *The Politics of Altruism: A Study of the Political Behaviour of Voluntary Agencies.* Geneva: Lutheran World Federation.

Lonsdale, J. (1981) 'States and Social Processes in Africa: A Historiographical Survey', *African Studies Review* 24 (2–3): 139–225.

McCarthy, K. (1990) *The Voluntary Sector Overseas: Notes From the Field.* Working Papers. New York: City University of New York, Center for the Study of Philanthropy.

Moe, T. (1984) 'The New Economics of Organization', *American Journal of Political Science* 11 (3): 734–49.

Quarles van Ufford, P., Kruit, D. and Downing, R. (1988) *The Hidden Crisis in Development: Development Bureaucracies.* Amsterdam: Free University Press.

Robinson, M. (1991) 'Development NGOs in Europe and North America: A Statistical Profile', *Charity Trends*: 154–65, Annual Report of the Charities Aid Foundation. Tonbridge: Charities Aid Foundation.

Rosenau, J. (1990) *Turbulence in World Politics: A Theory of Change and Continuity.* Brighton, Harvester/Wheatsheaf.

Salmen, L. and Eaves, P. (1989) *World Bank Work with Nongovernmental Organizations.* Working Paper No. 305. Washington, DC: World Bank, Country Economics Department, December.

Schneider, B. (1988) *The Barefoot Revolution: A Report to the Club of Rome.* London: Intermediate Technology Publications.

Shaeffer, S. (1992) 'Collaborating for Change: The Participation between Government, NGOs and the Community in Education and Development'. Paper presented at the South and East African Seminar on Collaboration for Educational Change in Non-Formal Basic Education, Kenya Institute of Education, Nairobi, Kenya, 21–29 January. Paris: International Institute for Educational Planning.

Smith, S. (1991) *OXFAM: Report of an Enquiry Submitted to the Charity Commissioners.* London: HMSO, May.

Smith, S. and Lipsky, M. (1993) *NonProfits for Hire: The Welfare State in the Age of Contracting.* Cambridge, MA: Harvard University Press.

Stevens, C., and van Thermaat, J.V. (1985) *Pressure Groups, Policies and Development: The Private Sector and EEC–Third World Policy.* London: Hodder and Stoughton.

TANGO (1991) *Tanzania Non-Governmental Organisations Directory.* Dar es Salaam: Tanzania Non-Governmental Organizations Association.

UNDP (1993) *Human Development Report.* Oxford: Oxford University Press.

van Rooy, A. (1991). 'The Politics of Devolving Development Aid'. Draft Working Paper. Oxford: Lincoln College.

Wallerstein, I. (1966) 'Voluntary Associations' in J. Coleman and C. Rosberg (eds) *Political Parties and National Integration in Tropical Africa.* Berkeley, CA: University of California Press.

Wallerstein, I. (1988) *The Politics of the World Economy: The States, The Movements and the Civilizations.* Cambridge: Cambridge University Press.

Whitaker, B. (1974) *The Foundations: An Anatomy of Philanthropy and Society.* London: Eyre Methuen.

Williamson, O. (1981) 'The Economics of Organizations: The Transactions Cost Approach', *American Journal of Sociology* 87: 548–77.

# 4

## KARUTI KANYINGA
## The Politics of Development Space
## in Kenya

State & Voluntary Organizations
in the Delivery of Basic Services*

The level and quality of basic services in Kenya are higher than in both Tanzania and Uganda (see Chapter 1), but public demand for and expectations of social services continue to outrun the state's delivery capacity. This has resulted in a mismatch between demand and supply. Both social and regional inequities in the services actually provided exacerbate the mismatch. Furthermore, regional disparities in the coverage of basic services have widened owing to pervasive political patronage. Decentralization measures, such as the District Focus for Rural Development (DFRD) introduced in 1983, have not only failed to correct the imbalance but also intensified the disparities (see Barkan and Chege, 1989; Ng'ethe and Kanyinga, 1993).

The rapidly increasing demand for services results from several factors: population growth that is among the highest in Africa – 3-4% per year in the 1980s, but now falling; deepening social stratification; differentiations of class demands; and high expectations based on past successful economic growth and therefore the state's past success in the ability to deliver. Although rich and poor have different service requirements, both expect improvements in quality and access, as argued by Oyugi (Chapter 7).

For decades, expansions in the supply of basic services have taken place through both the state and the voluntary sector (*inter alia*, non-governmental organizations, churches, people's organizations (POs) such as the *harambee* (self-help) groups and co-operatives), with donors contributing significant shares of the required funds. The private for-profit sector has contributed too. In the 1960s and 1970s, the state provided the bulk of services, while the voluntary sector confined itself mainly to relief and welfare. In the early 1980s, state contributions declined considerably, owing to the worldwide recession and its adverse implications for the Kenyan economy, Western pressure on the state to scale down direct involvement in service provision, a switch of donor support away from the state towards the voluntary sector, and the increased challenge of state legitimacy by both internal and external forces. Also the development

* The author wishes to thank Njuguna Ng'ethe for his help in writing this chapter.

philosophy of NGOs changed in the early 1980s, shifting from simple charity and relief activities to community development programmes that embraced institution-building and popular participatory approaches. The number, activities, and resources of NGOs increased tremendously. Moreover, the relations between the state and the voluntary sector became increasingly politicized.

This chapter focuses on the contributions of the voluntary organizations (especially NGOs and POs) to the provision of basic services (health and education) in Kenya during the 1980s and analyses relations between NGOs and the state. Two interrelated viewpoints inform this discussion: on the one hand, people view basic services as a principal component of development and see the state's main responsibility as one of providing such services. People also equate a high level and quality of services with successful development. On the other hand, post-colonial state legitimacy has centred on the ability of the state to enhance development as promised immediately after independence (see Chapter 1). Moreover, the post-colonial state became the main engine of economic growth and development. High expectations followed from this prominent role. Delivery of basic social services therefore influences the form of state–society relations in Kenya.

The concept of 'development space' is useful in analysing service provision in this complex and contested environment. In this chapter development space conceptually refers to the broad arena where socio-political and economic forces interact to shape the form of relations between state and non-state actors providing the services. We argue that, over the years, the development space has become highly politicized as a result of an increase in the number of NGOs, the nature of their activities, and the resources channelled through them. The fiscal constraints of the state to deliver services and therefore maintain legitimacy have added to the political prominence of the voluntary sector.

The analysis starts with a brief account of the political and economic setting of service provision in Kenya's development space. Then follows an analysis of the growth of the voluntary sector and its role in the local development framework, to provide the background for a sectoral analysis of the voluntary sector in service provision. Finally, the political implications of the analysis are drawn.

Makau (Chapter 5) deals in more detail with the provision of education. Anangwe (Chapter 6) analyses the provision of law and order in rural areas based on a case study of Western Kenya. Oyugi (Chapter 7) completes the analyses of service provision in Kenya by examining who benefits.

## Political and Economic Setting

The colonial state did not provide basic services equitably in Kenya. The central region, favourable to settler farming, had relatively better access to basic services than other areas. When independence came, it raised expectations for equitable distribution of basic services by the state. In Sessional Paper No. 10 of 1965, the government articulated the need and means of correcting the regional imbalances. As a landmark of independent Kenya's development policies, the document set the framework for better distribution of services (see Chapter 7), reaffirming the commitment of the state to create an enabling environment and a mixed economy in which partnership of the public and the private sector was crucial. It emphasized mobilization of domestic resources through collective voluntary initiatives as a means to self-reliance and redressing regional disparities. Nevertheless, these disparities and social differentiations continued to grow as the new political elites continued to accumulate wealth via the state and by means of diverting public resources to their areas. Close to the centre of 'state politics' were members of President Kenyatta's Kikuyu ethnic group which was also dominant in the developed central region.

The role of ethnicity in allocating resources continued to be dominant under President Moi. Ethno-regional groups allied to the political elites at the centre derived more benefits in terms of access to basic services, resulting in popular disenchantment in the neglected areas. The mixed market economy widened social differentiations amid slow economic growth and deeply entrenched political patronage. The DFRD, heavily influenced by provincial administrative officials, became a tool in the government's control of both economic and political activities. The provincial administrative set-up and the single political party (Kenya African National Union – KANU) machinery were used to repress the political dissent that accompanied disenchantment. Political patronage infiltrated *harambee*, causing increasing apathy in *harambee* activities.[1]

Skewed distribution of basic services, rising political repression, and failure to stimulate economic growth posed threats to state legitimacy throughout the 1980s. Moreover, slow economic growth prompted gradual adoption of Structural Adjustment Programmes as prescribed by the World Bank and the IMF. These emphasized the role of the state as creating an enabling environment for non-state agencies, the scaling down of state activities and introducing cost-sharing in public health and education services, among other measures. The government hesitated to carry out some of these measures till 1991 when donors intensified pressure to do so.

Economic performance has also influenced the level of basic services provided by the state. The 1960s witnessed comparatively good economic performance, in terms of growth, when gross domestic product (GDP) per capita rose at 3% per annum. It dropped to 0.3% per annum in the 1970s, and was mixed in the 1980s. GDP growth per capita in 1976 constant prices during the period 1980–85 stood at –3.5% per annum compared with 0.6% p.a. in the 1985–90 period.[2] Public expenditures fell by 1% p.a. during the 1980–85 period but grew by 5.9% p.a. in the 1985–90 period. Expenditures on education declined by 0.8% p.a. during the first half of the 1980s, but grew by 5.8% p.a. during the second half of the decade. Health expenditures fell by 5.4% p.a. between 1980 and 1985 but then grew by 3.8% p.a. for the rest of the decade. There was a

---

[1] For detailed discussion of the socio-political and development contexts of *harambee* (pulling together) see, among others, Ng'ethe (1979); Ngau, (1987); Thomas (1987); Barkan and Holmquist (1989); and Kanyinga (1993).

[2] Throughout the 1980s, fiscal performance was comparatively poor as the country experienced a recurrent budget deficit of between 4% and 11% (Semboja, 1992).

positive relationship between economic performance and public expenditures in the 1980s. When economic performance improved, public expenditure tended to rise and vice versa.

These figures throw some light on the growing outcry in Kenya that government expenditures on health and education have declined during the 1980s. This is not true as far as growth in education expenditure is concerned. It is more justified with respect to growth in health expenditures, which fell during the early 1980s, and rose more slowly than overall expenditures in the later part of the decade. But, if levels of expenditures are considered, the outcry is justified. Per capita expenditures in 1976 constant prices in education and health were lower in 1990 (at K.Shs. 91 and 27) than in 1981 (at K.Shs. 114 and 44). Thus recorded declines during 1980–85 were so severe that post-1984 growth rates did not restore previous real expenditure levels. The critics are therefore right on levels, but not on growth.

The mismatch between demand for services and their supply through the public sector has made the role of the voluntary sector in the delivery of such services more salient. Indeed, the observed relative decline of state-provided basic services raises the question: 'To whom is the state ceding its micro-development activities?' Attempts to address this question highlight the significance of NGOs and POs.

## The Growth of the Voluntary Organizations

In Kenya NGOs include the secular and formal (in terms of structure) organizations that are voluntarily and deliberately set up to help those people outside their membership in particular. *Harambee* self-help groups, widely spread throughout the country, exemplify the POs; intimacy, informality and service to members characterize the organization of such groups.

Nearly all categories of voluntary organizations claim to exhibit characteristics which include 'altruism, charity, efficiency, diversity, pluralism, popular participation, and autonomy' (Brodhead and Herbert-Copley, 1988). These characteristics, usually equated with NGOs' advantages over state institutions, have encouraged the view that NGOs not only ensure the survival of beneficiaries, but also promote sustainable development especially at the micro level.[3] However, the degree to which each particular organization exhibits these characteristics is a matter of debate.

### The Harambee Groups

As in most peasant societies, POs in Kenya are grounded in the indigenous lifestyles and values of the people. Rural life reverberates with the spirit of communalism, charity and voluntarism, all of which inform the establishment of

[3] Discussions on the relative importance and comparative advantages of NGOs over other micro development actors underline, among other things, that NGOs deliver quick returns; employ small-is-beautiful popular participatory methods; use flexible and effective development approaches; and are based at the grass roots where beneficiaries live: Hyden (1983); Drabek (1987); Streeten (1987); Brodhead and Herbert-Copley (1988); Fowler (1988); Bratton (1989).

POs throughout the world. In Kenya, this is manifested in the spirit of *harambee*, which has led to the growth of many self-help activities and associations that have become recognized as a central feature of the country's development process.

*Harambee* groups have taken a central role in local development, serving as the main focus of popular participation. Through *harambee*, communities mobilize their resources to implement and support basic service projects such as schools, health centres, water points and others (Ngau, 1987; Thomas, 1987). There are now over 30,000 registered *harambee* groups, most of which are women's organizations (Mazingira Institute, 1992).

Over time *harambee* has existed as one avenue through which communities, and their political elites, extract resources from the state (through matching funds) to complete and run development activities which they initiate. On the other hand, the state increases its legitimacy through this support for grass-roots activities. Politicians and government officials seeking a political base in the countryside therefore patronize *harambee* activities. Especially in more recent years attempts by the state to control the *harambee* have considerably changed the relationship and infused into it political values not related to the traditional spirit of voluntarism (see Chapter 1). This poses a serious threat to the voluntarism of the *harambee*.

The NGO community in Kenya maintains close contact with *harambee* groups, which it uses as a main avenue for reaching the grass roots. In some instances *harambee* projects are initiated with financial assistance from NGOs. Thus funds from NGOs and Western donors have induced the proliferation of *harambee* groups in both rural and urban areas.

## The Formalized NGOs

During the colonial period, the majority of NGOs in Kenya were charitable organizations, some of them religious bodies combining evangelical work with activities like education and social welfare. There were also urban-based welfare organizations formed by rural people living in the urban areas to guarantee survival in the new environment. However, secular NGOs were few in the colonial days.

With independence, many more organizations evolved with social welfare as their main objective. The floods and famine of the early 1960s, which ravaged many households, became the main focus of churches and an entry point for many relief organizations. Some indigenous NGOs like the National Council of Churches of Kenya (NCCK) and the *Maendeleo ya Wanawake*, an umbrella organization for self-help women's groups, greatly expanded their activities during this period. Secular NGOs emerged in the late 1960s and 1970s focusing, this time, on development activities such as the provision of water and health care. Some of these organizations, like the Co-operation of American Relief Everywhere (CARE), which came to the country in 1968, slowly shifted the focus from relief to development.

Since then, the country's development space has witnessed an unprecedented proliferation of NGOs. Despite disagreement among various sources about the exact numbers, they could be relatively larger than elsewhere in East Africa, if not in the continent. InterAction (1986) and Fowler (1989a) have estimated that the NGO population grew from 120 in late 1978 to over 400 ten years later. KNCSS (1988) figures were 135 for 1978 and 287 for 1988, half of them classified as foreign.[4] Fowler (1989a) estimated that the annual growth rate was 9% for indigenous NGOs and 11% for foreign NGOs during 1978–1988. By 1991 the number of NGOs stood at between 450 and 500.

Both internal and external factors accounted for this high growth. The market-based economic policies pursued by the political elites ever since independence and the latitude provided by the state to organize basic services through self-help initiatives have been critical. This induced the private for-profit and the voluntary non-profit sectors to engage in service provision.

Furthermore, donors now demand better accountability from states in the South. This has brought a much more favourable donor attitude to the voluntary sector than in the past (see Chapter 2). Donors now prefer NGOs for many types of service provisions, citing their efficiency, quick returns, effectiveness and grass-roots linkages. Moreover, donors – especially the IMF and the World Bank – now push for privatization, in which they see NGOs and POs as important actors. When services are privatized, beneficiaries will bear more of the cost of service provision, thereby reducing the fiscal and political burdens of the state.

These changes in donor policies in favour of the voluntary sector, deriving from disillusionment with past disbursements through the state sector and a surge in neo-liberal influence in the North, have led to increased funds for both foreign and local NGOs and to the growth of new ones. Foreign NGOs, which also receive substantial resources from their home governments, have sometimes channelled funds to the grass roots through local NGOs. Fowler (Chapter 3) analyses this trend in a global perspective and also illustrates the magnitude of the resources involved.

However, precise figures on NGO resources in Kenya are difficult to obtain because of inadequate records and generally unsystematized knowledge of NGO activities. Lekyo (1989) estimated that NGOs contribute between US$150m and US$200m annually. Preliminary results from Fowler (1989b) showed that budgetary figures for about 100 NGOs operating in the country were close to US$72m or above US$228m for the entire 400 NGOs, assuming the same size and activities. Indeed, the availability of donor funds has been such that 'any group that registers as an NGO can find funds for its operation somewhere in the North' (Kobia, 1985: 33). This observation would not only explain the growth of NGOs but also the existence of numerous 'hawking' NGOs that exist only in name or may be registered while awaiting donor funds, which they

---

[4] Foreign NGOs have their roots outside the country, while the indigenous ones are founded and controlled locally. Fowler (1985) and Ng'ethe (1991) show that this classification is not watertight: foreign NGOs have staff composed of local people, while indigenous NGOs depend entirely on funds from abroad.

solicit through elaborate project proposals fine-tuned to donor interests.

In sum, the 1980s witnessed increased growth and involvement of NGOs and POs in the country's development space. They supplemented state efforts in service provision. And, as demonstrated later, the state increasingly monitored the development space to ensure that activities by the voluntary sector were in line with official thinking. The District Focus for Rural Development (DFRD) became an important tool for regulating the development activities of both the state and non-state actors. The following section discusses how NGOs and POs were integrated into this essentially political framework.

## Voluntary Organizations and the Local Development Framework

The institutional framework for the provision of basic services and local development has undergone considerable changes since independence. In the late 1960s the state decentralized development planning by introducing District Development Committees (DDCs) and establishing Provincial Planning Officers (PPOs). The aim was to move the planning processes from the national offices of the Ministry of Economic Planning and Development to the provinces and districts so as to accelerate balanced growth and eliminate glaring regional inequalities (Makokha, 1985).

The more articulate decentralized strategy of the DFRD followed in 1983. This emphasized bottom-up strategies, thus providing a springboard for popular participation in development planning and implementation. The DFRD established local development institutions/committees at all levels from the district to the sub-location as channels of popular participation, but provincial administrative officers and departmental heads of the various ministries assumed prominent roles in the running of DFRD committees. Provincial administrative officers, for example, chaired committee meetings at all levels, and the District Executive Committee (DEC), comprising departmental heads, became the main decision-making body. This led to the concentration of decision-making powers in the hands of government officials. Only the most powerful local politicians had any influence in these new centres of power.

The state explicitly tried to integrate NGO activities into the DFRD. The Development Plan for 1989/93, for instance, noted that

> since NGOs have become increasingly involved in development activities their efforts will be strengthened by DFRD, through which NGOs, in collaboration with DDCs, community groups, and local authorities will enhance the process of local participation in the development projects (Republic of Kenya, 1989: 260).

But this can also be seen as an attempt by the state to keep track of NGO activities in order to co-ordinate (some say control) them, so as to avoid duplication of effort and wastage of resources. As a result, NGOs became members of District Development Committees and subordinate committees. At the same time, the government required the DDCs to approve NGO activities in the Districts, which the NGOs interpreted as an attempt to control them by providing opportunities for political influence and interference in their activities.[5] Some, especially the resourceful ones, feared that the DDCs could influence them away from needy areas to those preferred by the politicians. However, since the DDCs lacked legal authority to enforce compliance from NGOs, the extent to which NGOs are integrated into the DFRD is debatable. Some NGOs attend DDC meetings as a matter of routine or to present interests that require DDC attention, while others bypass the DDC and its subordinate institutions altogether.

The DFRD has also co-opted the *harambee* movement into the official local institutions. There are many explanations for this (see Chapter 5, and Kanyinga, 1993). The state perhaps regarded *harambee* as a safety valve to diffuse rising public expectations and also harness social divisions. Moreover, through *harambee*, local communities supplemented resources to match those provided by the state institutions, the mainstream churches, and private sector institutions.

## Voluntary Organizations and Basic Services Delivery

Development activities by the voluntary organizations spread across all sectors and parallel those of the state in many ways. Chapter 3 indicated the preference of local and foreign NGOs for the inclusion of food and nutrition, health, education, population, water and shelter in their programmes.[6] In pursuance of these objectives, NGOs stress the importance of people's participation in providing local materials and labour, among other things, in the construction of new projects, while NGOs provide the finance and inputs not available at local sites. Several factors account for the high priority given by NGOs to social development. They include the influence of donor preferences; a shift from relief to development work by many NGOs; and the high priority attached to these activities by the local communities, as manifested in the *harambee* efforts.

Other voluntary organizations pursue objectives similar to those of NGOs. The mainstream churches finance health care, provide water facilities and construct and maintain schools in their respective areas. Mission hospitals, health posts, schools and water points complement public services in the urban areas and the countryside. Islamic organizations have similar concerns. Next to the mosques are *madrasa* or nursery schools and other facilities for the Muslim communities. Cost-sharing is a central feature of most of the services provided by the religious bodies, as it has been for decades.

The strategies adopted by the voluntary organizations in these efforts depend

---

[5]  Some NGOs are uneasy about this requirement. The most articulate view it as an attempt by the state to dominate other actors in the development space and specifically to regulate those NGOs that try to meet perhaps the most socially and politically sensitive of all development needs, namely, basic services.

[6]  The KNCSS directories (1978) and (1988) also show these as the main priority areas of all NGOs.

on local traditions, their own organizational structures, and the availability of
resources. But NGOs generally tend to view development in human terms, as
raising human potential and capabilities through the provision of basic needs. In
recent years they have increasingly adopted a sectoral approach compatible with
their own view of how to establish a civic development culture characterized
by, among other things, group autonomy and group ownership of development
endeavour.

To make a detailed analysis of NGOs' impact by sector is difficult because of
lack of relevant data. NGOs rarely publish information on expenditure and,
when they do, it is either out of date or incomplete (operating costs are often
excluded, although they may be greater than construction costs). Indeed, there
are no systematic studies of NGOs' transparency in their operations or of their
actual capacity to deliver.[7] Few NGO beneficiaries have any idea of their bene-
factors' organizational structure, magnitude of the budget, or sources of revenue.
Nonetheless, there is no doubt that NGO involvement in the delivery of basic
services has been rising (see Chapter 3).

## Sectoral Activities

In 1990, the government attested to the significant role of NGOs, noting that
they mobilized foreign exchange worth K.Shs. 6.9 billion per annum (Republic
of Kenya, 1990a). It also estimates that NGOs and the private sector provide
about 40% of the country's health services and 33% of in-patient care (Republic
of Kenya, 1994: 231). The Minister for Health stated in 1989 that he expected
the share of the government's contributions to decline in the foreseeable future
to 50% with increased assistance from NGOs.[8] In addition, NGOs provide
between 40% and 50% of the family planning services. Here their role has been
explicitly recognized by the appointment of ten NGOs to the National Council
for Population and Development (Ng'ethe et al., 1988).

Examples of NGOs' contribution in specific rural areas provide an even
better picture of their expanding role. One NGO operating in two divisions
with a population of over 240,000 has provided over 80% of the total health and
education services within an eight-year period. The state has provided qualified
staff, albeit often rather late compared with the completion of the facilities
(Kanyinga and Makanda, 1991).

In the arid and semi-arid areas (parts of Eastern, Rift Valley, North Eastern
and Coast provinces) NGOs' support for basic services is perhaps more than that
provided by the government. NGOs provide water facilities, training in agriculture and livestock development, health care, and funds for the construction
and equipment of schools. They also provide relief supplies during droughts. In

---

[7] Anti-NGO sentiment, in some areas, cites NGOs as a 'secretive Pajero Community' with usually
high expenditures on luxurious cars and offices (Kanyinga, 1993). Some also suspect that they have
weak capacity and poor managerial skills to deliver services (Ng'ethe, 1991).

[8] Speech by the Minister for Health, Mwai Kibaki, when addressing staff of the African Medical and
Research Foundation (AMREF) in Nairobi. See *The Daily Nation*, 9 September 1989.

addition, they maintain school feeding programmes as a basic component of their activities – an essential part of the educational system in these areas because of recurring droughts, famine and general ecological difficulties. Some NGOs even attach foreign volunteer teaching staff to some of the schools because of the reluctance of government-employed teachers to accept postings to these areas, which are usually seen as a punishment for errant public servants. Even inducements such as compensatory 'hardship allowances' have failed to attract staff to these areas and NGOs have begun to substitute for them.

The NGO contribution, in partnership with government and the local communities, is even more pronounced in the field of technical education where they support about 45% of all the village polytechnics in the country (*The Daily Nation*, 24 September 1991), giving material, technical and financial support, among other things. The local communities provide the land and the labour, and the government assists in paying the instructors. It may also take over the projects or absorb some of the costs after the phasing out of the NGOs. In any event, the local communities use *harambee* to meet recurrent expenditures for these projects, since assistance from the government is insufficient and uncertain.

NGO activities in service provision are based on a general division of labour (see Chapter 5). Communities organize themselves to put up *harambee* schools and health centres. Some receive financial assistance from the mainstream churches, NGOs and other non-state bodies. Once the construction is completed, the government may take over the running of community schools and health centres or assist in staffing and meeting some maintenance costs, while the NGOs gradually phase themselves out. Moreover, the NGOs' role in some of the *harambee* basic service projects is limited to monitoring their funds. Their engagement with the project may end after the task they fund is completed.

*Harambee* groups mobilize resources for the provision of basic services but they need matching funds from NGOs, the state or donors to be successful. Overall *harambee* funding of development projects has been between 3% and 11% of total public funding, with educational projects taking the leading proportion of total *harambee* contributions (Republic of Kenya, 1989: 258–9; Chapter 5).

The NGO contribution to the provision of basic services is incontestable. What might be debatable is the size of the resources involved and how these compare with state resources. For the basic services as a whole, there is little doubt that NGOs and POs are micro actors compared with the state, no matter how large NGO and PO contributions might appear to be in individual projects, areas or activities. In such cases, the impact of NGO and PO activities may have political implications which may affect their relations with the state in the larger arena. But these relations would not be based on analyses of contributions of material resources alone. The state has the power to determine and direct the behaviour of other actors, including NGOs and POs. Looked at in this way, and in the light of NGOs' and POs' relatively 'small' budgetary outlays compared with the state, one should not, in theory, expect relations between the two to be marked by tension. Why, then, has this sometimes happened?

# A Question of Legitimacy: Relations Between State and Voluntary Organizations

It is noteworthy that in the first two decades of independence relations between the state and the voluntary organizations were generally cordial. The reasons for this include, first, that in the 1960s and 1970s the state's main concern was to meet citizens' expectations and fulfil the promises made at independence. To obtain political legitimation, the supply of basic services and development infrastructure became a main prerogative of the state. Good economic performance and generous foreign aid enabled it to meet these development challenges. Secondly, NGOs were relatively uncritical of the development administration and the governance situation at the time. Most of them were relief and welfare organizations; some were also affiliates of religious organizations. Also the government generally viewed voluntary organizations as agencies complementing and supplementing its own micro development activities. This required co-ordination to avoid duplication of effort, but not outright control.

The political framework for the voluntary sector changed considerably with the shift of political regimes – from President Kenyatta to Moi's second republic in 1978. An ideology emerged which was not only centralist in character, but also constrained the evolution of a civic development culture and an active civil society. President Moi rejuvenated the political party – KANU – which was more or less moribund during the Kenyatta period. Moreover, state and political patronage in the second republic increasingly eroded the relative autonomy guaranteed to the voluntary organizations by the Kenyatta regime, as Moi's political elites sought to cover for the state's relative inability to provide basic services. They transformed voluntary activities into avenues of political patronage and control of local politics, as the state tried to regulate the development space so as not to lose hold of its 'besieged legitimacy'.

Relations cooled in the late 1980s, as the state warily sought to 'control' voluntary organizations as it had done with several other civil society organizations. The 1990s witnessed an important watershed in NGO–state relations with the passing of the Non-Governmental Organizations Co-ordination Act in 1990. It may even be argued that the siege of NGOs, through legislation, was long overdue when it was finally attempted in 1991.[9] These trends are analysed in more detail below.

## Control or Co-ordination?

Changes in relations between the state and the voluntary organizations can be traced back to several events in the early 1980s. The state's capacity to deliver

---

[9] The Non-Governmental Organizations Co-ordination Bill 1990 was speedily introduced in parliament (then a single-party parliament) in December 1990, and received presidential assent in January 1991. Most NGOs interpreted this speedy process as motivated by 'control' rather than by attempts at co-ordination.

basic services and development infrastructure began to stagnate, as the effects of the 1980 and 1984 droughts became widely manifest. The voluntary sector also underwent changes during the same period. The number and activities of NGOs – mainly financed by donors – began to increase, possibly as a response to the droughts and famine. However, their activities remained unco-ordinated. Registration and co-ordination mechanisms were scattered among various government departments, and NGO growth outpaced the institutional ability of the KNCSS – the governmental body that traditionally co-ordinates voluntary organizations.

Moreover, as we have seen, voluntary organizations shifted from relief to integrated community development based on popular participatory approaches. The change required a relatively new approach because, unlike charity, such activities benefited a wider spectrum of people, including the middle class whose demands had significantly increased. In addition, the NGO leadership gradually shifted from volunteer 'charity workers' to the middle class who had not only the necessary organizational and political skills but also the strategic societal position to attract donor funds and challenge state legitimacy. Amid all these developments, popular expectations on what the state could deliver were rising. These were worrisome developments for the political elite, since the state's legitimacy was predicated on the ability to deliver. Meanwhile, relations between the state and the voluntary organizations remained cordial throughout the early 1980s.

By the mid-1980s political patronage in the delivery of development had become relatively widespread compared with the period before the inauguration of the DFRD in 1983. Patronage networks had now become the main avenue for distributing development resources. In consequence, political dissatisfaction grew in regions which lacked influential political elites at the centre of 'state politics' and were therefore bypassed when state resources were allocated. In some politically marginal areas, such as Central, Nyanza and parts of Eastern provinces, development activities by voluntary organizations supplemented the declining state support for basic services. However, patronage also infiltrated these activities, thereby constraining their development potential. More important, the provincial administrative officials and influential politicians took control of the organization of *harambee* activities and, as a result, 'forced contributions' became a main feature.

The voluntary organizations reacted against such political patronage in the administration of development. Relations with the state soured. The churches, in particular, opposed forced contributions to *harambees*, which brought them into conflict with the provincial administration and the political elites. Similarly, apathy and disenchantment with the state spread widely in areas where political patronage had infiltrated voluntary activities.

Other events also threatened both the legitimacy and the ideology of the state. In 1986 KANU introduced a queue-voting method for the party and national general elections, which made it easy to manipulate by the political coterie through the provincial administrative officials. Several NGOs, led by umbrella church organizations, opposed the queue-voting method and campaigned for its repeal through seminars both at the grass roots, where their activities were concentrated, and at the national level.

The state reacted by threatening to ban the 'subversive' NGOs (including church organizations), and called for strict monitoring, control, and co-ordination of their development activities and of their funds to 'ensure their activities were compatible with national interests' (Ndegwa, 1993: 11).[10] KANU co-opted the *Maendeleo ya Wanawake*, for example, perhaps as a way of monitoring the organizations's donor funds or as a means of mobilizing women into the ruling party, or even as a warning to the 'outspoken' NGOs. Indeed, one organization was banned in 1988 on security grounds. NGO registration and privileges such as exemptions from import duties were subjected to critical scrutiny on grounds of national interest. Unprecedented tension had slipped into the otherwise calm relations between NGOs and the state.

External factors also played a role. Throughout most of the 1980s, donor agencies, disillusioned with the government's performance, gradually sought partnership with the voluntary organizations and allocated more aid to them. In the late 1980s donors also sought to promote democracy and pluralism by supporting the voluntary sector and other organizations outside state control. Donor resources to the voluntary sector continued to bypass state institutions, while some donors reduced their aid to the government or froze it altogether. And, as NGOs became critical of 'state politics', KANU politicians accused the voluntary organizations, especially the NGOs, of using their funds for subversive activities. They argued not only for strict monitoring of NGOs but also for channelling donor funds to NGOs through the central government. Eventually the state reacted by seeking more 'co-ordination' of NGO activities, although 'control' rather than co-ordination may be a more appropriate term. This was not surprising, given that the NGOs were using donor funds to contest state legitimacy through delivery of services.

## The NGO Legislation of 1990

The deterioration in state–NGO relations culminated in the state's explicit attempt to co-ordinate and control NGOs through the Non-Governmental Organizations Co-ordination Act of 1990 (Republic of Kenya, 1990b). The Act was a highly articulate and formalized mechanism for restricting, co-opting and controlling NGOs. Drawn up without consultation with NGOs, 'the Act adopted very few recommendations made earlier by NGOs despite initial promises by the government to consult with NGOs in the drafting of the legislation' (NGOs Standing Committee, 1991).

Its main features included an NGOs Co-ordination Board with a comparatively heavy representation of government officials. No recourse to the judicial courts was offered to aggrieved parties. It also bestowed absolute executive and

---

[10]   See Ndegwa (1993) for a detailed discussion of the sequence of events leading to the legislation and struggles over it.

judicial powers on the minister responsible for NGOs. Co-ordination of NGOs was placed under the department of Provincial Administration and Internal Security in the Office of the President, lending credence to the view that the state looked upon NGOs with suspicion and mistrusted them. The legislation required NGOs to supply details of their organizational structure, operating budgets, sources of finance and annual project audit reports. The initial legislation also required them to apply for reregistration every 5 years, which meant that they had to tailor their development programmes to this time span. It also empowered the Board to suspend or deregister NGOs for any offences under the Act committed by individual NGO staff. The legislation defined NGOs loosely: it was debatable whether it covered churches and POs.

NGOs reacted by organizing themselves into a lobby in order to seek major amendments to the Act. They produced their own version of a Co-ordination Act, appointed an *ad hoc* Standing Committee to oversee lobbying activities and organized seminars and workshops to air and publicize their views.[11] This culminated in some major amendments to the Act, and a belated promise from the Attorney General to amend it further in order to include the interests of all parties.

The government initially resisted this NGO pressure and threatened to gazette the commencement date without further reference to NGOs. A group of donors intervened and negotiations for amendments began. If the Act had come into operation in its original form it would undoubtedly have had extremely negative consequences for the ability of NGOs to deliver services.

Current state–NGO relations in Kenya, therefore, seem to reflect competition for legitimacy. In this regard, NGO legitimacy is perhaps the more tenuous, intertwined as it is with the related issues of NGOs' organizational viability and, even more important, their accountability and reliance on donor funds. In other words, the legitimacy of the state seems to be the better guaranteed of the two.

# The State: No Immediate Withering Away

The state's capacity to deliver services has gradually declined or stagnated, due to the world-wide recession and domestic economic and political problems. At the same time, demands for services have been steadily on the increase, as has the deepening of social differentiations and regional disparities. These factors, together with the increased involvement of NGOs and POs in service provision, contributed to increased politicization of the development space and increased appetite on the part of the state to 'control' the voluntary sector. The contributions of voluntary organizations to specific sectors have been considerable, although in absolute terms this contribution remains small compared with that of the state.

---

[11]  Donor funds and contributions from NGOs enabled the NGOs Standing Committee to organize a series of National Workshops to educate NGOs on the legislation, to articulate their concerns and to draw up a common position with a view to seeking amendments. One of the National Workshops called for total repeal of the Act (Ndegwa, 1993).

The state's efforts to 'control' the voluntary organizations caused tension in their relations but also increased co-operation among the latter. The NGOs established a national network that not only co-ordinated their responses to the legislation but also turned out to be a useful structure for co-ordinating and exchanging development concerns. This networking provided them with the strength to make their resistance to the state more open on socio-political issues that affected them. This was an important outcome since, before the network was established, most NGOs were unable individually to challenge the state on such issues. The struggle also strengthened NGOs' links with the donors, as the latter intervened to protect these important partners.

The state's penetration of the people's organizations had adverse effects, however. *Harambees* became increasingly controlled from above, as a means both of enabling the state to extract peasant surpluses and of controlling the local politics of development. Apathy accompanied these legitimation measures, as *harambees* became more closely identified with provincial administrative officials and influential KANU politicians. These developments weakened the development potential of the voluntary organizations. Nevertheless, the political significance of the POs increased tremendously from the early 1980s. They became the locus of the local politics of development, and the entry points to the grass roots for the state political elites, NGOs and donors: hence their significance in the socio-political context of service provision.

Current development thinking by donors favours an increased role for NGOs and POs in the delivery of services, a development which is viewed with unease by the Kenyan state. Therefore relations between the state and the voluntary organizations are currently tense, a factor which will, no doubt, continue to affect the capacity of voluntary organizations to deliver basic services in the future. In this regard, the state is likely to continue to be the senior partner in the development space and especially in the management of relations with NGOs. How well these relations are managed will be one important determinant of the nature of the struggle in Kenya for development space and, quite possibly, for political space as well – both vital aspects of civil society.

## References

Barkan, J. with Chege, M. (1989) 'Decentralizing the State: District Focus and the Politics of Reallocation in Kenya', *Journal of Modern African Studies* 27 (2): 431–53.

Barkan, J. and Holmquist, F. (1989) 'Peasant–State Relations and Social Base of Self Help in Kenya', *World Politics* XLI (3): 407–30.

Bratton, M. (1989) 'The Politics of Government–NGO Relations in Africa', *World Development* 17 (4): 569–87.

Brodhead, T. and Herbert-Copley, B. (1988) *Bridges of Hope: Canadian Voluntary Agencies and Third World*. Ottawa: North–South Institute.

Drabek, A.G. (ed.) (1987) 'Development Alternative: the Challenges for NGOs', *World Development* 15 (Supplement).

Fowler, A. (1985) 'NGOs in Africa: Naming Them by What They Are' in Kinyanjui.

Fowler, A. (1988) *Non-Governmental Organization in Africa; Achieving Comparative Advantages in Relief and Micro-development.* Discussion Paper No. 249. Brighton: Institute of Development Studies, University of Sussex.

Fowler, A. (1989a) 'New Scrambles for Africa: NGOs and their Donors in Kenya'. Nairobi: Ford Foundation Regional Office.

Fowler, A. (1989b) 'Non-Governmental Organizations and Development in Kenya'. Paper presented in the Workshop 'Into the 1990s: NGOs During the Current Development Plan and Beyond', organized by IDS, University of Nairobi and the Kenya National Council of Social Services. Nairobi: Institute for Development Studies, University of Nairobi.

Hyden, G. (1983) *No Shortcuts to Progress: African Development Management in Perspective.* London: Heinemann.

InterAction (1986) *Diversity in Development: US Voluntary Assistance to Africa.* Washington, DC: American Council for Voluntary International Action.

Kanyinga, K. (1993) 'The Social Political Context of the Growth of Non-Governmental Organizations (NGOs) in Kenya' in P. Gibbon, (ed.) *Social Change and Economic Reform in Africa.* Uppsala: Scandinavian Institute of African Studies.

Kanyinga, K. and Makanda, W. (1991) *Situation Assessment and Goal Establishment for Foster Parents PLAN International – An Evaluation.* Meru: Foster Parents PLAN International Field Office.

Kinyanjui, K. (ed.) (1985) *Non-Governmental Organisations Contribution to Development.* Occasional Paper No. 50. Nairobi: Institute for Development Studies, University of Nairobi.

KNCSS (1978) *Directory of Voluntary Organisations in Kenya.* Nairobi: KNCSS.

KNCSS (1988) *Directory of (Non-Governmental) Voluntary Organisations in Kenya.* Nairobi: KNCSS.

Kobia, S. (1985) 'New and Old NGOs: Approaches to Development' in Kinyanjui.

Lekyo C. (1989) *Recommendation to the Government of Kenya on Supportive Policy and Legislation for Voluntary, Non-Profit Non-Governmental Organisations' Development and Welfare Activities.* Nairobi: KNCSS.

Makokha, J. (1985) *The District Focus for Rural Development: Conceptual and Management Problems.* Nairobi: African Press Research Bureau.

Mazingira Institute (1992) *Women and Development: A Kenya Guide.* Nairobi: Mazingira Institute.

Ndegwa, S.N. (1993) *NGOs as Pluralizing Agents in Civil Society in Kenya.* Working Paper No. 491. Nairobi: Institute for Development Studies, Universiy of Nairobi.

Ngau, P. M. (1987) 'Tensions in Empowerment: The Experience of Harambee (Self-Help) Movement in Kenya', *Economic Development and Cultural Change* 35 (3): 523–38.

Ng'ethe, N. (1979) 'Harambee and Development Participation in Kenya: The Politics of Peasants and Elites in Kenya with Particular Reference to Harambee Projects in Kiambu District'. Ph.D. Thesis, Ontario: Carleton University.

Ng'ethe, N. (1991) *In Search of NGOs: Towards a Funding Strategy to Create NGO Research Capacity in Eastern and Southern Africa.* Occasional Paper No. 58. Nairobi: Institute for Development Studies, University of Nairobi.

Ng'ethe, N. and Kanyinga, K. (1993) *The Politics of Democratisation Through Decentralisation in Kenya.* Nairobi: Institute of Policy Analysis and Research – IPAR.

Ng'ethe, N., Botros, F., Njau, P. and Gachukia, E. (1988) *Population Support for Non-Governmental Organisations (NGOs) and Government Ministries through the National*

*Council for Population and Development (NCPD): An Evaluation.* Nairobi: United Nations Fund for Population Activities.

NGOs Standing Committee (1991) *A Report of the NGOs Standing Committee on the NGOs Co-ordination Act of 1990: Concerns and Recommendations of NGOs.* Nairobi: National Council of NGOs.

Republic of Kenya (1989) *National Development Plan 1989–93.* Nairobi: Government Printer.

Republic of Kenya (1990a) *Hansard.* Nairobi: Government Printer, December.

Republic of Kenya (1990b) *Non-Governmental Organisations Co-ordination Act of 1990.* Nairobi: Government Printer.

Republic of Kenya (1994) *Development Plan 1994–96.* Nairobi: Government Printer.

Semboja, J. (1992) 'The Impact of Economic Recovery Programme (ERP) on the Provision of Social Services'. Report. Dar es Salaam: World Bank.

Streeten, P. (1987) 'The Contributions of Non-Governmental Organisations in Development', *Development: Seeds of Change* 4: 92–5.

Thomas, B.P. (1987) 'Development through Harambee: Who Wins and Who Loses? Rural Self-Help Projects in Kenya', *World Development* 15 (4): 463–81.

# 5

## B. M. MAKAU
## Dynamics of Partnership in the Provision of General Education in Kenya

Rapid expansion of general education in post-colonial Kenya has been possible largely because of the provision of resources by a partnership between the state, parents, community organizations, NGOs and private entrepreneurs. It is driven by the ideologies of the politically dominant class, the belief in education as a foundation for individual and national development, mobilization through the voluntary sector, and the constraints on public revenues. In this chapter three related questions are addressed: Why did the partnership develop? What salutary effects has the partnership had? What untoward outcomes has the partnership had and why?

## Origins and Changes of the Partnership

The present-day interdependence between state and voluntary sector in the provision of education is the outcome of a process that started early in this century. This section reviews (a) the influence of colonial policies on the provision of education and African responses to them, (b) the political imperatives to modify the colonial educational inheritance after independence, (c) how, since 1963, the burden of providing education has been shifted towards users, (d) the changing government priorities between primary, secondary and university education, and (e) the process of educational policy-making by political fiat.

### Colonial Legacy

Partnership in the provision of education developed from practices in the colonial state (Anderson, 1970; Mutua, 1975; Lillis, 1986; Otiende *et al.*, 1992; Eshiwani, 1993). Founded on a belief that the development of Kenya should be based largely on the immigrant communities (Berman, 1990), the colonial state gave little priority to the education of the indigenous people. While resources for providing education to all European (and a sizeable number of Asian) children in the colony were made available by the central government, it was argued that there were no resources to provide education to the great majority of African children.[1]

Christian missionaries were left to fill the gap. Cashing in on the drive to use education as a tool in propagating religion, the colonial government encouraged missionaries to establish schools for Africans. However, financial support for these schools from the missionaries' own resources, central government grants, and subscriptions from local authorities was not adequate. Thus, 'Parents and students were asked to contribute funds as well as labour for teaching materials, maintenance, equipment, furniture, school operations and construction' (Lillis, 1986: 2).

The growing partnership was expanded by the establishment of independent schools wholly funded on a self-help basis and managed by the Africans themselves. The independent school movement was a response to the very limited educational opportunities available to Africans, and to the fact that the education offered in mission and government schools for Africans was too narrow in its emphasis on practical learning at the expense of the broad-based intellectual growth fostered in schools for immigrants. The movement was also driven by the belief that the education provided by foreigners, particularly Christian missionaries, was inimical to African culture and traditions. By 1952 there were over 400 independent primary schools (Mutua, 1975). As discussed in Chapter 1, the African struggle for more education through self-help was closely associated with the nationalist struggle for independence and laid down a foundation for communal participation in educational development once independence had been won (Mwiria, 1985).

## Partnership in Financing State Institutions After Independence

By 1963 when Kenya achieved independence, education had become part and parcel of the nationalist movement. Second only to the alienation of land to European settlers, education was regarded as a sphere in which colonial rule had given a raw deal to the indigenous people. The new leaders, themselves the products of education, and the majority of the population strongly believed that education was crucial to the social and economic development of individual households and the nation. This belief made it imperative that, in order to sustain the support of the populace, the political leadership of independent Kenya had to pursue policies geared to the expansion and improvement of education.

Within the first decade of independence the state took several important steps in this direction. The ruling party explicitly stated that the government would be guided by the principle that 'every child in Kenya shall have a minimum of seven years free education' (Kenya African National Union, 1963 and 1969).

---

[1] However, the government set up a small number of primary schools for Africans to train artisans, clerks and other junior workers for the colonial service and the European settler-dominated economy.

The great majority of primary schools (formerly financed and managed by religious bodies and local authorities) were designated as public schools, i.e. eligible for some funding by the central government. The best secondary schools (already dependent on government grants for most of their resources) became government-maintained schools, i.e. eligible for government funding in relation to capital and recurrent expenditures. In 1970 the University of Nairobi, the country's first state university, was established.

However, in spite of the government's commitment to the expansion of education, a system financed wholly by the state did not emerge. The previous history of partnership, constraints in the public budget, the state's development policy in the macroeconomy, and the use of political fiat in educational policy-making combined to ensure that in all sectors parents, POs, NGOs and other bodies would be called upon to play a growing role in providing for education. Up to 1970 budgetary allocation by the state to education gave priority to the expansion of the post-primary sectors in order to facilitate the Africanization of middle- and high-level positions formerly held by expatriate personnel (Republic of Kenya, 1966). Consequently, the goal of universal free primary education received little concrete attention. For example, secondary schools received 13 times more recurrent funds per student than primary schools in 1969 (Olembo, 1985: Table 1).

By 1970 most middle- and high-level positions had been Africanized. This enabled the state to devote attention to the provision of universal primary education. In 1970, with the aim of advancing equity in the mode of provision, the central government took over from local authorities the financing (including the payment of teachers' salaries), planning and programming of all primary education. With this change, the recurrent expenditure allocation to primary education rose to K.Shs. 10.3m in 1970/71 (compared with K.Shs. 3.9m the year before), while the allocation to the secondary sector stagnated.

Two other measures pushed up both the primary allocation and the proportion of the total budget spent on education. First, with the aim of speeding up the attainment of universal primary education, two presidential decrees (promulgated in 1974 and 1978) abolished tuition fees in public primary schools. Second, with the aim of enhancing the nutrition of pupils, a presidential decree of 1979 introduced a state-funded scheme to supply milk to primary schools twice a week. The outcome of these measures was a sharp rise in the number of primary schools and enrolments. *Inter alia*, this growth meant additional state expenditure, particularly in relation to the resultant higher teacher salary bill. By 1981 the primary sector was consuming 65% of the total state allocation to education (Republic of Kenya, 1982a).

The state did not altogether neglect post-primary education. It continued to support a number of community-founded secondary schools and institutes of science and technology. Further, although in 1974 the government had intro-duced a loan scheme to enable university students to meet part of their education expenses, pressure on government funding was not eased because little was being recovered from borrowers after they had left the university. By 1981 the proportion of the total state budget allocated to education had risen to 32% (ibid.).

This rising state expenditure on education coincided with a down-turn in the economy, which started in the late 1970s and has continued into the early 1990s. Associated with the effects of a rapidly growing population, unfavourable terms of trade in the international marketplace, growing foreign debt, and inappropriate internal management policies and practices, the economic down-turn meant that the Treasury was not realizing adequate revenue to cover both social and economic development. Unless the rising expenditure on education was controlled, the government argued, it would no longer be possible to service the public debt and support the infrastructure necessary for economic development (Republic of Kenya, 1976, 1982b, 1986). Consequently, it was decided that the proportion of the public budget spent on education should be reduced and pegged at 29% in the future. This meant that the state would require its users to shoulder a heavier burden in financing public schools.

Secondary government-maintained schools were now forced to mobilize more resources for their needs from non-state sources (Makau, 1985). The 1984–8 Development Plan made it clear that public policy was moving towards more reliance on cost-sharing:

> ways and means will be found for passing on a larger share of the cost of post-primary education and training through cost sharing schemes to those who benefit from them and seeking support from local communities...the development of physical facilities and all boarding costs (in government maintained secondary schools) will be the responsibility of local communities and parents (Republic of Kenya, 1984: 150).

Paradoxically the state's assumption of a heavier burden of financing primary education had the effect of increasing parental and community contributions to the sector. Although nominal formal tuition fees were abolished (Nkinyangi, 1980), parents were now required to contribute more to build and expand schools. Moreover, the milk scheme diverted funds from the public provision of learning materials,[2] and parents now had to bear these costs.

During the 1980s the tendency for educational policy to be made by political fiat as opposed to being based on professional planning picked up an unprecedented tempo (Friedrich Nauman Stiftung, 1992). A rapidly growing population, a depressed economy, high unemployment among school-leavers, and a growing rate of social deviance had the combined effect of aggravating the ethnic, class and political tensions latent in Kenyan society. Beleaguered by these intractable problems, the political leadership became increasingly circumspect and suspicious of open debate in policy-making. In an effort to bolster its position, it saw education as sphere in which changes, touted as desirable and popular, could be introduced to expand opportunities in the economy.

Thus, in line with the launching of the District Focus for Rural Development in 1983 aimed at enhancing equity by devolving development planning to

---

[2] In 1986/87 the scheme providing each pupil with 0.4 of a litre of milk per week cost the government K.Shs. 16.5m as compared with an inadequate K.Shs. 8.4m spent on learning materials (Republic of Kenya, 1988).

the districts,[3] selection for secondary education was further localized: each state secondary school was required to select 85% (as opposed to 50% previously) of its new intake from feeder schools within the district. Two years later the whole school system was changed in response to growing unemployment.[4] Primary schools, upgraded from 7 to 8 years of education, were now required to teach pre-vocational subjects so as to prepare school-leavers for self-employment. To increase opportunities at the highest level of education, the selective 2-year upper secondary course was abolished and university education was expanded from 3 to 4 years. The enrolment in state universities rose from 8,900 in 1985 to over 40,000 in 1990.

These changes, made with little public debate or consideration of declared policy for controlling the state allocation to education, severely over-stretched the country's ability to pay for education. The requirement that the capital development of the vocationalized primary school curricula be funded outside the state budget forced parental and community contributions to hitherto unknown levels (Lillis, 1986; Makau, 1987). The rapid expansion of university education resulted in a situation where state expenditure on the sector was rising faster than the total allocation to the Ministry of Education; the emphasis shifted away from the already hard-pressed primary and secondary sectors.

Table 5.1 Estimates of Government Recurrent Expenditure on Education, 1985–90 (K.Shs.m)

| Year | Primary | | Secondary | | University | | Other | | Total | |
|---|---|---|---|---|---|---|---|---|---|---|
| | abs. | % | abs. | % | abs. | % | abs. | % | abs. | % |
| 1985 | 158 | 54 | 42 | 14 | 33 | 11 | 62 | 21 | 295 | 100 |
| 1990 | 293 | 51 | 88 | 15 | 124 | 22 | 72 | 12 | 577 | 100 |

Source: Estimates by Ministry of Education.

As shown in Table 5.1, in the course of five years the proportion of state recurrent expenditures on university education rose from 11% to 22% as compared with a decline in the primary education share, and a mere 1% increase for secondary education. Estimates of funds for development expenditures were also heavily skewed in favour of the university sector in the late 1980s. Recurrent and development expenditure estimates tell only part of the story, however. In practice, apart from teacher salaries which the state continued to cover, grants to most non-university state institutions, even though reflected in the estimates, were diverted to the development of the enlarged university sector. Moreover, in 1988 the government stopped supplying textbooks to primary schools, leaving this to the parents. The previous substantial amounts for salaries for non-teaching staff were also reduced. By 1992 little in the way of government grants was received in state schools.

[3]  See Chapter 7 for an analysis of this decentralization.
[4]  The previous 7–4–2–3 system (i.e. seven years of primary, four of secondary, two of higher secondary and three of university education) was replaced by an 8–4–4 system (i.e. eight years of primary, four of secondary and four of university).

With every change parents and communities had to dig deeper into their own pockets. As pointed out by Lillis (1986: 4) state, *harambee* (self-help) and private schools receive many resources from many sources:

> there is substantial community and 'private' expenditure on education which goes to meet recurrent and development costs. Such expenditure...consists of contributions made by private firms, education trusts, cooperatives, communities and individuals ...channelled into the education system through voluntary agencies, *harambee* committees, District Development Committees, private companies or bodies awarding bursaries to students.

A significant contribution has come from religious bodies, which have been the source of volunteer teachers, funds and advice, and of the approved managers of *harambee* and some of the private secondary schools (Roth, 1987: 36). In addition, NGOs have stepped in. By 1988 out of over 400 NGOs operating in Kenya, 181 (about 45%) were involved in assisting education and training (Lekyo and Mirikau, 1988). Intervention by the voluntary organizations has benefited from a growing tendency (since the late 1970s) for international donor development funding to be channelled to the Third World through NGOs.

## Growth of Non-State Schools

It has already been pointed out that at independence most Kenyan communities were convinced that education was the gateway to improved economic and social status. Fuelled by the example of Kenyans with post-secondary education who quickly moved into senior positions vacated by departing expatriate personnel and the leadership's constant reminders that education was crucial to national development, this conviction, in tandem with constraints in the public budget and the evolving strategy in the political economy, led to the growth of a large number of non-state secondary schools.

In discussing the origins of private schools in developing countries, James (1991: 5) states:

> Excess demand for education often exists when the capacity of the public school system is less than full enrolment, that is, the option of attending a free or low price public school is not available to everyone. If the private benefits from education are high (e.g., because of labour market rewards), many people who are left out of the public schools will seek places in private schools, as a 'second best' solution...the smaller the capacity of the public sector is, relative to the size of the age cohort, the larger will be the excess demand for the private sector.

In Kenya the demand for secondary school places has been far higher than the public sector supply since the 1920s. And since 1963 the country's leadership has encouraged partnership between the state, the voluntary sector and private entrepreneurs to expand opportunities in secondary schools for a growing proportion of primary school-leavers. The non-state actors have responded in two major ways. First, entrepreneurs have established profit-seeking secondary schools, particularly in urban centres. Second, communities, particularly in rural areas, have organized themselves to put up *harambee* secondary schools.[5] To cover both capital and recurrent resources, individuals have contributed 'local materials and voluntary labour, cash, professional advice, and professional assistance' (Roth, 1987: 36).

The *harambee* movement in education and other spheres of social development is in line with, and has been encouraged, by the *laissez-faire* development strategy adopted by the leadership (Barkan, 1984; Leo, 1984). Characterizing the leadership's view that the people's initiative (as opposed to manna from the state) is the proper route to development, Leo (1984: 151) states:

> Throughout the 1960s and the early 1970s, *hakuna cha bure* (Kiswahili equivalent of 'you can't get something for nothing') was repeated again and again on political platforms across Kenya. It became a central proposition in the individualist ideology underpinning Kenya's political and economic system...Again and again, the government – in its policies relating to land, education, health care, and many other areas – had served notice that people must be prepared to work for the benefits and amenities they hoped to enjoy.

A whole body of literature sees the leadership's encouragement of the *harambee* movement as going further than mere belief in *laissez-faire* as a mode of development. Barkan (1984: 10) argues that the *harambee* movement was seized upon by the leadership as a way of maintaining national unity by keeping ethnic and class antagonisms under control in the young nation. By 1969 further awakening of the populace through the development of multi-party politics had been abandoned in favour of a strong administrative state controlled by the executive. *Harambee*, characterized by competition between local areas (Roth, 1987), was used by the leadership as a device to absorb political energies. Politicians were encouraged to use *harambee* fund-raising to solicit for support, particularly at election time. The patron–client relationship, which replaced political activity through political parties, was lubricated by *harambee* donations from rich and powerful patrons. Many argue that promotion of development through *harambee* also served to diffuse the potential for social disruption emanating from inequalities in the society (Court, 1976; Court and Kinyanjui, 1978; Keller, 1980; Nkinyangi, 1980; Mwiria, 1985). The additional opportunities offered by *harambee* and profit-seeking private schools, and the use of performance in secondary school examinations as the gateway to high positions in the modern economy, have forestalled discontent by nurturing the illusion of a meritocratic society:

> education provides an opportunity for some to move from the lower to the upper ranks in society, and so tends to ease some of the incipient tensions associated with inequality. Furthermore, by offering a personal escape route from low status it tends to weaken interest in collective efforts by those who remain. To the extent that upward mobility is a reality for some, and is believed to be possible for all, it serves to disperse some of the incipient antagonisms of the disadvantaged towards the advantaged (Court, 1976: 64).

[5] In the early 1970s the government allowed communities to fund *harambee* classes attached to government-maintained schools (Eshiwani, 1983).

# Salutary Outcomes of the Partnership

The interdependence of state, voluntary sector and private entrepreneurs has made a rapid growth in school enrolment possible. It has, perhaps, also laid the foundation for a broader base for popular participation in educational matters.

## Rapid Growth of School Enrolments

Between 1963 and 1991 the number of primary schools rose from 6,052 to 15,196, while secondary schools increased from 151 to 2,647 (Republic of Kenya, 1988; *Economic Survey* 1992). Primary enrolments grew from about 892,000 to about 5.5 million (an increase of over 600%), and secondary enrolments from about 31,000 to 614,000 (an increase of 1880%). Parity between male and female enrolments has almost been achieved: in 1989 the proportion of females in primary school was 49%; in 1991 44% of the secondary school enrolment was female (*Economic Survey* 1992). These figures are impressive when compared with the stagnating or declining enrolments elsewhere in sub-Saharan Africa (World Bank, 1988).

## The Extent of Provision Through the Non-State Sector

In the primary sector expansion has been contained within the state ambit: as compared with an average of 16% for developing countries, only 1% of Kenya's primary enrolment is in non-state schools (James, 1991).[6]

In contrast, a large proportion of secondary enrolment has been in non-state schools. Between 1965 and 1979 Kenya's share of non-state enrolment rose from 29% to 60%, among the highest in sub-Saharan Africa (James, 1993). This reflects a key feature of educational provision in Kenya. From independence parents and communities regarded their investment in *harambee* schools as 'seed money': the expectation was that once a *harambee* school had been started, the state would step in and finance its further development. Wary of the political implications of a negative response to this expectation, the state responded by each year turning a number of *harambee* schools into government-assisted institutions, with the state undertaking to meet some of their expenses, e.g. the salaries of some or all of their teachers. Furthermore, a number of assisted schools were to achieve the status of maintained schools. The government response is clearly shown in Table 5.2: as compared with 36% in 1979, by 1988 only 17% of secondary students were attending schools which did not receive any assistance from the state.

What Table 5.2 does not show is that, in the course of the 1980s, the difference between government-maintained and -assisted schools began to disappear. As

[6] Non-state primary schools are private, i.e. they receive no financial support from the government. Among their founders are private entrepreneurs, religious bodies, charitable organizations, and international bodies (including embassies). Their number is small and most of them charge high fees, the quality of education they offer is by and large higher than is the case in state primary schools.

the expenses of capital development and non-teacher salary requirements in government-maintained schools were passed on to parents and communities, and more *harambee* schools were assisted with teachers paid by the state, the two categories of schools became indistinguishable in more than name. The Working Party on Education and Manpower Training for the next Decade and Beyond recognized this fact. Its recommendations on financing education (Republic of Kenya, 1988: 119), which the government accepted as policy, summarize the current operation of the partnership as follows:

> (a) the Government continues to provide facilities for maintained post-school institutions, special institutions and universities, while communities, parents and sponsors provide physical facilities in all other education and training institutions;
>
> (b) the Government continues to provide specialized equipment to public institutions, while parents provide books and supplementary readers, stationery and consumable materials;
>
> (c) the Government encourages the development of private educational and training institutions at all levels.

As indicated by recent statements by the Minister of Education, the government currently recognizes only two categories of schools, state and private, financed according to the above formula. The policy lays down that all *harambee* schools are to be staffed by government-paid teachers and thus become state institutions.

Table 5.2 Secondary School Enrolments by School Type, 1979–88 ('000s)

| Year | Government-maintained | | Government-assisted | | Unaided by government[a] | | Total | |
|---|---|---|---|---|---|---|---|---|
| | abs. | % | abs. | % | abs. | % | abs. | % |
| 1979 | 159 | 41 | 86 | 22 | 139 | 36 | 384 | 100 |
| 1988 | 264 | 49 | 183 | 34 | 94 | 17 | 541 | 100 |

[a] Includes both unassisted *harambee* schools and private schools.
*Source:* Republic of Kenya, *Economic Survey* (selected years).

## NGOs and Provision for the Under-Privileged

The involvement of the voluntary sector in education has often helped to bypass policy and bureaucratic bottlenecks. NGOs deal with policy questions as well as practical problems, 'redefining the issues and pioneering innovative solutions along the way' (Mazingira Institute, 1992: 6).

Two examples stand out. First, although the authorities recognize the importance of incorporating information technology into formal education, a combination of financial constraints and ambivalence in policy-making has prevented the state from making a definite move. Some NGOs and entrepreneurs are addressing the issue. For instance, during the 1980s, with government permission, funding from the Aga Khan Foundation, the Save the Children Fund and others was used to equip eight state secondary schools with computers (Scott, 1987; Makau, 1989). By integrating the computers into the ordinary curriculum, the initiative is demonstrating the potential of the technology in schools.

Second, some NGOs have spearheaded the development and implementation of a relevant curriculum in new ways. A case in point is the work of the Undugu Society of Kenya. Registered as an NGO in 1975 and backed by both overseas and local funding, the society has been addressing the issue of providing relevant basic education to destitute urban children. Currently Undugu runs four non-fee-paying schools with an enrolment of 470 (246 males and 224 females), with ages ranging from 12 to over 20. The curriculum, developed in consultation with the Ministry of Education, recognizes that the pupils have had no previous formal education and need to be better prepared for self-reliance in a hostile urban environment. During a four-year course, as compared with eight years in normal primary school, emphasis is given to equipping them with relevant practical skills (e.g. carpentry, crafts, and tailoring), basic literacy, and social skills. The programme provides flexibility: pupils are encouraged to state what they want to learn and attendance is tailored to accommodate those already in some employment. In recognition of its success, the government is interested in the expansion of the programme as one of Kenya's strategies for addressing basic education for all (Masiga, 1993).

In contrast to the Undugu programme, the Starehe Boys' Centre in Nairobi demonstrates that, if carefully planned and implemented, partnership between the state and NGOs can result in improving quality in normal schools. Founded in 1959 as a home for destitute children, with support from NGOs (particularly the Save the Children Fund) and individual donors, and staffed by teachers paid by the state, Starehe has developed to become one of the largest (over 1,000 primary and secondary pupils) and best-performing schools in Kenya.

As compared with the Ministry of Education, NGOs and other unofficial bodies are better placed to address the link between education and the socio-economic environment. NGO aid to education and training is often part and parcel of a larger project aimed at assisting integrated social and economic development. Projects, such as those funded by ActionAid (UK) and CARE International among other NGOs, have included development of income-generating activities, promotion of health (e.g. through provision of clean water, and training in nutrition and family life), as well as assistance to schools and needy children. UNICEF and FAO (through the World Food Programme) support NGOs that try to enhance the health and nutrition of pre-primary and primary school children, particularly in drought-stricken and impoverished areas.

Whereas the state has felt constrained to concentrate its resources on the majority of the school-age population, NGOs are free to choose where to invest their resources. Pre-primary education, which the state recognizes as important, has been dependent on non-state support. Currently 30% of children aged 3 to 5 are provided with pre-school education. The efforts of religious bodies and communities to build nursery schools have been complemented by support for curriculum development and teacher education from NGOs, such as the Aga Khan and the Bernard Van Leer Foundations. Similarly, non-state bodies are heavily involved in providing education for the disabled. In this respect the Salvation Army, the Kenya Societies for the Blind, for Deaf Children, and for the Mentally Handicapped are some of the outstanding partners of the state. Unofficial bodies have also worked closely with the state to provide education to communities in Kenya's arid and semi-arid lands (ASAL). Reminiscent of NGO support for education elsewhere in ASAL, a newspaper report explained the emergence of the arid Turkana District as the top performer in the 1992 primary school leaving examination as follows:

> The presence of donor agencies and non-governmental organizations has been the major factor behind excellent performance. They have provided all basic facilities like classrooms, dormitories, workshops, uniforms, exercise books and have even paid fees for needy pupils (*Daily Nation*, 13 March 1993).

Particularly prominent in the case of Turkana District has been the involvement of Christian churches and the Norwegian aid agency, NORAD.

## Growth of a Broad Base for Popular Participation

In the literature on development there is ample evidence that, in both the economic and the social spheres, development programmes are most successful when all stakeholders, in particular the beneficiaries, are actively involved in the planning and implementation processes (Mbithi and Barnes, 1974; Bernard, 1990; Shaeffer, 1992; UNDP, 1993). The partnership through which education is being provided has laid down a foundation for such involvement. Particularly important is the role played by Parent–Teacher Associations (PTA), school boards and committees, and *harambee* committees. With predominantly local membership, these bodies, as they have been called upon to mobilize for a rising share of the resources their schools require, have developed a growing interest in the schools' financial, administrative, and professional management (Roth, 1987: 36). Reports, such as the following, have become a regular feature in the daily press:

> Parents and teachers of [a named secondary school] in Kitui District on Friday chased away the school headmaster, *accusing him of mismanagement...the Parents and Teachers Association urged the local District Education Officer to intervene and transfer the headmaster*...Trouble started when the headmaster... allegedly refused to tell the members the whereabouts of shs. 118,000 meant for the completion of a dining hall...As tension gripped the meeting, [the headmaster] walked out in protest prompting angry parents to charge after him with sticks. He, however, fled to safety (*The Standard*, 26 July 1993). (Emphasis added.)

Of significance are the phrases in italics in this quotation. The PTA felt that it had a say in how the money it had raised was managed and utilized (no taxation without representation), but it had no authority to remove the headmaster. In essence, and speaking for all PTAs and other bodies who contribute to education, this particular PTA was advocating the development of a school system enabling all stakeholders to play a legal proactive role in the planning and management of education.

## Untoward Effects of the Partnership

As implied in previous sections, the operation of the partnership responsible for providing education has not been fully co-ordinated or systematic. This has resulted in a lower quality of the education provided, and has exacerbated inequity in its provision.

### Quality of Education

Because *harambee* and private secondary schools have shot up on the basis of grass-roots initiatives with minimal planning, their founders – almost everywhere beleaguered by resource constraints – have given little priority to the quality of education (Keller, 1980; Mwiria, 1985; James, 1986, 1991, and 1993; Lillis, 1986; Knight and Sabot, 1990). With reference to job opportunities for graduates of the Kenya education system, Knight and Sabot (1990: 299) observe that:

> The private rate of return to investment in secondary schools is markedly higher for children who attend government secondary schools than for those who attend *harambee* schools.

The main reason for this has been that the performance in the final examinations of *harambee* and most private schools has been poorer than that of government-maintained schools. Referring to the results of the 1984 Kenya Certificate of Education examination for secondary schools, Lillis (1986: 25) points out that:

> the top *harambee* school was 29th in the order of merit ... The next *harambee* school was 58th ... Only 17 unaided *harambee* schools were in the top 300.

The poor performance in *harambee* and private schools has been related to factors arising from their paucity of essential resources: inadequate supply of textbooks, lack of qualified teachers, unmanageably large classes, and inadequate physical facilities are major causes. Equally important is the fact that 'the intake into unaided schools is largely non-selective, representing the cadre of primary school leavers not selected to go to maintained schools' (Lillis, 1986: 24).

In spite of better performance by government-maintained schools, overall examination results have not been satisfactory. Table 5.3 summarizes the performance of all candidates in four key subjects in the 1989 Secondary Certificate examination.

Assuming that the examination was a fair test of the candidates, the low mean scores (e.g. 23.7 in mathematics where the total possible score was 200) and the low proportion (under 1%) of candidates who obtained B minus or better are significant. They indicate poor mastery of the curriculum. The B minus grade is supposed to be the lowest qualification for entry into a university department. In none of the four subjects did an adequate number qualify to fill the available places. The results in other subjects were not significantly better.

Table 5.3 Secondary School Examination Results, 1989

| Subject | Total candidates | Maximum marks | Mean score | Cand. with B– and better |
|---|---|---|---|---|
| English | 130,933 | 200 | 57.3 | 872 |
| Mathematics | 130,921 | 200 | 23.7 | 885 |
| Biological Sciences | 104,299 | 140 | 30.1 | 788 |
| Physical Sciences | 104,271 | 140 | 23.3 | 784 |

Cand. = candidates.
*Source:* Kenya National Examinations Council.

Unsatisfactory examination results are partly explained by the state's policy of passing on to parents and communities a heavier burden of financing state schools. Many of them were unable to mobilize resources for the physical facilities required for the new 8–4–4 curriculum introduced in 1985. Equally important, as the government grant for learning materials dried up, most schools decided that parents should purchase the materials on an optional basis. As a result, children whose parents could not afford basic textbooks have had to make do without a crucial tool in their learning.

Other indicators of quality show that all is not well. First, student indiscipline, particularly in post-primary institutions, has become a major problem. The student bodies in an increasing number of institutions express dissatisfaction (often violently) with, *inter alia,* poor boarding conditions, inadequacy of learning materials and facilities, unqualified and uncommitted teachers, and curtailment of student freedom. Secondly, the higher parental costs of education are forcing an increasing number of children to leave school prematurely. Thirdly, partly because the resources available have been inadequate for the teaching of science and technology, most secondary school students have been channelled into the liberal arts. The result is growing unemployment of university graduates, even though there are openings in careers related to science and technology (Republic of Kenya, 1989).

## Equity

The *laissez-faire* development strategy adopted by the leadership and the use of *harambee* as a political tool may have assisted in the maintenance of social tranquillity in the short run. However, to the extent that lasting social tranquillity is dependent on the reduction (if not eradication) of inequalities, the illusion of extended opportunity represented by low quality *harambee* and private secondary schools must be judged as short-sighted and an evasive approach to building a fair and just society. Similarly, the approach adopted in the provision of education to pre-primary children and under-privileged groups would seem to have precluded concerted long-term action. While NGOs have played a commendable role, the fact that the government has not been at centre stage has meant that public policy on the provision of education to these special groups has been diffuse. As a consequence, the current provision is patchy and continues to be characterized by inequalities.

The policy of passing on more of the costs of school education to beneficiaries and thus enabling the state to shift more of its resources to university education has the effect of exacerbating inequity. Equity would be better served if priority were given to primary education. Research shows that the public (as opposed to private) return on investment in education is much higher in primary education than in secondary and higher education (Psacharopoulos, 1985). In advocating a higher allocation of state resources to the primary sector, Mingat and Psacharopoulos (1985: 3) argue that:

> it is primary education, which can be regarded as both a fundamental right of the individual and a sound economic investment, that needs to be further expanded – given its high social returns... and its relatively low cost unit.

State provision should aim in particular at raising quality. Providing primary schools with essential learning facilities and materials through the allocation of state resources (as opposed to reliance on parental and community contributions) should guarantee that all pupils, and particularly those from poor backgrounds, have the tools for competing for a place in secondary school (Psacharopoulos *et al.*, 1986; Roth, 1987).

Another important reason for the state to give priority to primary education is the finding, common in the literature (Mingat and Tan, 1984; Makau, 1985; Mingat and Psacharopoulos, 1985; Knight and Sabot, 1990), that, as compared with the poor (who are the majority in most developing countries), the higher socio-economic echelons of society are better represented in post-primary education. Equity would be better served if public policy took into account that

> students in higher education are more likely to come from better socioeconomic backgrounds (and could afford to bear a greater share of the cost of their education) and, again on average, will realize higher incomes from their studies. They could therefore reimburse the state for at least part of the financial support they received while studying (Mingat and Psacharopoulos, 1985: 3).

At the secondary level, accelerating class differentiation is leading to poorer families being priced out of education. This phenomenon is closely associated with rising user charges. By the mid-1980s it was evident that rural smallholders, the landless, the low-paid, petty traders and craftsmen could no longer afford the user charges demanded by government-maintained secondary schools

(Makau, 1985). By early 1993 the combined effects of non-payment of government grants to state schools and a depressed economy had led to inability among many parents to pay fees. One newspaper reported that nearly half the 1992 primary school-leavers who qualified for entry into government-maintained secondary schools had been unable to take up their places because of lack of school fees (*The Standard*, 20 February 1993). According to another newspaper, the problem was more acute for those admitted into boarding schools, where the annual fees ranged between K.Shs. 16,000 and 20,000, an increase of 400% since 1987 (*Daily Nation*, 12 February 1993). Boarding schools dominate the top rungs in performance in public examinations. Thus, students whose parents are unable to pay the fees in these schools have to seek places in day schools or discontinue their schooling. In advocating selective bursaries for poor students, Knight and Sabot (1990: 300) point to the equity implications of the current situation:

> There is some reason to believe that the students from uneducated and poor backgrounds who are forced to withdraw from the school system because of the rise in fees will be the most able, since students who gain access to government secondary schools without having the advantage of educated parents are likely to be unusually bright. If the increases in fees are uniform, relatively bright but poor students may terminate their education and be replaced by less able students from higher-income families who would otherwise have gone to *harambee* schools.

## Conclusion

In this chapter it has been argued that the partnership responsible for the provision of education emanated from the interaction between the ideologies of the politically dominant classes; the belief in education as a foundation for individual and national development; the interests of social organizations (such as religious bodies), NGOs, POs, and private entrepreneurs; and the constraints on the public budget.

Collaboration between the state and non-state bodies has increased educational opportunities far beyond what would have been possible if the state had been the only provider of education. The partners of the state – the NGOs and POs – have played an important role in the provision of education to pre-primary children and disadvantaged groups, and in experimenting with approaches aimed at enhancing relevance and quality in education. Moreover, the partnership has contributed to the creation of a broad base on which systematic popular participation in the development of education could be built in the future.

However, the operation of the partnership has had some untoward outcomes. The close association between macropolitical considerations and educational policy-making has hindered the emergence of a systematic partnership. In particular, the tendency for political fiat to replace professional planning and open debate as the basis of educational policy-making has made it difficult for the country to develop strategies which effectively address quantitative growth, quality, and equity in the provision of education.

It is also noteworthy that Kenya, more than Tanzania and Uganda, has pursued a deliberate policy of linking the provision of education to voluntary sector initiatives. Some success has been achieved through this. But it is also clear that there are major equity and quality problems that cannot be adequately addressed by increased reliance on the voluntary sector – or by privatization. There are clear limits to the partnership in education.

# References

Anderson, J. (1970) *The Struggle for the School: The Interaction of Missionary, Colonial Government and Nationalist Enterprise in the Development of Formal Education in Kenya.* Nairobi: Longman.

Barkan, J.D. (ed.) (1984) *Politics and Public Policy in Kenya and Tanzania.* Revised Edition. New York: Praeger Publishers.

Berman, B. (1990) *Control and Crisis in Colonial Kenya: The Dialectics of Domination.* Nairobi: East African Educational Publishers.

Bernard, A.K. (1990) 'Learning and Intervention: The Informal Transmission of the Knowledge and Skills of Development'. Paper presented at the World Conference on Education for All, Jomtien, March. Ottawa: IDRC.

Court, D. (1976) *The Education System as a Response to Inequality in Tanzania and Kenya.* IDS Discussion Paper No. 217. Nairobi: Institute of Development Studies, University of Nairobi.

Court, D. and Kinyanjui, K. (1978) *Development Policy and Educational Opportunity: The Experience of Kenya and Tanzania.* Paris: IIEP.

Eshiwani, G.S. (1983) *Factors Influencing Performance Among Primary and Secondary School Pupils in Western Province of Kenya: A Policy Study.* Nairobi: Kenyatta University College, Bureau of Educational Research.

Eshiwani, G.S. (1993) *Education in Kenya since Independence.* Nairobi: East African Educational Publishers.

Friedrich Nauman Stiftung (1992) *Blueprint for a New Kenya: Post Election Action Programme.* Nairobi: Friedrich Nauman Stiftung.

James, E. (1986) 'Differences in the Role of Private Educational Sector in Modern and Developing Countries'. Paper presented at an international conference on Economics of Education, June, Dijon, France.

James, E. (1991) *Private Finance and Management of Education in Developing Countries: Major Policy and Research Issues.* IIEP Orientation and Training Report No. 5 on Issues and Methodologies in Educational Development. Paris: IIEP.

James, E. (1993) 'Why is There Proportionately More Enrollment in Private Schools in Some Countries?' World Bank Working Paper No. 1069. Washington, DC: World Bank.

Keller, E.J. (1980) *Education, Manpower and Development: The Impact of Educational Policy in Kenya.* Nairobi: Kenya Literature Bureau.

Kenya African National Union (1963) *What a KANU Government Offers You: Manifesto for the May General Election.* Nairobi: Printing and Packaging Corporation.

Kenya African National Union (1969) *KANU Manifesto for the October General Election.*

Nairobi: The English Press Ltd..

Knight, J.B. and Sabot, R.H. (1990) *Education, Productivity and Inequality: The East African Natural Experiment.* New York: Oxford University Press.

Lekyo, C.M. and Mirikau, A. (1988) *A Directory of Non-Governmental (Voluntary) Organizations in Kenya.* Nairobi: Kenya National Council of Social Service.

Leo, C. (1984) *Land and Class in Kenya.* Toronto: University of Toronto Press.

Lillis, K. (1986) 'Community Financing of Education: Issues from Kenya'. Paper presented at an international conference on Economics of Education, June, Dijon, France.

Makau, B.M. (1985) *Equity and Efficiency in Financing Secondary Education in Kenya: Key Issues in State-Community Partnership.* IDS Working Paper No. 429. Nairobi: University of Nairobi.

Makau, B.M. (1987) *The Management and Financing of Secondary Education in Kenya – The Effectiveness of Policy at the School Level.* Report of a study funded by IDRC. Nairobi: University of Nairobi.

Makau, B.M. (1989) 'Computers in Kenya's Secondary Schools: Case Study of an Innovation in Education.' Report. Ottawa: IDRC.

Masiga, E.S. (1993) 'Education of the Disadvantaged and Girls'. Paper presented at the 8th World Bank Education Credit Workshop, Mombasa, 29 November–3 December. Nairobi: World Bank.

Mazingira Institute (1992) *Women and Development: A Kenya Guide.* Nairobi: Majestic Printing Works.

Mbithi, P.M. and Barnes, C. (1974) *A Conceptual Analysis of Approaches to Rural Development.* IDS Working Paper No. 154. Nairobi: Institute of Development Studies, University of Nairobi.

Mingat, A. and Psacharopoulos, G. (1985) 'Financing Education in Sub-Saharan Africa', *Finance and Development* 22 (1): 35–8.

Mingat, A. and Tan, J.P. (1984) *Who Profits From the Public Funding of Education? A Comparison by World Regions.* Washington, DC: World Bank, Education and Training Department.

Mutua, R.W. (1975) *Development of Education in Kenya: Some Administrative Aspects, 1846–1963.* Nairobi: East African Literature Bureau.

Mwiria, K. (1985) *Harambee Schools and the Ideology of Educational Opportunity.'* Discussion Paper No. 4008. Nairobi: Kenyatta University, Bureau of Educational Research.

Nkinyangi, J.A. (1980) 'Socioeconomic Determinants of Repetition and Early School Withdrawal at the Primary School Level and their Implications for Educational Planning in Kenya'. Ph.D. dissertation, Stanford, CA: Stanford University, School of Education.

Olembo, J.O. (1985) *Financing Secondary Education in Kenya.* KERA Research Report No. 2.2. Nairobi: Kenyatta University, Bureau of Educational Research.

Otiende, J. E., Wamahiu, S.P. and Karugu, A.M. (1992) *Education and Development in Kenya – A Historical Perspective.* Nairobi: Oxford University Press.

Psacharopoulos, G. (1985) 'Returns to Education: A Further Internal Update and Implications', *Journal of Human Resources* 20 (4): 584–604.

Psacharopoulos, G., Tan, J.P. and Jimenez, E. (1986) *Financing Education in Developing Countries: An Exploration of Policy Options.* Washington, DC: World Bank.

Republic of Kenya (1966) *Development Plan 1966–70.* Nairobi: Government Printer.

Republic of Kenya (1976) *Report of the National Committee on Educational Objectives and*

*Policies*. Nairobi: Government Printer.

Republic of Kenya (1982a) *Report of the Working Party on Financing Higher Education*. Nairobi: Government Printer.

Republic of Kenya (1982b) *Report and Recommendations of the Working Party on Government Expenditures*. Nairobi: Government Printer.

Republic of Kenya (1984) *Development Plan 1984–88*. Nairobi: Government Printer.

Republic of Kenya (1986) 'Economic Management for Renewed Growth', *Sessional Paper No. 1*. Nairobi: Government Printer.

Republic of Kenya (1988) *Report of the Presidential Working Party on Education and Manpower Training for the Next Decade and Beyond*. Nairobi: Government Printer.

Republic of Kenya (1989) *Development Plan 1989–93*. Nairobi: Government Printer.

Republic of Kenya (selected years) *Economic Survey*. Nairobi: Central Bureau of Statistics.

Roth, G. (1987) *The Private Provision of Public Services in Developing Countries*. New York/Oxford: Oxford University Press.

Scott, R.J.P. (1987) *Directory of Computers in Educational Institutions in Kenya, 1987*. Nairobi: University of Nairobi, Institute of Computer Science.

Shaeffer, S. (1992) *Collaboration for Educational Change: The Role of Teachers, Parents and the Community in School Improvement*. Paris: IIEP.

UNDP (1993) *Human Development Report*. New York: Oxford University Press.

World Bank (1988) *Education in Sub-Saharan Africa: Policies for Adjustment, Revitalization, and Expansion*. New York: Oxford University Press.

World Bank (1989) *Sub-Saharan Africa: From Crisis to Sustainable Growth – A Long-Term Perspective Study*. New York: Oxford University Press.

# 6

## AMUKOWA ANANGWE
## Maintenance of Law & Order
## in Western Kenya

The State
& Voluntary Organizations

An inquiry into the maintenance of law and order in the rural areas of an African polity raises fundamental issues about the scope and role of the state and the voluntary sector.[1] The central argument in this chapter is that the maintenance of law and order in rural Kenya depends largely on the effectiveness of the latter, whilst the role of the state is complementary rather than critical. Arising from this argument are two fundamental questions. Have the role and scope of the voluntary sector in the maintenance of law and order been underestimated, whereas those of the state have been overestimated in Kenya so far? What are the implications of the unequal contributions of the state and the voluntary sector for the security arrangements in the rural areas?

It is often argued that the voluntary sector in Africa is weak, or that there are few civil institutions of any strength (Hyden, 1983: 119). In contrast, the African state is perceived as being hegemonic and omnipotent, or, as Ake (1973: 358) suggests, there has been a political tradition of statism and a clearly associated pattern of political authoritarianism. Flowing from this position is a general conclusion that the voluntary sector is overshadowed (Bratton, 1988: 18; Fowler, 1991: 53–4).

A totalitarian perception of the African state cannot, of course, be completely ruled out, given the complexities of the political processes and governance in Africa. However, such a perception may be more apparent than real and probably more applicable in the few urban areas, particularly the capital cities, than in the rural areas. If non-governmental organizations have encountered problems with the state, as Bratton and Fowler suggest, this may be attributed to their location and their high profile in the capital cities where the state is strongest. On the other hand, as the Kenyan experience seems to suggest, what is in place in the rural areas is a 'soft state'[2] – a situation that exhibits characteristics

---

[1] The notion of 'law and order' can be interpreted from several perspectives; in the context of this chapter it describes a state of tranquillity in a form that is deemed desirable from the standpoint of the rural population and to the extent that the concerns of the statutory law are also met.
[2] The concept was coined by Myrdal (1968: 65) to describe the behaviour of the state in Asia. Hyden (1983: 60–3) has attempted to apply it generally to Africa.

such as (a) lack of effective government presence and control except where special circumstances (e.g. 'rebel' activities) warrant unusual state attention; (b) rampant ignorance of statutory laws and regulations on the part of the rural people, who obey the laws only to the extent that they are in harmony with local customs and customary law; (c) public policies that are known only vaguely by the rural population and are also poorly implemented by the state; (d) local officials who may be heard of but rarely seen by most rural people, apart from those few who bother to visit government offices, or when these officials engage in what Chambers (1983) calls 'rural development tourism'. Such a conception of the state in the rural areas is not far from what Zolberg (1966: 66) and Bienen (1967: 134) posed in the 1960s when they asserted that the African state lacked sufficient political resources and, hence, its authority was limited and ineffectual even in those domains where it claimed the legal right to make decisions.

The soft nature of the African state obliges African leaders to concentrate resources in their priority areas, or crisis points, usually in the urban areas,[3] whilst the rest of the society, particularly in the rural areas, is left to its own devices. Moreover, a large part of rural society in Kenya operates according to a logic that is underpinned by indigenous social organizations, self-help groups, affective networks, customary laws as well as modern NGOs, both local and foreign. As in the case of one rural district (Machakos), there are groups that are organizationally independent in the rural political process. These rural groups function:

> Through the manipulation of traditional structures and techniques a very large portion of the rural population is swayed from national politics; they thus perceive the party and other national organizations and programmes as alien institutions (Mutiso, 1977: 294).

Similar observations of autonomous actions by other rural communities in Kenya have been highlighted by Lamb (1977: 171–82) in Murang'a District, and Anangwe (1991) in the pastoral districts.

In the subsequent analysis of the maintenance of law and order in Western Kenya since independence, these arguments are developed further.

## The Administrative Context in Western Kenya

The state attempts to maintain law and order in Western Kenya against the backdrop of a structure of government that is quite weak at the grass roots in the rural areas. The structure covering the whole country has three branches of government: judiciary, legislature and executive. The judiciary plays a part in the maintenance of law and order through its network of nine courts in some urban centres, but its function is largely passive and confined to the hearing of

---

[3] The notion that there is urban bias in resource allocation in Africa and other Third World countries is popular amongst some scholars. See, for example, Chambers (1983: 7–10). There are also problems of physical access (Anangwe, 1990: 411–16).

cases that are brought before it by the executive branch; it does not engage in policing. The legislature performs the legislative function.

## Civil Servants

The major part of the structure is the executive branch which holds political sway in the state arena generally, and maintains law and order in particular. The executive comprises the President, the Cabinet, central government ministries, local government, and state corporations. Outside the capital, its influence is exercised by civil servants deployed in the various field departments and in institutions such as schools and health centres.

Western Province is one of seven in Kenya. It has four Districts (Kakamega, Bungoma, Busia and Vihiga), each further divided hierarchically into divisions, locations and sub-locations for administrative purposes. The Provincial Commissioner is the administrative head with his headquarters at Kakamega, while each district and division is headed by a District Commissioner and District Officer respectively. There were 14,490 civil servants stationed in the districts in Western Kenya in 1984, with half of them in Kakamega District – the provincial headquarters (Republic of Kenya, 1984: 37). Whereas the provincial and district headquarters are adequately manned, below the district level civil servants are few, and they become fewer the lower the level in the field administrative hierarchy. Below the divisional level few government ministries are represented, with the exception of provincial administration and the ministries responsible for agriculture and livestock.

Surveys show that there is a lopsided distribution of field officials in Kenya ranging from a high concentration at provincial headquarters and few at the lower levels. In Western Kenya, apart from the 50% at the provincial headquarters at Kakamega, there are 42% at the district headquarters in Bungoma, Busia and Vihiga, 7% at the divisional headquarters, and only 1% or less at the locational levels.[4] Furthermore, there are only 11 police stations, 9 police posts and 6 patrol bases, quite a distance apart and staffed with far too few policemen (*Western Province Annual Report,* 1980: 26). In other words, the administrative infrastructure for maintaining law and order is weak at the grass roots. Government presence is seriously felt only at the district headquarters and their immediate surroundings, and in some divisional headquarters in the more developed parts of the districts. A weak police presence obviously hampers the state's ability to prevent and detect crimes in a locality. To the extent that these functions are crucial to maintaining law and order in Western Kenya, the current police presence is obviously not adequate, given the small numbers of policemen *vis-à-vis* their enormous responsibilities to prevent and detect crime in the rural areas.

## Chiefs

The locational and sub-locational levels headed by chiefs and their assistants are the weakest link in the government structure at the grass-roots level. Their ability

---

[4] Own estimates.

to exercise their authority as government agents is highly dependent on the good will and acceptance of their function by the local community. For the chiefs and assistant chiefs are first and foremost part and parcel of the rural community. They are recruited from amongst the local adult males and, unlike other civil servants, are usually not liable to redeployment away from their localities. This obliges them to be sensitive to the wishes of the community in which they live so that they do not become social misfits themselves.

Indeed, very often they tend to assess official directives from their administrative superiors with local concerns in mind.[5] When such directives do not meet the local criteria, they offer passive resistance by failing to implement them effectively. Although the Chief's Authority Act, enacted during the colonial era, was meant to endow them with wide-ranging powers to control various aspects of rural life, it has in many ways remained a dead letter since independence in 1963 (Republic of Kenya: 1970, chapter 128, sections 10 and 11). For example, in 1980 President Moi directed the provincial administration to stamp out illicit brews such as *chang'a*, but the local brewing continues unabated. Chiefs and assistant chiefs know who the local brewers are but they take no appropriate measures to implement the presidential directive, because the local brews are popular in the rural areas and are also the main source of income for some families. Many chiefs and their assistants have therefore been persistently accused of incompetence and have often been threatened with summary dismissal by their administrative superiors. Yet in only a few instances are such threats ever carried out because the state realizes how difficult it is to find replacements; new recruits have ultimately not behaved differently from their predecessors.

Thus, the maintenance of law and order in the rural areas has been largely dependent on the collective effort of the rural people themselves through their own institutions.

## The Role of Voluntary Organizations

Given the thinness of the governmental structure at the grass roots in Western Kenya, the maintenance of law and order since pre-colonial days has been based on collective action by the rural population. This principle is no less relevant to modern law-enforcement arrangements which are built on the assumption that it is the bounden duty of every citizen to keep the peace.[6] A modern police force is a recent phenomenon, a colonial creation that came into being at the beginning of this century. A collective system, in which every member of a local

---

[5] Smith (1967: 62) makes a similar observation about the limitation on the use of field officials as agents of the central authority. Very often field officials develop their loyalties to the communities they serve.

[6] For example, before the introduction of the police force in England and Wales at the end of the eighteenth century, the male population had a responsibility to produce any of their members who had committed crimes, or they would be expected to pay compensation collectively to the local authority (Wegg-Prosser, 1979: 1–2)

community is responsible for each other's conduct and for the internal peace of the locality, has been an integral part of the survival mechanisms in African societies, which have always had indigenous institutions and modalities for maintaining customary law and meting out sanctions against offenders. These arrangements still survive in a significant form, despite direct or indirect colonial and post-colonial attempts to eclipse them.

## Historical Roots of Indigenous Institutions

The major ethnic group in Western Kenya is the Luhya. Small ethnic groups such as the Kalenjin and Teso occupy parts of Bungoma District. These ethnic groups grow maize along with some cash crops such as cotton, sugar cane, tea and coffee. The profile of the local economy in Western Kenya is similar to that of other parts of Kenya; it is largely based on peasant agriculture, and is characterized by widespread poverty (Jaetzold and Schmidt, 1982; UNICEF, 1984).

The Luhya have been organized on a clan basis and patrilocally for a long time. However, until its collapse in the latter part of the colonial era, the Wanga Kingdom, established at the end of the sixteenth century, placed most of Western Kenya under a centralized state (Were, 1967: 99–186). By the nature of kingdom politics, one group became the royal clan and over time established its hegemony over the vanquished clans and tribes (Anangwe, 1990: 500). Because of the expansive nature of the Wanga Kingdom, it became necessary for the *Nabongo* (the King) to rule the distant parts through vassals on whom he bestowed the royal insignia. Indeed, there were several such vassals in most parts of Western Kenya who tended to dominate local affairs and whose role was supported by royal authority and occasional use of force by the *Nabongo* (Makila, 1976: 206–15).

Although the Wanga Kingdom came to an end during colonial rule, political behaviour reminiscent of that era still persists, for the colonial rulers adopted a similar pattern of rulership. The local District Commissioner literally assumed the role of the *Nabongo,* and appointed colonial chiefs who, in the eyes of the local population, were seen in the same light as the royal vassals. Similarly, present-day chiefs and assistant chiefs tend to assume the traditional mantle, although they are government appointees. If they perform their responsibilities well, each of them tends to be treated respectfully and perceived by his subjects as *Omwami* (leader), an imagery of the former Kingdom. Moreover, even today respected elders are informally earmarked as the custodians of the interests of their villages; they play a leading role in village matters and apply customary values and norms, not the statutory law of which they may in any case be ignorant.

All this is not to suggest that the whole of Western Kenya is traditional. Modernization (e.g. Christianity and education) has also occurred, initially through the missionaries in the earlier part of this century but later espoused by the colonial and post-colonial states as an integral part of development efforts.

The result has been the establishment of a set of institutions (e.g. political parties, co-operatives, self-help committees) and practices that have taken traditional social structures and processes as their main point of departure.

The real issue is not whether or not the new holds more sway in the rural areas than the traditional way of life, but rather that modern, Christian and traditional ways find joint expression in the responses and adjustments to problems in general, and the requirements for law and order in particular. This takes place against a backdrop of futile attempts by the colonial and post-colonial states to assert their authority over the rural areas, where voluntary agencies have enjoyed considerable space all along. In the following sections three vital institutions in the rural areas of Western Kenya, namely the village community, the local church and youth groups, are analysed.

## The Village Community

A village community may be perceived as a corporate group, often related by lineage or marriage, that resides in a locality, and whose members frequently engage in face-to-face interaction, experience similar problems and share resources and facilities (Anangwe, 1991: 12). A village is differentiated on class, gender and age bases, but these cleavages do not necessarily generate social conflicts. Such conflicts are moderated by the acceptance of mutual social responsibility, a clear division of labour and the assignment of roles in the social structure which seem to be accepted by everyone, apart from a few social pariahs. For example, in Western Kenya the household is usually male-headed (except where wives assume the roles of their husbands for one reason or another); wives accept the leadership of their husbands, at least overtly, and the young people assist their parents. In terms of division of labour, the man is the policy-maker, the defender of the homestead and the undertaker of more difficult tasks (e.g. clearing the bush on the smallholding and building the house), while the wife takes care of the domestic chores as well as providing labour on the smallholding; children participate in the domestic chores invariably. At the village level, the gender division of labour also holds sway; the men assume the leadership and make the major decisions affecting the village, whilst the women and children may participate marginally in the decision-making process, if not simply to follow what the men have decided.

At the helm of the male-dominated decision-making system in the village in Western Kenya is the *Liguru*. This institution is a carry-over from the era of the Kingdom of Wanga when royal agents were appointed to oversee village affairs. The colonial and post-colonial administrations perpetuated the institution when they continued to rely on it as their link with the villages. Today, the *Amaguru* (plural of *Liguru*) are not civil servants but are, in fact, elected or selected through consultation with the village community. They tend to be the major actors in the maintenance of law and order at the village level and also serve as the main conduits between the villagers, on the one hand, and the state, par-ticularly the chiefs and their assistants, on the other. The *Liguru* relays villagers' problems and demands to the state (for example, reporting crimes to the assistant chief or the police, arresting suspects with the help of his male aides, and taking them to the police station). On the other hand, the *Liguru* also conveys official communications from the state to the villagers in his area of jurisdiction, through village *barazas* (meetings).

Numbering about 1,000 in Western Kenya, the *Amaguru* are more loyal to the village community than they are towards the state. When the community loses faith in a *Liguru,* he is often simply replaced by another appointee acceptable to the village. Each *Liguru* holds regular village *barazas*, usually under a tree, where most of the villagers congregate voluntarily to discuss village problems and find solutions, although the men do most of the talking whilst the women and the young people simply listen. During a *baraza* issues that may result in lawless acts are dealt with transparently; offenders are fined or admonished, while the accusers are sometimes charged a token fee payable in cash or kind. The villagers hold these meetings in high esteem, as evidenced by the large attendance.[7] In addition, matters are discussed and decisions reached fairly through consensus rather than by administrative fiat, and without resort to state intervention.

Disobedience of the decisions of the village meetings would be taken as a sign of disrespect, requiring more severe sanctions to be meted out. In that case, criminal matters would be reported to the police by the *Liguru*. In the case of civil disputes, a complainant might be encouraged to seek redress in a court of law with the support of the villagers. If it is a misdemeanour (unlawful act of a not very serious sort), the offender would be publicly ridiculed, or even ostracized. Probably the worst sanction is to be stigmatized and be the talk of the village in a disparaging way. To be excluded from normal social intercourse is, for most villagers, very serious. For example, other villagers would not respond enthusiastically to helping a ridiculed villager with a funeral. Villagers also believe that such people become a target for ill-will or witchcraft. Of course, this is not to suggest that none of the villagers in Western Kenya commit offences; they do, but not so brazenly against their fellow villagers.

## The Local Churches

Christianity is the dominant religion in Western Kenya, as exemplified by the deep-rootedness of the church in the province. The various local churches have a strong following and still maintain credibility in the eyes of the people. The church is the only organization besides the ruling party that claims any mass following in African countries, particularly in the rural areas.[8] The church has played an extensive role in the modernization process in Kenya. As Ngugi wa Thiong'o (1972: 31) asserts:

[7] The author has attended several of these meetings; depending on the importance of the matters to be discussed, the attendance can be as large as the whole village.

[8] Hyden (1983: 117–18) notes that this is the situation in Africa generally.

The coming of christianity also set in motion a process of social change, involving rapid disintegration of the tribal set-up and the framework of social norms and values by which people had formerly ordered their lives and their relationship to others.

In essence, being a Christian meant shifting allegiance away from the African values and rituals, and towards a European way of life that was deemed to be superior and co-terminous with Christianity (Mutiso, 1975: 3–13).

Indeed, the introduction to Western education in the rural areas was usually associated with certain Christian denominations (see Chapter 5). Whereas the missionaries may have started formal education as an integral part of evangelization and civilization in Africa, going to school was an eye-opener for the African; the students not only acquired writing and reading skills but were also socialized in Western values and norms more or less as Christianity had done, inasmuch as both drew their praxis from the European culture. Like Christianity, the Western education tended to weaken the interest of its graduates in traditional values.

There are approximately 3,000 churches in Western Kenya today. For example, in an ordinary village of 1,000 people and within a radius of a half kilometre, there may be three churches of different denominations. The majority of rural people belong to one of the major church organizations in Kenya such as the Catholic, Anglican or Baptist Churches, the Salvation Army, the Quakers, the Seventh Day Adventists, the Church of God, the Sinai Mission, the African Divine Church, the Legio Maria, or the Pentecostal Assembly, to name but a few. The spiritual influence of the local churches in the villages is quite strong; most people are baptized, and Christian prayers are offered in the morning, before each meal, before going to bed, and during important functions in many rural households. Most rural people have imposed on themselves a six-day working week without official legislation. To be seen to be seriously working (e.g. ploughing or thatching a hut) on a Sunday is regarded as against Christian belief. Finally, a church priest is expected to preside over burial ceremonies; a dead person buried without a Christian ceremony is regarded as hellbound. Hence, the priests of the various churches are treated with respect and accorded a high profile.

Against this background, church morality makes a positive contribution to the maintenance of law and order. The relevance of fundamental Christian principles, as elucidated in the Bible, to law and order is obvious. The churches in Kenya preach love and peace; 'To love one's neighbour is to respond to his needs and care for him' (National Council of Churches of Kenya, 1983: 9). The concept of neighbour refers not only to the person who lives next door, but to any person with whom one comes in contact.

The real question is whether these principles govern the lives of the rural people in Western Kenya. No doubt, some Christians may simply pay lip-service, while breaching Christian principles in their daily lives. However, a significant proportion of people do attempt to lead Christian lives; they keep Bibles in their homes, believe in daily prayers, and attend church services regularly. In short, the churches inculcate amongst their followers values that facilitate the effective maintenance of law and order in the rural areas.

## Party Youth Groups

Youth groups – frequently associated with the ruling party, the Kenya African National Union (KANU)[9] – function in theory to popularize the Party's policies and programmes, and to ensure successful party mobilization. In practice, they engage in self-help and voluntary work that are little related to Party work. Furthermore, they have sometimes been involved in local issues in ways that may not promote Party goals. Their activities at the local level are often oriented towards law and order. They frequently behave like private armies of local party bosses who use these Youth League committees in a highly decentralized way, with little supervision from the Party headquarters in Nairobi. The allegiance of the committees to the Party *per se* may therefore be questionable; in any case, only a few of the young people are paid-up members of the Party, and they may know very little about the Party programmes and policies. During the transition to multi-partyism in Kenya, the new political parties have provided for similar youth groups in their constitutions, but they have yet to establish them extensively in the rural areas as KANU has done. So youth groups of this kind in the rural areas remain largely a KANU affair.

Coupled with the ambiguous position of the KANU Youth League committees is the weak party–state relationship in Kenya, as in many one-party states in Africa, and this was particularly the case under the Kenyatta regime (Okumu, 1984). The Party's role under the Moi regime has been somewhat different, particularly before the advent of multi-partyism. The regime attempted generally to revitalize KANU as an instrument of control rather than as a vehicle for transmitting popular demands to the government. However, the success of these attempts has been somewhat hampered in the past by the decentralized nature of the actual Party arrangements, except when special circumstances with a bearing on national politics have warranted the intervention of Party headquarters in Nairobi in local party affairs. For the most part, the direction of the Party activities in the districts is left to the branch chairmen, who tend to use the Party branches as personal machines for managing conflicts of a local nature. As a result, some branch chairmen have tended to assume the mantle of district bosses with a political clout more to do with their critical locus in the patron–client nexus underpinning the Kenyan state than with the provisions of the KANU Constitution (Anangwe, 1990: 179–80). Such district bosses may often have used the Party merely to consolidate their local power bases. With the advent of multi-partyism these tendencies are disappearing rapidly, as KANU headquarters tries to reshape the Party into an instrument for inter-party competition by supervising the branches and sub-branches, and centralizing the

---

[9] Under article 14 of the KANU Constitution, Youth League committee members should be aged between 18 and 35 years, although it is not unusual to find older members (KANU, 1979). Most of them are unemployed. There are youth committees at sub-location, location/ward, constituency and district levels. They have existed for about three decades.

policy-making process. Against this changing background, the role KANU Youth League committees have played in the maintenance of law and order can be understood generally not so much as an extended arm of the state as their being civil actors contributing positively to resolving local problems.

In Western Kenya the KANU Youth League committees engage in the maintenance of law and order in the villages and at public meetings, helping in the apprehension of criminals as well as the waging of campaigns against drug abuse. As the police in Western Kenya acknowledge, the 'KANU Youth' have also been quite helpful in providing information about crimes (Republic of Kenya, 1981: 9). Such a favourable view of the 'KANU Youth' is no different from the perception of ordinary Kenyans, as the Saitoti Report asserts following countrywide interviews with the public:

> It was further stated that many Kenyans today record with appreciation the role the majority of the youth league members are playing in the maintenance of law and order (KANU, 1990: 112).

## Importance and Political Implications

The impact of the voluntary sector (village communities, local churches and the KANU Youth League committees) on the maintenance of law and order in Western Kenya is considerable. Because government influence in the rural areas – apart from exceptional circumstances – remains largely symbolic, the role of the state has always been marginal. The maintenance of law and order in these areas is predicated upon the ability of the voluntary sector to shoulder this responsibility effectively. That has indeed been the case, although not without pitfalls, of course, and it may remain so for quite some time.

Can the voluntary sector be a substitute for the state in the maintenance of law and order? So far it has been the mainstay of law and order in the rural areas, largely because the rural society is held together by affective networks and communal values and norms. However, the recent onslaught by capitalist forces on rural societies has been immense. For example, the introduction of cash crop production (e.g. sugar-cane growing in Kakamega District) has engendered social differentiation, resulting in class formation and a weakening of traditional institutions, that does not augur well for rural order. 'Development' has meant that the traditional social fabric is weakened. Instead, new relationships are being created that require new mechanisms for maintaining law and order. For instance, new measures and institutions (e.g. private security firms, sophisticated security gadgets, private detectives) for law and order are emerging, and many of these are beyond the capability of rural communities. Already many rural communities are being overwhelmed by organized crime syndicates in the rural areas (e.g. '*Muzumbiji*' and 'Angola' hoodlums in Kakamega District and armed robbers in Busia and Bungoma Districts) which require armed policemen to intervene.

Nevertheless, the current role of the voluntary sector in Western Kenya implies that to a large extent it determines not only the arrangements for law and order but also the perceptions about lawful and orderly situations. Inasmuch as this is the case, the state becomes a dependent sector, often open to influences from the voluntary sector in matters of law and order. In other words, the reality in the rural areas raises fundamental questions about the popular view that the state in Kenya is omnipotent, as this may be more apparent than real. Consequently, arrangements for law and order need to be built on different assumptions. Measures to improve the maintenance of law and order in the rural areas should be geared towards building up the capacity of the rural communities to defend themselves, particularly in areas where traditional mechanisms for conflict resolution and social control may be less effective than before.

## The Role of the State

If the responsibility for the maintenance of law and order has been shouldered overwhelmingly by the voluntary sector, what has then been the role of the state? The state (defined narrowly as the government) has had both indirect and direct inputs in the maintenance of law and order in Western Kenya.

Its indirect role is related to education. Started by the missionaries, as already mentioned, education is now a major responsibility of the state, albeit in close partnership with the voluntary sector as described in Chapter 5. The school today is an important agent of socialization as well as an institution for inculcating law-abiding attitudes amongst rural communities in Kenya in a similar fashion to Christianity.

Moreover, to the extent that the causes of crime (e.g. thefts, robberies and housebreaking) are attributed to lack of employment or the prevalence of poverty, as some sociologists suggest (Odegi-Awuondo, 1978: 8; Nzisa, 1985: 11–12), then the efforts of the state in rural development may contribute to the enhancement of security. The public services the state provides include education (mentioned above), agricultural extension services, health services, agricultural credit, and an improved road network. All this may help to minimize the occurrence of crime by providing opportunities for a better standard of living. Without such activities rural poverty would be exacerbated, and would render rural people susceptible to lawlessness and disorder.

Apart from the public services, the state is also a key employer. Between 1963 and 1984, the civil service establishment grew by over 300% (Republic of Kenya, 1984: 30) – much faster than employment in the private sector. In terms of the wage bill, the amount involved was considerable; for example, in 1984 outlays on salaries amounted to 60% of the Ministries' recurrent budgets (Republic of Kenya, 1986: 32). Although accurate provincial figures are hard to come by, it is estimated that Western Kenya's share was about 10% of total public sector employment and 2.5% of the population in the province in 1984. In short, the public sector has generated employment for many who, without the public sector jobs, might have become criminals of one kind or another.

The direct role of the state in maintaining law and order is related to policing and the administration of justice through the courts. In Western Kenya, the number of crimes handled by the police has run into thousands and the crime figures have been rising on average by 8% annually since 1979 (*Western Province Annual Reports*). The major crimes committed there have been assaults, thefts, burglaries, robberies, theft by servants, and other offences against property and the penal code. The most serious crimes (such as murder and manslaughter) are usually reported to the police, unless they occur in situations of mob justice or civil disorder, or the bereaved families decide to keep them quiet.[10]

The basis of police work is the statutory law, particularly the criminal procedure code which enumerates a number of wrongs that are deemed to be criminal offences (Republic of Kenya, 1978). In addition, there are other written laws, the breach of which may constitute an offence. Many of the Kenyan laws are colonial in origin, and hence fundamentally English in nature (Jackson, 1975: 74), although there have been post-colonial enactments that reflect indigenous perceptions. To the extent that the statutory law is incompatible with certain aspects of rural life in Western Kenya, there is a tendency for courts and chiefs also to resort to customary law, especially in civil disputes. In such cases, the police have a very limited role to play.

## Relationship with the Voluntary Sector

Obviously the state depends on the public to prevent and report crimes, as argued above. It is not a zero-sum game. In recognition of this fact President Moi – during the early years of his rule – directed the police to cultivate cordial relationships with the public in order to succeed in maintaining law and order. The police acknowledge this, as the 1980 *Western Province Annual Report*, p. 9, states:

> It is gratifying to note that the members of the public have volunteered to give police information following an assurance from His Excellency the President that their information will be treated as confidential and protected at all times. We shall continue to welcome and protect our informers and the source of information for the benefit of all concerned.

In order to strengthen its capability, the state has made deliberate attempts to co-opt the public in its law-enforcement arrangements in the rural areas. In the first instance, although *Amaguru* are not civil servants, the state tends to treat them as if they were part of the official administrative hierarchy in the field; in return, the *Amaguru* have at times behaved like government agents.

There are also situations where the state has compromised statutory in favour of customary law in order to resolve rural conflicts, particularly in land cases. Indeed, such cases illustrate the extent to which the state can bend to customary practices. Since 1967, land disputes have been heard by the magistrates' courts

---

[10] The traditional ways of compensating bereaved families in kind or through payment of 'blood money' are no longer practised. See similar analyses by Penwill (1986) and Snell (1986).

under an essentially capitalist law that accorded sanctity of individual ownership of land a high premium (Republic of Kenya, 1967: chap. 10). This proved unworkable, given the complex land-tenure systems in the rural areas. The law was therefore amended in 1981 to bestow on a panel of elders the jurisdiction to hear and resolve land disputes. Once the panel makes a decision, it is neither subject to appeal nor are the magistrates allowed to alter it. In fact, the latter are supposed to enter their judgements when such cases are referred to them strictly in accordance with the decisions of the panel.

The panel is composed of either two or four elders under the chairmanship of the local District Officer. For the purposes of constituting the panel, elders are deemed to be

> persons in the community, or communities to which the parties by whom the issue is raised belong who are recognized by customs in the community or communities as being, by virtue of age, experienced or otherwise, competent to resolve issues between parties and where there are no elders, or where the parties cannot agree upon the choice of elders, then the expression shall mean such persons as the District Commissioner shall appoint (Republic of Kenya, 1981a, chapter 14, section 9F).

One empirical study shows that elders are currently involved in settling land disputes according to the Act. Customary law and family considerations frequently override some of the provisions in the statutes regarding land ownership. Furthermore, the cases are being disposed of faster and at less cost than before (Oloo and Yatich, 1986: 12–13).

Other attempts by the state to co-opt the voluntary sector in the maintenance of law and order in the rural areas have also targeted the KANU Youth League committees. In the case of Western Kenya, the police have, as already noted, acknowledged the assistance of these committees. They have not only given valuable information about crimes but have also arrested criminals and handed them over to the police. If suggestions have been made that these committees should be properly trained on how to maintain law and order and be paid allowances for their services (Republic of Kenya, 1981: 111), it is because they have carved a niche for themselves in this respect.

The danger of this close relationship is also obvious. Sometimes the state has used these committees so much that they are regarded as having usurped 'the role of the police force' (KANU, 1990: 111). Some sections of the public have objected to this, particularly when the committees took sides in local feuds and used their influence against those to whom the establishment was ill-disposed. In such cases, they have behaved as if they were a department of the government working in tandem with the police and the chiefs and their assistants.

The state has been less successful, especially in Western Kenya, in its attempts to co-opt the church than it has been with the other voluntary agencies. This is because of differences not so much over the need for peace and security as about how these values should be achieved. The state–church relationship has appeared confrontational at times when the church has taken moral or biblical stances[11] in contrast to secular practice which the state prefers. Nonetheless, such differences do not usually generate so much conflict that law and order are compromised.

Nevertheless, the bottom line in all this is that rural people report to the state only those crimes that they choose to report, and remain silent about others. Consequently, the number of reports that reach the police centres are fewer than the number of crimes that actually occur and are known by the rural people. For example, during the inter-ethnic clashes in Western Kenya in mid-1992, the Luhya and Kalenjin communities engaged in bloody feuds along their borders, resulting in the destruction of life and property.[12] Because the killings and arson were committed by popular consent and collective action by one ethnic group against the other, it became desirable for either ethnic group in the border areas, on the one hand, to cover up acts of violence committed by their own members, and, on the other hand, to point an accusing finger at the other community. Normally, the perpetration of such crimes even by close relations, let alone an ethnic group, would result in the matter being reported to the police and the culprit being arrested. In the circumstances under which the Luhya and Kalenjins clashed, however, it became difficult for the police to discover from either community who the murderers and arsonists were, although the local people knew who amongst their own members had committed these crimes. In short, the rural people choose what crimes to report to the police, and which ones to cover up.

## Conclusion

The central argument in this chapter is that the maintenance of law and order in rural areas in Kenya depends on the effectiveness of the voluntary sector, whilst the role of the state is more complementary than critical. This argument departs significantly from the popular view that the state in Africa, or in Kenya for that matter, is hegemonic and overshadows the voluntary sector. Future arrangements aimed at improving law, order and security in rural areas should take cognizance of the crucial role of the voluntary sector and of the fact that the state is weak in rural areas. However, such arrangements should also take account of the rapid social differentiation that capitalist penetration is bringing about, and of the growing attempts by the state to co-opt the voluntary sector in law and order activities. Moreover, when violence in rural areas is instigated from above, then the limits of the capacity of voluntary agencies to maintain law and order are reached.

[11] It is the church's view that the state must submit itself to God, and that the governing authorities are God's servants. Obviously, such a view does not find favour with the governing authorities who, in the quest for stability, security and power, may be obliged to engage in some political practices that could be deemed to be unchristian. See National Council of Churches of Kenya (1983: 65). See also Chapter 11 of this book for a discussion of state–church relations in Tanzania.

[12] These clashes were instigated by the Kalenjin politicians and chiefs against the non-Kalenjins for political reasons. See *The Weekly Review*, 25 September 1992:11–15.

There is also a need to reassess the role the voluntary sector has been performing and under what conditions. To postulate that the participation of the voluntary sector in rural life has been hampered by the growth in the state sector may be a myth, if not a partial perception of a highly complex reality. The basis of such a myth may be the tendency to let urban perceptions tamper with an inquiry into such a phenomenon in the rural areas.

# References

Ake, C. (1973) 'Explaining Political Instability in New African States', *Journal of Modern African Studies* 2 (3): 347–459.

Anangwe, A. (1990) 'The Politics of Decentralization in Kenya'. Ph.D. Thesis, University of Manchester, Manchester.

Anangwe, A. (1991) 'A Review of Indigenous Ways for Communities to Cope with ASAL Conditions in Kenya Through Joint Efforts'. Paper prepared for the World Bank ASAL team under the auspices of a plan of action for community participation. Nairobi: World Bank Regional Office.

Bienen, H. (1967) 'What Does Political Development in Africa Mean?' *World Politics* 20 (1): 128–41.

Bratton, M. (1988) 'Beyond the State: Civil Society and Associational Life in Africa', *World Politics* 41 (31): 407–30.

Chambers, R. (1983) *Rural Development: Putting the Last First*. London: Longman.

Cliffe, L., Coleman, J.S. and Doornbos, M. (eds) (1977) *Government and Rural Development in East Africa: Essays in Political Penetration*. The Hague: Martinus Nijhoff.

Fowler, A. (1991) 'The Role of NGOs in Changing State–Society Relations: Perspectives from Eastern and Southern Africa', *Development Policy Review* 9 (1): 53–84.

Hyden, G. (1983) *No Shortcuts to Progress*. Nairobi: Oxford University Press.

Jackson, T. (1975) *The Law of Kenya*. Nairobi: East African Literature Bureau.

Jaetzold, R. and Schmidt, H. (1982) *Farm Management Handbook of Kenya*. Nairobi: Ministry of Agriculture.

KANU (1979) *The KANU Constitution*. Nairobi: KANU Headquarters.

KANU (1990) *Report of the Review Committee*. Chaired by Professor George Saitoti. Nairobi: KANU Headquarters.

Lamb, G. (1977) 'Promoting Agrarian Change: Penetration and Response in Murang'a, Kenya' in Cliffe *et al.*

Makila, F.E. (1976) *An Outline of the History of the Babukusu*. Nairobi: Kenya Literature Bureau.

Mutiso, G.C. (1975) *Kenya Politics, Policy and Society*. Nairobi: East African Literature Bureau.

Mutiso, G.C. (1977) 'A Low Status Group in Centre–Periphery Relations: Mbai Sya Eitu' in Cliffe *et al.*

Myrdal, G. (1968) *Asian Drama: An Inquiry into the Poverty of Nations*. New York: Twentieth Century Fund and Pantheon Books.

National Council of Churches of Kenya (1983) *A Christian View of Politics in Kenya*. Nairobi: Uzima Press.

Nzisa, K.V. (1985) 'The Attitude of Women Criminals Toward Custodial Treatment'. B.A. Dissertation, University of Nairobi, Nairobi.

Odegi-Awuondo, C.B. (1978) 'The Probation Service in Kenya: Its Organization, Functioning and Effectiveness'. M.A. Thesis, University of Nairobi, Nairobi.

Okumu, J.J. (1984) 'Party and Party–State Relations' in J. Barkan (ed.) *Politics and Public Policy in Kenya and Tanzania*. New York: Praeger.

Oloo, C.M. and Yatich, P.B. (1986) 'The Magistrates Jurisdiction Amendment Act, No. 14 of 1981, Its Success and Bottlenecks: A Study of Nakuru District'. Research paper in partial fulfilment of the requirements of APA No. 32/86. Nairobi: Kenya Institute of Administration.

Penwill, D.J. (1986) *Kamba Customary Law*. Nairobi: Kenya Literature Bureau.

Republic of Kenya (1967) *The Magistrates Courts Act*. Nairobi: Government Printer.

Republic of Kenya (1970) *The Chief's Authority Act*. Nairobi: Government Printer.

Republic of Kenya (1978) *Criminal Procedure Code, Chapter 75*. Nairobi: Government Printer.

Republic of Kenya (1981) *The Magistrates Jurisdiction Amendment, Chapter 14*. Nairobi: Government Printer.

Republic of Kenya (1984) *Report of the Census of the Kenyan Civil Service*. Nairobi: Government Printer.

Republic of Kenya (1986) 'Economic Management for Renewed Growth'. *Sessional paper No. 1*. Nairobi: Government Printer.

Republic of Kenya (various years, 1979–1991) *Western Province Annual Report*. Kakamega: Provincial Commissioner's Office.

Smith, B.C. (1967) *Field Administration: an Aspect of Decentralization*. London: Routledge and Kegan Paul.

Snell, G.S. (1986) *Nandi Customary law*. Nairobi: Kenya Literature Bureau.

UNICEF (1984) *Situational Analyses of Children and Women*. Nairobi: Central Bureau of Statistics.

wa Thiong'o, Ngugi (1972) *Homecoming*. London: Heinemann.

Wegg-Prosser, P. (1979) *The Police and the Law*. London: Oyez Publishing Ltd.

Were, G.S. (1967) *A History of the Abaluhya of Western Kenya c. 1500–1930*. Nairobi: East African Publishing House.

Zolberg, A.R. (1966) *Creating Political Order: The Party-States of West Africa*. Chicago: Rand McNally & Co.

## 7

WALTER O. OYUGI
Service Provision in Rural Kenya:
Who Benefits?

Historically, the Kenyan state has been a major provider of many basic-needs services to the people in both rural and urban areas. Some of the services in question include: health care, education, water and sanitation, law and order, employment, agricultural extension, access roads, urban housing, a variety of welfare services, etc. In the provision of most of these services, the state has been joined by many voluntary organizations. During the colonial period, the missionary organizations, in particular, played a significant role and they have continued to do so to the present day. In the course of time, however, other actors have emerged as service providers. These include popular institutions (such as the co-operative societies, self-help organizations, etc.) and foreign NGOs.

This chapter surveys service provision in rural Kenya since independence and examines in particular: the socio-political context of service provision, the roles of the various providers, the organizational context within which the services are provided. Finally an attempt is made to address the question: who benefits? To illuminate the arguments advanced in the analyses, the provision of two major services, health care and education, are discussed in some detail. Other services are also focused upon where necessary.

## Access and Equity

What do the two concepts mean in the Kenyan context? The idea of providing facilities such as schools, health centres, etc. is, of course, intended to improve the provision of services to those in need. To receive a service, one has to gain access to it. Access thus implies an action as well as a means of obtaining a service. Its structure can either facilitate or frustrate one's efforts. Indeed, as Schaffer and Lamb (1981) put it, to understand access means coming to terms with the gates, lines and counters of institutional allocations; the problems of eligibility; the problems of waiting, ordering and priorities; the problems of items and packages of the services allocated. Put differently, the structure of the institutional–organizational delivery system affects access situations directly.

If a service is to be made available: who gets priority, who waits and under what conditions, and in what manner is that which is available to be distributed or shared out? This is where the criterion of equity comes in. Equity is a value. The Heinemann dictionary defines it as justice and fairness. And, it could be added, it is justice and fairness in the distribution and allocation of resources or services. Schaffer and Lamb (1981: 2) contend that, as concept and practice, equity is above all political. It is, they add, an ideological construct about distribution, about the apportionment of resources in society and therefore political in the sense of an intervention in the struggle of political ideas. The roles of the state and of the institutions created to deliver the services are therefore critical. So are the roles of the dominant socio-economic groups in a given society. The interplay among these forces could lead to what Schaffer and Lamb (1981: 3) call the *irony of equity*:

> public action may be intended to correct an equity arriving (arising?) from the operation of institutions and rules (e.g. markets, agencies, laws, household structure). It does so characteristically and unavoidably however, by setting up fresh institutions and new bodies of roles which have their own ironic outcomes of exclusion and inequality: and the process can continue indefinitely.

The operational meaning of the two concepts becomes clearer in the discussion of the Kenyan experience.

Independent Kenya inherited a structure of access that was characterized by regional and human inequalities. There was urban bias, and the interest of the immigrant races in every aspect of life reigned supreme. The recognition of the inherited structure of inequality was to lead the new government to the enunciation of a number of egalitarian-related principles in *Sessional Paper* No. 10 of 1965 on African Socialism. It is discussed in further detail below, but of relevance here is the emphasis on the need for a strategy of development that would guarantee: freedom from exploitation, equal opportunity for advancement and equitable distribution, balanced development of urban and rural areas, intra-regional balance and attendance to the needs of vulnerable groups. All these principles have been reiterated in all the development plans produced since then, as exemplified in the following statements:

> it is a major aim of the government to prevent economic development being concentrated in the towns at the expense of rural areas. But it is also a major concern to ensure that some districts, particularly those which are poorer than the others, do not continue to lag behind (Republic of Kenya, 1970: 14).

Twenty years later, the emphasis still remains:

> The main objective of the spatial dimensions of policy is dispersing development activities to as many parts of the country as possible (Republic of Kenya, 1989a: 75).

And for intra-group equity another policy document declared:

> In the provision of basic needs, the government will allocate development expenditure as equitably as possible. Individuals will receive roughly equal weight, except for special (vulnerable) cases needing above average public service (Republic of Kenya, 1979: 18).

Again, how the state intended to achieve the objective of equity is to be found in the development plans. During the First Plan period, the emphasis was on capacity-building and development of the institutions and personnel needed in service provision in the rural areas. A self-help strategy addressed the first objective, while the second remained a continuing preoccupation of the state. In the Second Plan period, rural development itself emerged as the strategy. The government stated:

> the key strategy in this plan is to direct an increasing share of the total resources available to the nation towards the rural areas. The government believes that it is only through an accelerated development of the rural areas that balanced economic development can be achieved... (Republic of Kenya, 1970: 2).

This orientation was to be continued in the Third Plan, emerging in the Fourth Plan as the *Basic Needs Strategy,* organized around the theme alleviation of poverty, with education, health care and water being singled out as essential to improving the quality of rural life (Republic of Kenya, 1979: 2–18).

The need for equity in the provision of basic needs was again stressed. And in the Sixth Plan (1989/93), the emphasis on participation for progress, pointing to the complementary roles of government and people in their individual and corporate capacities, emerged as an added emphasis on self-help development, apparently in furtherance of the policies of structural adjustment (especially cost-sharing).

In spite of the existence of these policies and strategies, inequality still remains a major problem in the structure of access.

## The Socio-Political Context

To appreciate the dynamics of service provision in Kenya, it is necessary to comprehend the socio-political setting within which access and equity questions are addressed. The nature of this setting has been the subject of conflicting perceptions and interpretations – especially in the last two decades. An outline of the basic tenets of the debate, as they relate to the subject matter of this chapter, is presented below.

The first view tends to focus on the *development ideology of the state* as it has emerged, especially since its articulation in the earlier-mentioned 'African Socialism and its Application to Planning in Kenya' (Republic of Kenya, 1965) – the document that President Kenyatta often referred to as 'Our Development Bible'. The document reaffirmed the faith of the state in a mixed economy in which the public and private sectors would join hands in the interest of national development. The centrality of individual initiative was stressed, and the role of the state in development was generally perceived to be one of assisting individuals and groups to engage in rewarding economic ventures.

In this effort, partnership with foreign capital was welcome and the state did in fact pass the Foreign Investment Protection Act in 1964 encouraging such investment. This open-door policy, and the partnership in development between foreign and indigenous capital which was later to develop from it, created a new structure of relationship characterized by dependence. At the level of the state, this dependence manifested itself in the intensification of foreign penetration of the Kenyan political economy (Langdon, 1981), leading to the emergence of what critics have characterized as neo-colonialism (Leys, 1974). As a form of behaviour, neo-colonialism involves the surrender of the state prerogative on policy imperatives to foreign forces. Therefore, donor influence on policy-making in Kenya through technical assistance has been quite pronounced (Oyugi, 1973).

Indeed, a major feature of the above dependence is the emergence of the *class character of the state,* whereby the state becomes an instrument mainly serving the interests of the power holders. According to this perspective, the Kenyan state serves especially the interests of the affluent, urban-based propertied class who in addition have extensive property also in the rural areas – especially land and businesses. Whether its economic base is increasingly local and usually state-supported, or auxiliary (meaning foreign-supported), this class tends to be insensitive to the emerging structure of inequality in the country (Sandbrook, 1980). The result is rising urban–rural differentials, the persistent inequitable allocation of resources between the urban and rural areas or, put differently, the relative neglect of the rural areas. The problem of the provision of services in the rural areas must therefore find some explanation in the ideological or class character of the Kenyan state.

The second view explains the problems of the provision of services as the 'social structure' of Kenyan society. According to this view, *ethnicity* is a major mediating factor in the allocation of state resources and this influences the provision of services (Bienen, 1974; Berg-Schlosser, 1992). An extension of this position maintains that, in a situation where the state is controlled by a given ethnic group or groups, resources would tend to flow in the direction of their areas. Indeed, it has been suggested that, under the regime of President Kenyatta, the Kikuyu were a favoured group (Leonard, 1984). Similar observations have been made about the position of the Kalenjin during the Moi regime. Preferential treatment of an ethnic group or groups naturally leads to regional disparities because of the association of specific ethnic groups with certain geographical areas of the country. Even in the case of assistance by foreign donors studies show a tendency to favour the areas of those in power (Mbithi and Rasmussen, 1977). But ethnicity does not operate in isolation. One observer contends that ethnicity cannot be explained without linking it to class-based behaviour (Berg-Schlosser, 1992).

More recently, however, a less ideological position has been advanced to explain the structure of access in Kenya and the rest of Africa. The phenomenon of *personal rule* puts an individual actor at the centre of political patronage with a patronizing role in the sphere of resource allocation (Jackson and Rosberg, 1982). As a national patron, the personal ruler 'can see far and wide' and reward or withhold patronage according to his/her socio-political preferences. As shown later, such methods have been put to good use in the self-help movement, thereby making it highly dependent on selective patronage.

In the rest of this chapter it is argued that the socio-political context in which services have been promoted has had a direct bearing on both the structure of access and its magnitude and quality.

## State, NGOs and POs in Service Provision

The provision of services in Kenya is a function shared between the government (central and local) and the voluntary sector. Among the NGOs, church organizations are prominent, but POs are the backbone of much of Kenya's service provision, as will be shown below. The present division of labour has, however, evolved over time.

During the colonial period, the local authorities provided the bulk of the services both in the urban and in the rural areas, and the central government merely played a complementary role through a grant mechanism intended to strengthen the hands of the local authorities in the process. In the rural areas, the important services provided by the local authorities (African District Councils) included: health care, primary education, rural secondary roads, construction and maintenance of markets, water supply, some aspects of agricultural and veterinary services, etc. But the provision of law and order was a function shared between the central government and the traditional authorities – with the latter operating according to the framework set by the centre to suit the new colonial situation. The services provided by the local authorities varied both in quality and scope – depending largely on the abilities of the individual councils (Oyugi, 1983).

In many cases, councils relied on non-governmental organizations, notably the churches, for running the services. But the physical facilities were more often than not provided by the local communities. This situation was inherited at independence and survived with many difficulties during the first decade of independence.

The demand for more and better services in the post-independence period led to the establishment of more facilities (schools, health centres, community water points, social halls, etc.) through self-help activities, all requiring matching resources from the government. The situation soon got out of hand and the local authorities could neither staff nor equip the new facilities. The decline in service quality and quantity forced the central government to intervene in 1970 by taking over the running of the three major services: primary education, health and secondary roads, which claimed 70% of the council's recurrent expenditure (Colebatch, 1974a and 1974b). And in 1974, following the creation of the Ministry of Water Development, all water projects hitherto managed by the local authorities were progressively taken over by the Ministry. The only notable function that the rural councils continued to provide thereafter was the construction and maintenance of marketplaces. Thus, the provision of basic-needs services from the mid-1970s became the sole responsibility of the central government in collaboration with NGOs and the local communities.

## Education

In the field of education, the state has been exclusively responsible for all the professionally orientated activities such as: the training of teachers at all levels (a few private primary teacher training institutions have emerged recently), research and curriculum development, examinations, and special education in both rural and urban areas.

What used to be parochial missionary schools during the colonial period were immediately 'desegregated' after independence; and the private sector has never found it economically attractive to establish primary schools in the rural areas. Such schools only exist in the major urban areas, and cater mainly for the children of the elites, both indigenous and expatriate. So today the state remains the main supporter of primary education in the rural areas, but the local communities, through *harambee* (self-help) efforts, have been providing the physical facilities since before independence. Indeed, the massive expansion in primary and secondary education that is the pride of the nation today is largely attributable to direct popular participation stretching over several decades. Besides putting up the facilities, the parents also bear a large part of the recurrent expenditure in primary education. They pay for books and uniforms and contribute to school funds for buying equipment, mainly furniture, and the maintenance of buildings – all this in spite of official policy according to which access to primary education is supposed to be free (Noormohamed and Opondo, 1989; Republic of Kenya, 1989a). However, the massive expansion of primary education has also imposed a heavy demand on the government in terms of teachers' salaries. Since the mid-1970s, payment of salaries has been the major concern of the state.

A different situation emerges in secondary education. During the colonial period, the provision of secondary education was shared between the state and the missionary organizations, with the latter owning the majority of the schools. These schools did, however, benefit from a variety of grants disbursed by the central government, and bursaries allocated through the local authorities, with the latter mainly playing an agency role on behalf of the central government. Denominational schools continued in some form until 1968 when they were abolished by Act of Parliament. A few private (for-profit) schools also existed during the colonial period. Whereas at independence in 1963 there were only 32 such schools in the whole country, in 1987 the number had risen to 353. On the other hand, the number of government-aided schools over the same period increased from 119 to 635.

But the huge expansion in secondary education in the rural areas was caused by the *harambee* movement. Whereas at independence no such schools existed, by 1987, the number stood at 1,497 (Republic of Kenya, 1989b: 215). And they have provided alternative opportunities for many young Kenyans, otherwise excluded through a highly competitive admission system, to gain access to state-aided schools. For instance, in 1982 while the government-aided schools admitted 16% of primary school-leavers and the private schools another 8%, the *harambee* schools admitted 26% (Noormohamed and Opondo, 1989). The irony of the *harambee* schools is that they were usually undercapitalized and therefore lacked both facilities and staff, and this did affect the quality of the education they provided. In 1990 the distinction between government-aided and *harambee* secondary schools was abolished and all public schools were redesignated as national, provincial or district schools for the purposes of admission.[1] But since the government has stopped giving development grants to schools and has instead handed over the responsibility to parents, national and provincial schools continue to enjoy relative advantages over the district ones (most of which are former *harambee* schools) since the children of those able to pay are unlikely to be in district schools. All have, in theory, equal claim on government resources. Chapter 5 provides a detailed analysis of education services.

## Health

Another service whose provision the state shares with other organizations is health care, organized around the following activities: curative and preventive health, health promotion, rural health, research and training. These activities are carried out in a variety of facilities scattered throughout the country, ranging from fully fledged hospitals to village dispensaries. There has been tremendous growth in the number of these facilities since independence. For example, the number of hospitals increased from 148 at independence to 264 in 1989. The number of beds and cots increased from 11,430 at independence to 32,534 in 1989.[2]

The state is the major provider of these health facilities nationally. By the mid-1980s it owned 68% of beds and cots, about 51% of the hospitals, about 87% of the urban health centres and clinics, about 78% of the rural health centres and clinics, about 78% of the rural health centres and 81% of the rural dispensaries and clinics (Ministry of Health, 1986: 7). The ownership structure has not changed much since then. In terms of expenditure the public sector is still by far the largest contributor, providing 50% of recurrent and development expenditures. The remaining percentage is shared between the missionary organizations and the private market (Republic of Kenya, 1989b: 236). The dominant role of the state is quite evident from these statistics.

Provision of education and health services is, as shown above, strongly dependent on the voluntary sector. The self-help movement, in particular, has steadily contributed over the years to the alleviation of the scarcity of facilities,

---

[1] National schools recruit pupils from all over the country on a district quota basis; provincial ones from all districts in the province but with no quota system; district schools recruit from within the district.

[2] Republic of Kenya (1990: 178). The statistics presented here should be treated with some caution as the designation of what a hospital is has varied over the years. For example, statistics made available to the writer by the MOH Statistics Division in November 1993 refer to 92 government hospitals and 100 NGO hospitals as at that date!

thereby enabling the government and the communities to provide services whenever resources are available. However, this strong involvement of the *harambee* movement in service provision has far-reaching implications for access and equity. These are discussed in detail later. For the question which remains to be answered is: to what extent does the government delivery system ensure effective delivery of services at the existing service points?

## The Government Delivery System

The ministerial structure has been the key framework of service delivery in Kenya dating back to the colonial period. Every ministry with a service to provide in the rural areas has a hierarchy of field offices at the various administrative levels (the province, district, division, location and sub-location) of the centralized bureaucracy. Each level is directly responsible to the one immediately above it. Two major problems that affect service delivery through the government delivery system are discussed below. One is the resistance to change in existing bureaucratic practices. The other arises from the centralization and departmentalization of the delivery system. Both help to illustrate the 'irony of equity' mentioned above: new institutions or attempts to change the roles of the existing bodies have their own outcomes of exclusion and inequality.

### Bureaucratic Inertia

For the first two and a half decades of independence, the various ministries kept intact the centralized system of field administration inherited at independence, which required all important decisions affecting development in the field and financed by the central government to be taken at the centre. This orientation was in practice accentuated after independence. It denied field-level officers the discretionary powers to shape the nature of service provision.

The requirement that programmes and projects to be implemented in the field had to be centrally approved often led to delays in implementation. More unfortunately, it gave the centre the power to use the act of approval as a means of frustrating those areas that were not in good favour with the system. Diverting funds earmarked for projects in one district to those of another, especially on ethnic and regional grounds, was reportedly quite common. And, even where commitment to implement a given project existed, piecemeal (often quarterly) release of funds had the effect of slowing down the work momentum. In the end, the delay in project completion had a direct effect on service provision.

Apart from such bureaucratic bottlenecks, the delivery system in many areas was also quite weak at points of contact with the clients or beneficiaries. The problem of inequitable distribution of staff (already mentioned in the 1979/83 *Development Plan*) resulted in some areas having low project implementation rates and poor service provision. This was compounded by the problem of staff morale arising from: lack of, or poor, accommodation for staff, especially those operating below the district level; budgetary constraints which limited the ability of staff especially at the district and divisional levels effectively to supervise the frontline workers who were actually involved in service delivery. In many departments such as Health, Agriculture, Livestock Development, Community Development, etc., the problem of morale was further aggravated by lack of career prospects and progression for virtually all frontline workers. Schemes of service were non-existent and even in-service training was rarely carried out or did not exist at all in many departments. The centralizing culture of administration affected service provision in another way. It created fear on the part of subordinates to take initiatives or to be creative and innovative. Weaknesses inherent in the operative policies and directives could not be modified on the spot for fear of violating existing working procedures.

Indeed, resistance to changing the existing bureaucratic practices has been a major cause of poor service delivery in the rural areas. Many efforts have been made since independence to modernize the organizational delivery system but each time these have met with resistance. The experience of the Ministry of Health in this regard is a case in point.[3] During the first two and a half decades of independence the procurement, management and delivery of medical supplies in the Ministry of Health was centralized at the then Central Medical Stores (the name has since been changed to Medical Supplies Co-ordinating Unit (MSCU).

However, after the launching of the District Focus for Rural Development strategy in 1983 – which aimed at decentralization of administrative decision-making to the districts, as discussed below – district medical personnel were given the authority to purchase a number of drugs. The allocations were disaggregated among the various districts, with the MSCU retaining only a small revolving fund for purchasing 'buffer stocks' that could be delivered to end-users in emergencies or during times of acute shortage. Each hospital or medical officer of health was therefore required to keep an account with the Unit for this purpose. But it was not long before problems were experienced. With Authority to Incur Expenditure (AIE) devolved to the district heads under the DFRD strategy, some medical officers used money intended for drugs to buy other supplies (e.g. detergents, brooms, etc.) whenever money voted for such purposes ran out before the end of the year. In some cases, medical officers found it difficult and more costly to procure important drugs and equipment in local chemists; the costs of the supplies when procured locally were generally very high. And the districts did not have the capacity to subject the drugs supplied locally to quality control. In addition, there were also reported cases of collusion between some suppliers and the medical staff to defraud the government. The allocations were therefore being depleted even faster than before and in some cases as early as during the first quarter of the year.

---

[3] The analysis benefits from information received from my colleague Mr Oginga Nyinguro (a former officer at the Central Medical Stores), and earlier discussions with Dr Kanani, formerly Senior Deputy Director of Medical Services and now on the staff of the Faculty of Medicine, University of Nairobi. See also Oyugi (1992b) for detailed analysis of the management of Health Services in Kenya.

'In–house' studies conducted after the decentralization effort confirmed the existence of widespread shortages of all kinds of medical supplies, especially at the hospitals. This was contrary to expectations. Against this background, the Ministry reversed the decentralization experiment in 1988 by setting up a Procurement Committee at the centre and co-opting all the Provincial Medical Officers as members. Under the new system, drugs are being procured directly from the manufacturers, with the MSCU acting as some kind of a warehouse, from which the various allocations are dispatched by the Ministry to the end-users.

It should be noted, however, that these developments have not affeced supplies to the health centres and dispensaries. The kit system (kits containing the medical requirements of a health centre or dispensary, determined by the incidence of various diseases in the respective areas) had remained under central control and were simply delivered to the provinces and districts for onward distribution to the receiving institutions.

The important lesson from the experience of the Ministry of Health is that, if not well planned, deconcentration can lead to inefficient and ineffective delivery of services to the intended beneficiaries. In retrospect, however, it should also be noted that the urgency with which the DFRD strategy was pushed through might have contributed to the failure of the Ministry to anticipate problems and to plan to avoid some of them. But the problems experienced in the districts also gave the headquarters the excuse to resume the power they had only reluctantly delegated. Bureaucratic resistance to changing existing practices is a major cause of poor delivery.

## Centralization and Departmentalization

The hierarchial structure of service provision discussed above is generally mediated by some lateral interaction of participating agencies. The framework set up for this by the government is the committee system. During the colonial period the committee system was quite weak. Called 'team meeting', it was mainly orientated towards law and order; development matters were discussed only incidentally.

The decision in 1966 to establish a hierarchy of Development Committees to co-ordinate government development business in the field was expressed in the revised first *National Development Plan of 1966/70*. The Committees were to operate at every level of the field administrative units. They were required to initiate, discuss and approve all proposed development projects – especially those initiated through self-help efforts at the grass-roots level. The committees appear to have stalled in 'taking off', and, when they were finally established towards the end of the decade, they turned out to be utterly ineffective (Jackson, 1970).

In order to strengthen the co-ordination of service provision, the government decided in 1974 to strengthen these committees by appointing an officer – the District Development Officer (DDO) – to be in charge of them on a more regular basis. A one-man secretariat was initially established, but later grew into what is today known as the District Planning Unit manned by a number of professionals (a planner, a statistician, an assistant DDO, etc.) But much still depended on the interests of the individual line ministries, which were still responsible for the financing of project recurrent expenditures. Throughout the 1970s the efforts of the Ministry of Planning and National Development to improve the quality of development planning and implementation through the district planning exercise yielded few, if any, positive results (Oyugi, 1986, 1992a). Most of the important organizational innovations intended to strengthen service delivery systems continued to be carried out departmentally. Combined with the expanding volume of services provided by the central government, this helped to weaken the function of service provision.

A new and more determined attempt to address the twin evils of centralization and departmentalism inherited at independence was launched in 1983 with the District Focus for Rural Development strategy. This required ministries to delegate most of their decision-making powers to the districts, especially regarding those development programmes and projects that were district-specific (Republic of Kenya, 1987). A District Development Committee (DDC) was established as the major vehicle for the management and implementation of rural development. All development agencies, both governmental and voluntary, were obliged to process their development projects through these committees, the idea being to ensure that only projects that could provide direct services were implemented.

The management of financial resources for district-specific projects was also to be devolved. This was intended to improve the timeliness of financial disbursement upon the approval of a project. In addition, the deployment of more senior staff to the districts was intended to improve the rate of project implementation as well as the quality of service provision at the existing facilities.

As was to be expected, the central ministries received the new directives with misgivings. The programme threatened to deprive them of their most powerful weapon, finance, hitherto used to control the behaviour of field officers. It also threatened to remove from their hands the patronage and 'kickbacks' that go with the award of tenders for projects. Initially, attempts were made to frustrate the programme, but a push from the then Office of Development Co-ordination in the Cabinet Secretariat forced the various headquarters to relent.

There were similar misgivings on the part of the County Councils. The requirement of the DFRD strategy that all council projects be vetted by the DDCs before being forwarded to the Ministry of Local Government for funding was resented. So was the requirement that the methods to be used by a local authority for raising revenue from within the district should have the concurrence of the DDC (ibid.). After some time, the councils began to complain that the new system was not working in their interest, having failed to assist them in mobilizing additional resources for service provision (Smoke, 1987).

The new strategy also required that, in identifying projects and programmes to receive donor support, donors, central ministries and the External Resources Department of the Ministry of Finance would have to undertake their negotiations in line with the principles of the DFRD, and that such negotiations would have to give high priority to district-specific projects already approved by the respective DDCs (Republic of Kenya, 1987: 4–5). In reaction, many donor agencies as well as NGOs expressed instant misgivings, with some going to the extent of threatening to pull out of the country if the position was not reversed (Oyugi, 1992a). For many of them, the policy appeared potentially to threaten to deprive them of their freedom to determine the beneficiaries of their patronage as well as the nature and flow of their assistance. The available evidence tends to suggest some kind of compromise: donors have continued to support what they consider to be priority projects and areas (e.g. UNICEF's continued support for the six districts with the highest incidence of child mortality nationally; Danish support for water projects, etc. in the arid and semi-arid lands (ASAL); Finnish support of water projects in Western Kenya, etc.), while taking care to integrate them with the on-going local district development programmes.

Meanwhile, the DFRD approach appears to have succeeded in making development funds available at the district level once the estimates have been approved. Most of the decisions pertaining to district-specific development programmes are also being taken at the district level. And, unlike before, the departmental heads as well as the local political leaders now regard the deliberations of the DDCs as being critical to the success of local development efforts. The equity implications of this fairly successful deconcentration of bureaucratic decision-making are, however, mixed, as discussed below.

## Who Benefits?

It is quite clear that the self-help movement has made a major contribution to the expansion of service facilities in the rural areas of Kenya. But the ideology of self-help has not been without its own disadvantages and/or unintended consequences. Earlier on, there was reference to the factors that influence the allocation of resources in the country: class orientation, political patronage and ethnic preferences. All of them have found some expression in the self-help movement, though in varying degrees, as will be shown below.

The previous discussion has also shown that the mere availability of facilities as such does not necessarily guarantee access to services, though it increases such chances. The government delivery system has, either by design or by default, caused widespread inequalities in service provision. The inequity has had both regional and human dimensions, as will also be shown below.

### Access and Equity Implications of Harambee

The movement succeeded partly because of the government's operative policy, in the 1960s and part of the 1970s, of assisting in the completion of projects as well as assuming the responsibility for running them upon completion. These were, however, lofty intentions that the government soon realized it could not live up to. In practice, therefore, self-help projects functioned well only in areas with a strong economic base.

Moreover, the class character of the self-help movement is reflected in the fact that over the years it has, more often than not, been captured by the rich and the influential for their own parochial and occasionally wider political ends. In the heyday of the movement, no project emerged without a prominent person or persons being in the background. For the rural poor, it has emerged in many areas as a form of regressive forced taxation used to provide services which in many countries are primarily the responsibility of the state.[4] The accentuation of the movement since independence could also be explained in terms of the reluctance of the state to tax the rich (especially their non-salary incomes) sufficiently to generate extra funds for the state provision of services. More importantly, *harambee* has served to divert accountability or blame for lack of development from the state to the people themselves!

As already indicated, political patronage has been central to the operation of the movement. From its inception in the early 1960s, the movement has been a captive of the politicians, used either as a launching pad for leadership bids or as an instrument of power consolidation. The richer the politician, the greater the amount and frequency of patronage. At the level of the wider community, the greater the number of wealthy patrons, the greater the number of self-help projects that get completed. Therefore, the movement can contribute and has in fact contributed to regional inequalities (more on this below). And, since, in the Kenyan context, geopolitical regions are associated with specific ethnic groups, it has been observed by others that the movement has also contributed to ethnic disparities. Indeed, the policy of project takeover that operated in the 1960s and part of the 1970s had the effect of concentrating government support in those areas where the communities were capable of completing projects. During the period in question, Central Province and the people living there appear to have been the main beneficiaries. And, since power was held at the time by the people of that province, donors who wanted state patronage tended to channel their support there too (Mbithi and Rasmussen, 1977; Thomas, 1985).

The role of ethnic identity in the *harambee* movement has been incidental in the sense that the main funders of a *harambee* project in any given community usually happen to be members of that community. Only where the local patron has national connections does a project benefit from 'outside' assistance. This 'outside' assistance appears to have declined in frequency since the death of President Kenyatta. Under his leadership, wealthy and politically ambitious Kenyans enjoyed the freedom to patronize *harambee* projects all over the country as they chose. Kenyatta himself encouraged, but never directly gave, generous contributions to the movement. Instead, he let others do it. But under President Moi the situation has been different (see also Chapter 1). The freedom of the would-be national patrons has been circumscribed via a practice which expects

---

[4] For a different interpretation see Barkan and Holmquist (1989).

them to contribute through him or in functions presided over by him. And there have been so many such *harambee* functions presided over by President Moi since he came to power that even the rich and generous have usually found it taxing to act as guests of honour outside their own communities.

## Rural–Urban Imbalance

This imbalance[5] manifests itself especially in the existing opportunities for access in the form of the availability of better facilities and better qualified personnel. In the field of primary education, for example, the urban areas enjoy better facilities than those found in the rural areas. Moreover, changes in the educational system in 1985 (see Chapter 5) meant that the extra facilities required for the additional primary-level class were provided much earlier in the urban areas than was the case in the rural areas. Part of the explanation here is that the working parents in the urban areas, in collaboration with the municipal authorities, were in a better position to provide them in comparison with the relatively disadvantaged rural parents.

But one particular area of education where inequity is especially pronounced is pre-primary education. Until quite recently, the provision of pre-primary education was largely confined to the urban areas, and was carried out by the councils, the NGOs (notably the churches) and the private sector, the latter primarily serving the interests of the urban elite. Since this is not yet a major concern of the central government (beyond assisting since 1984 with the training of teachers), it has turned out that the curricula being followed vary widely. To the extent that attendance at pre-primary school is now a prerequisite for admission to standard one in many urban-based schools, pre-primary education has more or less become mandatory. But this is not the case in the rural areas. Yet, when the two groups join standard one, the curriculum is a common one (except for the languages).

Although there are pre-primary schools in many rural areas today, they remain poorly capitalized and are generally manned by untrained staff. By 1986 up to 69% of staff were untrained nationally with the situation being worse than that in many areas (Gakuru *et al.*, 1987); in Embu District, 70.6% were still untrained, in Baringo 78.4%, and in South Nyanza 90.3% (Odada and Otieno, 1990: 77 and 173). The inference to be drawn is that the pre-primary education being provided in the rural areas is relatively inferior to that being offered in the urban areas.

The situation in the health sector is even worse (World Bank, 1988: 23–32). Doctors are concentrated in the urban areas – notably in Nairobi and Mombasa. Whereas nationally there was one public doctor per 46,987 people, in Nairobi and Mombasa, the ratios were 1:2,246 and 1:6,852 respectively. For the rural

---

[5] A full analysis of the nature of rural versus urban balance in development and the provision of services would require a wider focus on factors accounting for the differential, such as investment patterns, income-generating opportunities, etc. However, the present discussion is limited to the provision of education and health.

districts the ratio varied between 1:12,360 and 1:212,800. When all doctors (public and private) are taken into account, the ratio for Nairobi is 1:650, for Mombasa 1:1,118, and for the whole country 1:11,448. Public hospitals are also urban-based. Although the rural population have access to them, in many cases the distances covered by patients from different corners of the district can be long, costly and off-putting. The evidence available also tends to suggest that there has been much less expenditure on rural-orientated health services than in the urban areas in spite of the stated redistributive policy of the government. After a detailed analysis of the expenditure pattern from 1979 to 1988 by the Ministry of Health, the World Bank (1988: 23) concluded:

> It is evident that ministry priorities are not being translated sufficiently well into budgetary estimates, and the latter often have little influence on actual expenditures. The result is that the ministry's policy of priority for rural, preventive and promotive services is not being reflected in corresponding disbursements of funds; district and provincial hospitals continue to have first call on expenditure.

The situation is made even worse by the poor rural health delivery system already discussed.

## Regional Imbalance

Kenya has eight geopolitical regions including Nairobi. For administrative purposes, they are officially referred to as provinces. Analysis of equity on a provincial basis is usually a tricky exercise in Kenya. There are distortions caused by the presence of large urban areas in some provinces, and not in others. The figures for Coast Province, for example, are usually distorted by the large concentration of service activities in Mombasa Municipality.

Again there is distortion from the nature of the ethnic composition of some provinces. Consideration of ethnic factors is important because, as already discussed, it is a major influence on resource allocation. Whereas resources flowing to Central Province could immediately be associated with the flow to a specific ethnic group (i.e. the Kikuyu), the same is not true of other provinces which are multi-ethnic in composition. For example, an attempt to explain the flow of resources to the Rift Valley must also come to terms with the conspicuous presence of other 'non-Rift Valley' ethnic groups, especially in the former white-settled districts (Nakuru, Uasin–Gishu, Trans-Nzoia and parts of Kericho). Province-level data also hide a lot of intra-provincial disparities. Nonetheless, a few illustrative data will be provided.

In the health sector, the government has set 4 km or less as the reasonable distance a patient should have to travel to a health-care facility. Table 7.1 is indicative of the range of inequality that exists.

A number of dimensions of inequality can be abstracted from this table. First is the provincial differential, with North Eastern and Central Provinces at extreme opposite ends. The dominant position of Central Province can be explained partly by the unintended consequences of self-help participation (which favours the richer areas) already discussed and also by the relative political good will and therefore material advantage that this province enjoyed from the state and other actors during the first two decades of independence.

Table 7.1 Percentage of Non-city Population within 4 km of a Government or Mission Health Care Facility

|  | Achieved 1984 | | Planned 1988 | |
|---|---|---|---|---|
|  | Province | Range[a] | Province | Range |
| North Eastern | 9 | 5–17 | 11 | 5–19 |
| Coast | 45 | 21–71 | 45 | 22–71 |
| Eastern | 49 | 12–77 | 52 | 12–79 |
| Rift Valley | 49 | 7–76 | 52 | 9–80 |
| Nyanza | 67 | 40–82 | 71 | 44–83 |
| Western | 73 | 52–81 | 75 | 57–82 |
| Central | 79 | 44–88 | 83 | 56–92 |
| Total Kenya | 59 | 5–88 | 62 | 5–92 |

Source: MOH (1986: 46).

[a] Extremes of percentages between the districts that comprise the province.

The wide inter-district variation in access in both Rift Valley and Eastern Province can also be explained. The northern part of Rift Valley is mainly arid and semi-arid lands settled mainly by nomadic peoples. In Turkana, for example, one health centre serves 166,000 people in comparison with a national average of 72,000 (Republic of Kenya, 1979: 128). Similarly parts of Eastern Province are also arid and semi-arid (Kitui, parts of Machakos, parts of Embu, Isiolo and Marsabit).

In his analysis of the existing literature on regional inequality in Kenya, Bigsten (1981) concluded that, with regard to access to public services, Central Province got the most money (after Nairobi and Mombasa) followed by Rift Valley, while Western, North Eastern and Nyanza Provinces got the least per capita. Focusing on expenditure on education, health and roads, he concluded further that the most developed regions got the largest share of public resources (p. 185). These observations were at the time consistent with the conclusions reached by others, namely, that the incidence of poverty is concentrated in Nyanza, Eastern and Western Provinces – the areas with 78% of all Kenyan poor households (House and Killick, 1981).

## Inter- and Intra-Group Inequities

The income disparities between the various income groups in Kenya are said to have worsened over the years. As the economy has grown, income distribution has become more skewed in favour of the rich (Collier and Lal, 1980; Ayako, 1989).

In relation to service provision, the structure of inequality has had a direct bearing on access. The concentration of income-earning groups in the urban areas helps to explain why privately owned facilities (education and health, in particular) are concentrated in the major towns. This, in turn, has had a direct bearing on the quality of services provided in the rural areas. Rarely do most of the sick in the rural areas (mainly served by paramedics) come into contact with doctors. And usually, when they do, it is when it is too late for a doctor to be of any help!

Indeed, the effect of income disparity in access to health services has been clearly highlighted by a World Bank study (1988). It reports that more than 80% of the country's out-of-pocket expenditure on health was made by the 12% of the population living in urban households with a monthly income of K.Shs. 1,500 or more; the lower urban income group (22% of urban households earning less than K.Shs. 1,500 per month) accounted for only 2% of this expenditure and had an average annual health expenditure of K.Shs. 51 per head. According to the same source, the rural population, which constitutes 85% of the total population, accounted for only 16% of the reported expenditure, amounting to an average annual health expenditure of only K.Shs.12 per head. The report concludes that the poorer town-dwellers and rural people – who cannot afford private health services – depend mainly on government facilities or on traditional medicine for health care. However, the irony, as we indicated earlier, is that the government sector has been too inefficient and ineffective to provide the services needed. Resorting to traditional medicine is an act of despair.

As if income differential were not enough, the government has also accentuated the inequities in the medical services by allowing public service employees private medicare as a fringe benefit. Some 2.2% of MOH recurrent expenditure (or K.Shs. 34.7m) was, for example, spent on it in 1984 (World Bank, 1988: 12). The seriousness of this becomes apparent only when one considers that only 5% of the Ministry's recurrent expenditure is spent on what is classified as 'rural health services'.

But there is also a structure of inequity built into the benefits. For, whereas all grades of government employees are entitled to claim for in-patient services at some selected private facilities, including drugs purchased on their prescription, senior civil servants in the lower super scale and above[6] can claim for services rendered by private practitioners. It should also be noted that the majority of the 'fringe benefits group' also benefit from the National Hospital Insurance Fund.

The poor have also been adversely affected by the Structural Adjustment Programmes which the government has been implementing since the early 1980s. The 'adjustment' policy of price decontrol, for instance, has led to intolerable price increases, thereby rendering goods and services inaccessible to the poor. In the field of health services, the price increases have been accompanied by the requirement, since the turn of the 1990s, that patients pay for all hospital services. Although a 'subsidy' element has been built into the cost structure, available information suggests that access by the poor is being adversely affected (Odada and Odhiambo, 1989; Oyugi, 1992b).

The problem of inequity in the health services emphasizes the point that,

[6] About 4.3% of a total of 207,107 employees (Republic of Kenya, 1984: 31).

where the elites in charge of ensuring that health services are efficiently and effectively run have no stake in them, it is very unlikely that they will be bothered by whatever shortcomings may arise in their delivery. In a nutshell, then, one could state that the task of service provision has been quite insensitive to the structure of inequity that exists between the various income groups as well as between different regions of the country.

## Conclusion

It is necessary to present a brief summary of the service provision situation before drawing some conclusions which are inherent in the analysis presented.

Many institutions have been involved in building the capacity for service provision in the rural areas of Kenya. But the state, through its various agencies (ministries, local authorities and parastatals) and the rural communities themselves, emerges as the major actor. Therefore, the efficient and effective provision of services depends on the organizational strength of the state agencies and of the rural communities. These are, however, found to be rather weak on many fronts: the state often lacks the resources required to maintain the facilities and to provide the services; the little that may be available is often inefficiently managed, thereby depriving the people of the expected services. And, because of the widespread poverty in the rural areas, the people's own efforts cannot provide a credible alternative to that of the state.

There is yet another problem to consider. It concerns the discrepancy between the officially stated goals and the operative policies. Many egalitarian goals have been stated in virtually all the important government policy documents since independence; yet some of the actions which have been taken have had the opposite effect of contributing to the build-up of inequities at the regional, ethnic and inter-personal levels. And this has had adverse effects on equitable access to public and private services.

The conclusion to be drawn is that the nature of the state has been a contributory factor. The policy of individual-centred development that has been operative since independence is ideologically non-egalitarian. And the concentration of privileges in the hands of a few people in positions of authority and power has had the added effect of building up regional and ethnic disparities, as men of wealth, authority and power struggle to influence the flow of resources to areas of personal and group preference. In this sense, therefore, class and ethnicity have converged to explain the structure of access, especially in rural Kenya, in favour of communities that happen to be well connected at any given time.

This situation is unlikely to improve in the short or medium term. The structural adjustment policies now in operation following donor countries' intervention in the country's economic management have, and will continue to, hit the rural poor hardest. This has to be so because the notion of cost-sharing seems to be premised on a false assumption, namely that there is residual capacity on the part of the poor to continue taxing themselves beyond what they have managed so far! Many sectoral studies contained in the Odada and Otieno volume already cited are unanimous that the policy is bound to deprive the poor further of access opportunities. The reality of the matter is that, in rural Kenya today, there is simply no alternative to the state when it comes to service provision.

In the meantime, efforts to restructure the organizational delivery system with a view to improving the quality of service delivery keep running into problems. Again, one can only attribute the difficulties to the existing bureaucratic culture which cherishes hierarchical relations as well as acquisitive values that are anti-developmental. These twin problems explain the inefficient and ineffective provision of services. Decisions get delayed and resources once released are diverted to illicit purposes. A further irony of access, as Schaffer once observed, is that it really can be 'degraded' by those in positions of authority! This is the problem in Kenya.

# References

Ayako, A.B. (1989) 'Cost Sharing in Kenya: Macro-Economic Setting and Research Methodology Issues' in Odada and Odhiambo.

Barkan, J.D. and Holmquist F. (1989) 'Peasant State Relations and the Social Base of Self-Help in Kenya', *World Politics* 41 (3): 359–80.

Berg-Schlosser, D. (1992) 'Ethnicity, Social Class and the Political Process in Kenya' in Oyugi.

Bienen, H. (1974) *Kenya: The Politics of Participation and Control.* Princeton, NJ: Princeton University Press.

Bigsten, A. (1981) 'Regional Inequality in Kenya' in Killick.

Colebatch, H.K. (1974a) 'Local Councils and Local Services', *IDS Bulletin* 6 (1): 13–24.

Colebatch, H.K. (1974b) 'Local Services in the Government Process in Kenya', Unpublished D.Phil. Thesis, Sussex University, Brighton.

Collier, P. and Lal, D. (1980) *Poverty and Growth in Kenya.* World Bank Working Paper No. 389. Washington, DC: World Bank, May.

Gakuru, O.N. et al. (1987) *Evaluation of National Centre for Early Childhood Education (NACECE) and District Centres for Early Childhood Education (DICECE).* Nairobi: Kenya Institute of Education.

House, W. and Killick, T. (1981) 'Inequality and Poverty in the Rural Economy, and the Influence of Such Aspects on Policy' in Killick.

Jackson, R. (1970) 'Provincial Planning' in G. Hyden, R. Jackson and J. Okumu (eds) *Development Administration: The Kenyan Experience.* Nairobi: Oxford University Press.

Jackson, R. and Rosberg, C.G. (1982) *Personal Rule in Black Africa.* Berkeley, CA: University of California Press.

Killick T. (ed.) (1981) *Papers on the Kenya Economy.* Nairobi: Heinemann Educational Books.

Langdon, S. (1981) *Multinational Corporations in the Political Economy of Kenya.* London: Macmillan.

Leonard, D. (1984) 'Class Formation and Agricultural Development' in J.D. Barkan (ed.) *Politics and Public Policy in Kenya and Tanzania.* Nairobi: Heinemann.

Leys, C.T. (1974) *Underdevelopment in Kenya: The Political Economy of Neocolonialism.* London: Heinemann, now London: James Currey.

Mbithi, P.M. and Rasmussen, R. (1977) *Self-Help in Kenya: The Case of Harambee*. Uppsala: Scandinavian Institute of African Studies.

Ministry of Health (1986) *Expenditure and Financing of Health Sector in Kenya*, draft. Nairobi: Government Printer.

Noormohamed, S.O. and Opondo, F. (1989) 'Cost Sharing in Education' in Odada and Odhiambo.

Odada, J.E.O. and Odhiambo, L.O. (eds) (1989) *Report on Proceedings of the Workshop on Cost Sharing in Kenya*. Nairobi: Ministry of National Planning and Development and UNICEF.

Odada, J.E.O. and Otieno, J. (eds) (1990) *Socio-Economic Profiles*. Nairobi: Government Printer.

Oyugi, W.O. (1973) 'Role of Technical Assistance in National Development' in Y. Tandon (ed.) *Technical Assistance Administration in Eastern Africa*. Uppsala: Dag Hammarskjold Foundation.

Oyugi, W.O. (1983) 'Local Government in Kenya: A Case of Institutional Decline' in P. Mawhood (ed.) *Local Government in the Third World: The Case of Tropical Africa*. Chichester: John Wiley.

Oyugi, W.O. (1986) 'Kenya: Two Decades of Decentralization Efforts', *African Administrative Studies* 26: 133–61.

Oyugi, W.O. (1992a) 'Decentralized Development Planning and Management in Kenya: An Assessment' in P. Chitere and R. Mutiso (eds) *Working with Rural Communities*. Nairobi: University of Nairobi Press.

Oyugi, W.O. (1992b) 'Bureaucracy and Management of Health Services in Kenya' in S.K. Asmeron *et al.* (eds) *Bureaucracy and Development Policies in the Third World*. Amsterdam: Free University Press.

Oyugi, W.O. (ed.) (1992c) *Politics and Administration in East Africa*. Bonn & Nairobi: Konrad Adenauer Foundation.

Republic of Kenya (1965) 'African Socialism and its Application to Planning in Kenya'. *Sessional Paper* No. 10. Nairobi: Government Printer).

Republic of Kenya (1970) *Development Plan 1970/74*. Nairobi: Government Printer.

Republic of Kenya (1979) *Development Plan 1979/83*. Nairobi: Government Printer.

Republic of Kenya (1984) *Report on the Census of the Kenya Civil Services*. Nairobi: Government Printer, October.

Republic of Kenya (1987) *District Focus for Rural Development*. Revised edition. Nairobi: Government Printer.

Republic of Kenya (1989a) *Development Plan 1989/93*. Nairobi: Government Printer.

Republic of Kenya (1989b) *Statistical Abstract*. Nairobi: Government Printer.

Republic of Kenya (1990) *Economic Survey 1990*. Nairobi: Government Printer.

Sandbrook, R. (1980) *The Politics of Basic Needs*. London: Heinemann.

Schaffer, B. and Lamb, G. (1981) *Can Equity be Organized? Equity, Development Analysis and Planning*. Paris: UNESCO and Gower Publishing Co.

Smoke, P. (1987) *Financing Local Government in Kenya*. Report to Ministry of Local Government. Nairobi: Ministry of Local Government.

Thomas, B. (1985) *Politics, Participation and Poverty: Development Through Self-help in Kenya*. Boulder, CO: Westview Press.

World Bank (1988) *Kenya: Review of Expenditure Issues and Options in Health Financing*. Washington, DC: World Bank, February.

# 8 GASPAR K. MUNISHI
## Social Services Provision
## in Tanzania

The Relationship
between Political Development Strategies
& NGO Participation

Tanzania is, by many indicators, one of the poorest countries in the world (see Chapter 1). Nevertheless, the country has gone on record with respect to its concern and its dedication to develop and ensure an equitable distribution of the essential social services, especially education and health care. Poor as it is, the government has endeavoured to provide such social services, by and large, free of charge to all.

An important partner in service provision has been the non-governmental organizations. Their importance has varied from one period to another, reflecting the changing socio-political and economic developments of the country. There were times when the NGOs were more involved in the provision of social services, but later on the government became the most important provider.

In order to understand these changing involvements, it is necessary to contextualize these processes within the framework of the country's political development, understood as the processes by which populations become aware and concerned and wish to participate in the governance of a territory. Strategies to bring this about include political mobilization, penetration into otherwise politically disengaged populations, integration of splinter groups into the central body politic and cultivation of political acceptance (legitimacy among the various groups of the population). The provision of free social services in Tanzania is an important means of enhancing and facilitating these strategies.

In this chapter the role of service provision by the government and the NGOs is traced over time. More specifically the chapter addresses the following issues. Did the government's entrenchment in the provision of social services come about by design or by default? Under the conditions existing at various points in the country's development history, was this indulgence necessary or not? Why did the government take on more tasks in service provision, while its funds were financially limited?

The chapter focuses on two important sectors, namely health and education. It is in these sectors that popular demand is high, that both NGOs and the government are actively involved, and that data are more readily available. The analyses cover the 1960–86 period and raise issues for the subsequent period.

141

The donor factor is considered, though in less detail. Ishumi (Chapter 9) deals extensively with education and takes a different and longer perspective. Mwaikusa (Chapter 10) deals in detail with the provision of law and order in Tanzania, while Sivalon (Chapter 11) scrutinizes the role of the Catholic Church in service provision. All the chapters on Tanzania deal with the mainland only.

## Social Services Provision Before Independence

To understand the post-independence development of social service provision it is useful to start with a brief account of service provision under colonial rule.

The colonial administrative oligarchy encouraged 'separate development' on the basis of race and class. Services such as schools were organized separately for the rulers (Europeans), the Asians (a commercially dominant group) and the Africans (peasants and labourers, many of whom worked in lower-level civil service positions). Indeed, colonial education policy emphasized class orientation in addition to 'social tinting' (i.e. colour prejudice), not only to match the racial configuration of rights, obligations and expectations, but also to meet the aspirations of a few African elites who were likely to challenge the oligarchic administration.[1] This racial and class policy was institutionalized by maintaining separate development 'plans' for the different races in the territory.

Whereas colonial education emphasized a separate and class-focused system, mainly focused on European and Asian needs, some religious organizations, especially the Christians, spread their faith along with the provision of education, irrespective of race and class. Consequently, the role of the religious NGOs in (partly) filling the gap in service provision left by the colonial government was very important for the education of Africans. On the eve of independence 70% of African primary school children went to schools run by the religious institutions, while 30% went to government schools. The colonial government recognized the importance of these institutions in the provision of African primary education by helping their schools through grants-in-aid. It is also worth noting that total enrolment at independence was limited (some 360,000 Africans in 1958, of which 67% were boys).[2]

The role of religious NGOs at higher levels of education was equally central. Although the colonial government put more emphasis on secondary than on primary education, NGOs still outnumbered government contributions in terms of schools and pupils enrolled (45% of African pupils attending secondary education went to government schools compared with 55% who attended NGO-owned schools, according to Tanganyika Territory Report (1958: 369)). As was the case for mission-owned primary schools, the colonial government provided grants-in-aid to NGO secondary schools and established in this way a close co-operation with the voluntary sector.

[1]  There were, for example, schools for the children of chiefs, such as the Tabora school.
[2]  Data refer to Tanzania mainland only (Tanganyika Territory Report, 1958: Appendix XXII, p. 363).

The situation in the health sector was similar. By December 1958, the government owned 58% of all hospital beds compared with 42% owned by religious NGOs. However, access was influenced by racial and class policies. Europeans mainly got treatment at government-owned units.[3] Furthermore, government services were concentrated in urban locations (where most Europeans lived), while most NGO hospitals were located in rural areas where the poor road network and lack of reliable means of transport made the running of hospitals a difficult undertaking.

The difference between government- and church-provided health services becomes even more pronounced when dispensaries and health districts are compared. NGOs owned 81% of the primary health care facilities compared with 19% owned by the government in 1958. Again, the NGO facilities were mainly located in rural areas while those of the government tended to cater for urban people.

Thus, on the eve of Tanganyika's independence, the religious NGOs played a critical role in the provision of education and health services. Moreover, whereas the government services had an elitist, urban and racial bias, the NGO services had a popular and essentially rural focus (90% of the population lived in rural areas). Deep dissatisfaction with the colonial administration's service provision was therefore often expressed by local politicians during the fight for independence. Criticizing the colonial administration, and promising that the (new) independence government would do better where the colonial government had not delivered the goods, strongly influenced the process of political mobilization by the nationalist party, the Tanganyika African National Union (TANU). Also subsequent policies and the development and management of social services in the post-independence era were directly affected by the African nationalists' colonial experience.

## Political Imperatives, Ideology and Social Services Development After Independence

During the first years after independence (1961–7) the new nationalist government had no clearly stated ideology of development. It did not even seriously challenge the status quo ante. Capitalism remained the unchallenged economic principle, which meant that those already in privileged positions would continue to enjoy and/or have more added unto them (on the biblical 'Matthew principle'). But continuation of the 'Matthew principle' would alienate the new independence government from the majority of the rural poor (Africans) who had supported the cause and course for independence. When 'their' independence had been won, they expected to enjoy services ('fruits of independence') hitherto unavailable to them owing to the racial and class biases of the colonial government. On the other hand, the independence government

---

[3] For example, between 1 December 1957 and 30 November 1958, 2,851 Europeans were treated or admitted at the government-owned facilities compared with 336 admitted to the NGO facilities.

would not be serving its own cause for political survival if it openly pointed the finger at those who were in the privileged positions in society.

In addition to this complex problem, the new nationalist government was faced with another serious difficulty: how to gain political legitimacy over dispersed and differing tribes. Indeed, there were then 'tribes' (which were miniature nations in their own right) like the Barbaig and the Ndorobo who had significant political, economic, social and cultural distance from not only the central government in Dar es Salaam, but also from the other 'nations' in the territory. Means and ways had to be found to mobilize and integrate such peoples into a new and wider conception of a modern nation-state. The development and distribution of social services was one of the strategies to penetrate such societies.

Gradually the new government began to pursue four related strategies in response to these problems: state-driven provision of services; exclusion or reduction of the religious NGOs from their hitherto dominant role in service provision; attempts at mobilizing self-help for service provision; and – in 1967 – the attempt to base the country's development effort on 'socialism'. Obviously a significant expansion in basic services was needed to fulfil the promises made during the struggle for independence. To achieve this, the state took the initiative in development programmes in what was essentially a statist approach. It created new institutions where there were none, or took over the existing private ones in an attempt to assert its presence and enhance popular recognition. The structures and the establishment of institutions were vehicles for development. The state was regarded as the central hub for development and the people were seen as (passive) recipients. People's private initiatives through NGOs and POs were gradually incorporated or were made to conform to statist dominance of the development activities.

This changing role for the government and NGOs in the delivery of social services resulted from the need for political mobilization, national penetration and integration by the independence government. It was based on the logic that beneficiaries of services are likely to appreciate, recognize, support and pledge partial or total allegiance to the provider. This assumption seems to have been crucial for the government's use of the social services as one of the means for political penetration in order to increase its political territoriality and constituencies. It is through creating schools, health units, water supply systems, etc. and making these amenities easily accessible to the majority of the poor population that the government enhances its own recognition and legitimacy. It follows, moreover, that a government using this approach may create social services even in areas already adequately supplied by the non-governmental units. If the means can justify the ends of political survival and recognition, then even nationalizing NGO-held units in politically strategic areas is not out of the ordinary within the above logical framework of understanding the relationship between social services distribution and political development. This shift towards a statist approach to service provision was especially pronounced after the Arusha Declaration of 1967 (TANU, 1967), as discussed below.

Self-help was the third element in the post-independence strategy for service expansion. It was encouraged by the government with its promise to take full responsibility for running social service facilities completed by self-help groups. This encouraged people to initiate locally based projects such as water dams, trenches for irrigation canals and piped water, schools and especially health centres and dispensaries. In most cases these efforts were initiated by local 'political action groups' under the leadership of some local politicians e.g. the Member of Parliament. This is indeed what partly contributed to the rapid growth of government-owned health-care units and schools in the late 1960s and 1970s.

In 1967 the ruling party issued the Arusha Declaration – an 'improved version' of the country's framework and principles to guide the development of and access to the social services, representing the party's philosophical (ideological) position. It required the development of social and other services to adhere to the principles of 'socialism' and self-reliance, which fitted quite well with the spirit of service provision through self-help, but with the presupposition that the state was the driving force. Consequently 'state socialism' reinforced the state's dominance of development and the delivery of social services in the country. It aimed at enhancing the legitimacy of the government of the day rather than at developing the people. This is not socialism in the Marxist sense (Munishi, 1991a); rather, it is something akin to populism or Fabianism.

The Arusha Declaration itself gave the government a mandate to undertake all sorts of nationalization in order to ensure regional and social equality in the distribution of social services. Moreover, it stated that the government had to commit itself to fight against three national ills or enemies, namely disease, poverty and ignorance (including illiteracy). This commitment entailed a rapid increase in the establishment of schools, dispensaries, hospitals, water system units, etc. However, within the context of the Arusha Declaration, self-help became a highly dubious and contradictory concept. Without self-help, resources for service provision would be totally inadequate. On the other hand, the popular and NGO initiatives were regarded as supplemental and transient, as the state was presumed to be the benevolent provider of the essential social services. The extensive involvement of donors in the area of social services raised further questions about the concept of self-reliance. Social services such as education, water and health became highly donor-dependent after 1967 (Therkildsen, 1988; Munishi, 1991b).

This brief account of the interplay between Tanzania's ideology, the political imperatives of the new post-colonial regime and social service provision provides the context in which the expansion of health and education services can be traced.

## Provision of Health Services

Tremendous strides have been made in improving health service delivery since independence – especially with respect to health staff and lower-level health facilities (Table 8.1). The expansion of hospitals has been much slower.[4]

Most government dispensaries and health centres were located in rural areas hitherto largely neglected by the colonial administration. This was a gap-filling measure. The populist ideology of the Arusha Declaration emphasized rural development, indeed marrying well with the desire of the political elites for national mobilization and integration. There is one major explanation for the high rate of primary-level units. Dispensaries and health centres were smaller units and cheaper to construct. Most of them were built on a self-help basis by villagers who (after construction) called on the government to provide personnel, equipment and drugs, etc., free of charge to consumers. The independence government readily responded in most cases, as shown in Table 8.1.

Table 8.1 Expansion of Government Health Services

|     | Indicators | 1961 | 1971 | 1980 | 1984 | 1991[a] | 1994[a] |
|-----|------------|------|------|------|------|---------|---------|
| 1. | Population (000s) | 10,268 | 20,500 | 18,080 | 20,683 | 25,000 | 27,100 |
| 2a. | Medical Doctors (MD) | 415 | 579 | 889 | 1,065 | n.a. | 1,134 |
| 2b. | Population per MD | 24,724 | 23,300 | 20,300 | 19,421 | n.a. | 23,898 |
| 3a. | Medical Assistants (MA) & Rural Medical Aids (RMA) | 580 | 833 | 3,710 | 3,974 | 6,436 | n.a. |
| 3b. | Population per MA + RMA | 17,703 | 16,200 | 4,900 | 5,205 | 3,884 | n.a. |
| 4a. | Rural Health Centres (RHC) | 22 | 89 | 239 | 239 | 276 | 276 |
| 4b. | Population per RHC | 466,700 | 151,700 | 75,700 | 86,540 | 90,580 | 98,190 |
| 5a. | Dispensaries | 875 | 1,452 | 2,600 | 2,644 | 3,024 | 3,024 |
| 5b. | Population per Dispensary | 11,700 | 9,300 | 7,000 | 7,820 | 8,267 | 8,962 |

*Source:* United Republic of Tanzania, 1969.

*Notes:* [a] Estimated.    n.a. Not available.

The national target was to have one Rural Health Centre per 50,000 people by the year 2000. By 1994 performance had come as close as one per 98,190 people, a big stride compared with 151,700 in 1971 and 466,000 in 1961 – but still far from the target. The target for dispensaries was one for every 10,000 people by 1980. That target was met, although the expansion in the number of dispensaries has not kept up with population growth since then.

There is a lack of data on the provision of services through NGOs.[5] In principle, the government did and still does have an implicit policy of avoiding

---

[4] Thus the growth rate in the development of government hospitals between 1975 and 1988 was only 0.3% p.a. compared with the establishment of health centres and dispensaries which grew at 5.4% p.a. over the same period. This reflects the government's policy of emphasizing growth at the primary rather than at the tertiary level (Jamhuri ya Muungano wa Tanzania, 1990: Table 69).

[5] However, as noted earlier, NGOs run a substantial proportion of the country's hospitals (42% in 1958, but declining relatively since then).

locating health units in places already well provided by NGOs.[6] This principle is adhered to if political calculations do not become paramount, in which case, for the cultivation of political constituencies, government units have been located in areas already provided by the NGO units, contrary to the government's own principle.

Moreover, nationalization included the takeover of two hospital complexes, namely Bugando hospital, owned by the Catholic Church, and Kilimanjaro Christian Medical Centre, owned by the Lutherans. They became government (zonal) referral hospitals. Other moves included converting church-owned hospitals into 'designated' government units where the NGOs saw their authority being eroded by government policies and other forms of control. However, this did not seem to disturb the normally good relations between the state and the churches, as Chapter 11 argues.

In 1977 a law was passed with the major objective of making health-care provision an obligation of the government. It also stated that health services could not be regarded like (other) market commodities, thereby proscribing private medical practice in Tanzania (mainland). This became effective from 1981. However, it did allow 'authorized organizations' (which included the armed forces, parastatals and religious entities) to own and establish health-care units. This legislation reinforced the government's involvement and commitment to deliver health care, while providing for some limited NGO participation. It was further reinforced in 1986[7] by specifying that 'authorized' meant registered trustees who were non-profit-oriented.

The nationalizations and the legislative moves slowed down the NGOs in opening up new facilities. The government aimed to assume an almost absolute role and control in the delivery of health care. Certain missionary or church organizations continued to own their units, and cautiously built a few new ones, as they were 'authorized organizations'. But the pace was slower than previously, because the tedious bureaucratic registration procedures made it more difficult to register a facility than to build one. The hurdles were numerous – at the district, regional and ministry levels. The Health Secretary for the Catholic Archdiocese of Dar es Salaam, for example, lamented that he had been to the Ministry of Health 30 times during 1991 to get his units registered, and had even been obliged to seek the Cardinal's help in obtaining provisional permits.[8] Indeed, some units had to operate without registration and others used the registration certificates of different units, while awaiting their own. This, in turn, made control, co-ordination and supervision of health services difficult for the government. A further problem arose because of the blurred distinction between NGOs for profit and those for 'service'. It encouraged the private for-profit units to hide under the wings of the 'authorized' organizations.

Nevertheless, the operations of NGOs in health-care delivery have continued

6   Their services are available to consumers for a fee, and the government has a policy to aid the NGO facilities by bed and salary grants.
7   Government Notice, number 421, of 15 August 1986.
8   Interview with Rev. Fr. Horbus, Health Secretary for the Catholic Archdiocese of Dar es Salaam, at Kiwalani Yombo Dispensary in May 1992.

to be significant throughout the post-independence period, despite the government's intensive participation. Under the current economic liberalization policies and the Structural Adjustment Programmes, private health-care services are again allowed to operate.[9] Furthermore, government health-care services are on sale to consumers under the new policy of cost-sharing, although this is against the government's populist ideological commitment to deliver essential social services free of charge to consumers.

## Provision of Education Services

Religious NGOs were very active in the provision of education in the pre-independence era, as already discussed. Their involvement continued to grow in the immediate post-independence years, until the Arusha Declaration of 1967, which marked the start of deliberate government efforts to mobilize all ways and means to bring education under total official control. This was achieved by the nationalization and centralization of the social services delivery. The principal motive for this shift was the need to ensure rapid planned educational development to meet the government's primary goals of equity in service provision and Africanization.

The Education Act No. 50 of 1969 furthered the moves towards a single education system. It also aimed to bring all educational units receiving public funds (grants-in-aid) under the control of the government. This was in effect a process of centralizing, not only the NGO schools, but also those managed by the local governments.[10] And, just as with the health-care units, schools built on a self-help basis by various POs were handed over to the government.

Prior to the 1969 legislation, church-owned units reported to a church-appointed Education Secretary. This was changed in 1969 when church-owned school heads had to report directly to the central government's District Education Officers. Also all financing and management of church-owned units was taken over by the government. This move was aimed at enabling the government to determine entry and examination policies in order to further equity in service provision.

Two other policies increased the government's involvement in the provision of education, namely the decentralization policy of 1972 and the universal primary education policy of 1974. With decentralization district councils as locally elected bodies were abolished and replaced by government-controlled local administrations. Ministry headquarters' personnel and other resources to execute programmes were transferred to lower levels (regions and districts) to work on behalf of the central government. They were the government's local hands that were supposed to plan (with?) for the people at the district level, taking into account what the local populations needed, with the government as

---

[9] Legalized in 1991.

[10] At independence local government schools accounted for 89% of the enrolment of African primary school children in the public sector schools compared with 11% in central government schools (Tanganyika Territory Report, 1958: 362).

the benevolent provider of free education for all. This further slowed the pace of NGO participation.

But NGO participation in service provision was not completely halted. Defined as authorized and government-approved organizations with non-profit motives,[11] they continued to provide education services, particularly at the post-primary level. In fact, the importance of NGOs in secondary education grew over time as the public schools increasingly failed to cope with the demand, while the number of pupils graduating from primary schools increased dramatically over the period (Table 8.2). Thus, 28% of primary school-leavers were admitted to secondary schools in 1963, but only 15% were successful in 1990.

As a result of increased pressure for secondary education, the NGO contribution rose consistently – and contrary to government policy. NGO secondary schools accounted for 28% of admissions in 1965, and 58% in 1990. This means that NGOs were making a major contribution in dealing with the problem of primary school-leavers. Chapter 9 provides a detailed analysis of secondary education.

Table 8.2  Primary School-Leavers and Selection into Secondary Schools (1965–90)

|      | Completed primary schools (1000s) | Selected for secondary schools (%) | Share entering private/NGO schools (%) |
|------|------|------|------|
| 1965 | 29   | 28   | 28   |
| 1970 | 65   | 16   | 31   |
| 1975 | 138  | 11   | 40   |
| 1980 | 213  | 8    | 44   |
| 1985 | 429  | 6    | 54   |
| 1990 | 307  | 15   | 58   |

Source: Ministry of Education and Culture (1992).

In the end the government changed its secondary school policy in the face of increasing and unmet demand. Starting in mid-1984, NGOs' school intakes have rapidly risen. The trend intensified during the liberalization (1986–1990) period and this explains why the intake of secondary school students has increased significantly.

# The 1990s: Government Needs Voluntary Sector More Than Vice Versa

The above analyses have demonstrated that the provision of education and health services has been undertaken by both the government and NGOs, but

---

[11] Such as the Tanzania Parents Association (TAPA), marketing co-operatives, some religious organizations, etc.

that their importance has varied over time. In the pre-independence era the NGOs – operating mainly in places where government-provided social services were not available – tended to focus on the needy. During the post-independence period the NGOs tended to complement government efforts. Now, in the 1990s, people are increasingly setting their expectations on, and supporting, social service provision by the voluntary sector.

Also, the government – through the various Structural Adjustment Programmes – is now inclined to allow NGOs and the private sector to provide social services (although not primary education) at cost, and to permit them to expand as they see fit. This may have a definite impact on equity and access to services for the poor.

But what else can the government do? The budgets for the social services shrank during the first half of the 1980s, and the sustainability of the observed recovery in the later part of the 1980s is uncertain (Chapter 1). At the same time the costs of providing services have risen. The government has reported, for example, that the costs of producing a primary school, a secondary school and a university graduate have grown at 35%, 20% and 18% per annum, respectively, during the period 1977–87 (Ministry of Education, 1989: 14). Yet demand for this service at all levels has been rising. These factors make the support of free-of-charge public social services very precarious and intricate.

For a long time the government has depended heavily on foreign assistance to sustain the social services. There are two problems with this source. The reliability of aid is questionable, especially in recent times when competition with Eastern Europe for Western funds has intensified and aid fatigue has set in. But the second problem may be even more important from a policy standpoint.

Dependence on foreign assistance to the extent that 50–70% of government investment budgets for the ministries of health, education and science, technology and higher education originate from donors (United Republic of Tanzania, 1991) is somewhat absurd and highly precarious. It may easily undermine the sustainability of such services. Indeed, the government has silently and sometimes openly acknowledged its hopes that the private and the voluntary sectors may increase their roles in service provision in order to lessen the burden which the state can no longer carry. Thus, in the 1992 Budget Speech the voluntary sector was given important prominence (United Republic of Tanzania, 1992). The government therefore is simply stating openly what has in fact been happening, namely, that the NGOs have made a very significant contribution, and that more is expected of them, given the limited government resources. But, as shown in Chapters 1 and 3, most service-providing NGOs are as dependent on donors as is the state.

One may ask then: Why is the government giving up on its earlier commitments to provide social services to everybody free of charge? The question is especially pertinent, given the past importance of this policy for the party's wider goals of political development, penetration and integration of the country. One way of answering it is to argue that most of the government's basic goals of political penetration and national integration have been achieved to a great extent. The fingers of the ruling political party and the finger tips of the government have been felt in the remotest of places in Tanzania. Further penetration may be unnecessary, given the immense costs involved, although a total withdrawal of government-provided free social services may eventually undermine the ruling party's political legitimacy. However, this course of events is no longer on the cards, owing to changes in the politico-economic system of the country during the three decades of independence. Economic pluralism promoted through the Structural Adjustment Programmes' calls for political pluralism (as introduced in 1992) as well as the pluralism of those organizations that are to participate in the provision of social services. No doubt the role of the NGOs and the private for-profit organizations will increase in the 1990s and beyond.

## Conclusion

Social service provision in Tanzania has developed in three phases. The social service provision of the pre-independence era favoured the urban elites and was racially based. The underprivileged African population did not receive its proportionate share. Its provision was left to NGOs, mainly the missionary organizations. By independence they ran a substantially larger number of schools and dispensaries than the government, especially in the remote areas of the country.

At independence the new government abhorred the elitist and racially inclined colonial policies. Instead, it pursued a populist stance, erroneously referred to as socialism. The purpose was to use social services to reach all tribes, races and classes, so as to further mobilization, political penetration and national integration. To achieve these equity objectives and political goals, the government adopted the policy of centralization (both in resource mobilization and in allocation), while the population accepted the provision of essential social services as the well-deserved 'fruits of independence'.

During the first decades of independence the role of NGOs in service provision declined in both absolute and relative terms. While there were clear policy indications as to what the government would do, it was silent on the role of NGOs and other potential participants in service provision. Instead, most of the NGO infrastructure was taken over by the state and used as channels through which the government provided the 'fruits of independence' to the supportive population.

The financial implications of this policy, coupled with the poor economic performance of the mid-1970s to mid-1980s made it impossible for the government to satisfy its whole clientele of social service consumers. Silently, but surely and probably usefully, the NGOs were allowed to take on a larger role in service provision. The case of the mushrooming NGO-sponsored secondary schools attests to this conclusion, as does the recent agreement with the churches to take over schools and hospitals that were nationalized two decades previously (see Chapter 11).

Thus in the 1990s the government has shown the green light to private operators and NGOs. It is officially banking on their participation in the provision of social services. This move is not accidental. Rather, it is evidence of an evolution which has seen the government's capacity to provide social services dwindling, while the NGOs (often backed with donor funds) and other private entities have come in to save the situation or to fill in the gaps. The green light for the private and the voluntary sector is indeed a *fait accompli*. It results from the social service evolutionary process over the period of the 1960s to the 1990s. But it is also a consequence of the politico-economic liberalization policy moves now afoot in the 1990s.

# References

Jamhuri ya Muungano wa Tanzania (1990) *Hali ya Uchumi wa Taifa katika mwaka 1989.* Dar es Salaam: Government Printer.

Ministry of Education (1989) *Education for All: Meeting Basic Learning Needs to the Year 2000.* Dar es Salaam: Ministry of Education.

Ministry of Education and Culture (1992) *Basic Education Statistics in Tanzania.* Dar es Salaam: Ministry of Education and Culture.

Munishi, G.K. (1991a) 'The Ideological Basis of the Arusha Declaration' in J. Hartmann (ed.) *Rethinking the Arusha Declaration.* Copenhagen: Centre for Development Research.

Munishi, G.K. (1991b) 'A Social Welfare State Development: The Basis, Rationale and the Challenges of Policy Reforms'. Paper presented at a conference on the Crisis of Social Service Delivery in Tanzania, University of Dar es Salaam, 3–4 April 1991.

Tanganyika Territory Report (1958) London: HMSO.

TANU (1967) *The Arusha Declaration: TANU's Policy of Socialism and Self Reliance.* Dar es Salaam: TANU.

Therkildsen, O. (1988) *Watering White Elephants.* Uppsala: Scandinavian Institute of African Studies.

United Republic of Tanzania (1969) *The Second Five-Year Plan for Economic and Social Development.* Dar es Salaam: Government Printer.

United Republic of Tanzania (1991) *Makadirio ya Maendeleo ya Wizara na Mikoa* (Estimates of Development Expenditures for Ministries and Regions), Part A, Vol. 4. Dar es Salaam: Government Printer.

United Republic of Tanzania (1992) *Hotuba ya Waziri wa Fedha, Prof. K. Malima katika Bunge tarehe 18 Juni 1992* (Speech by Minister of Finance, Prof. K. Malima, in Parliament on 18 June 1992). Dar es Salaam: Government Printer.

# 9

## ABEL G. M. ISHUMI
## Provision of Secondary Education
## in Tanzania

Historical Background
& Current Trends

In Tanzania, education is one arena of social service provision in which, over a historical period of time, several agencies have participated for varying reasons. The agencies include the state, the religious missionary societies, philanthropic organizations and, recently, local community development associations. The relationship between the state and the voluntary organizations has not always been stable, consistent or predictable. It has been influenced in many instances by the political, ideological and economic conditions prevailing in the different periods over the last 130 years.

This chapter is divided into six parts, covering the historical background to education in Tanzania; the changing state–NGO relations after 1967; the emergence in the 1980s of community organizations to promote secondary education; a case study of a self-help education project; issues of quality and sustainability; and conclusions.

## Historical Background

Formal Western-type education in Tanzania was first introduced by European Christian missionaries, with the first-ever school in Tanganyika set up by the Holy Ghost Fathers in 1862 at Bagamoyo. These practical efforts by Christian missions in establishing formal education preceded those by the colonial administration by as many as three decades (by six and a half decades in Kenya; and two and a half decades in Uganda). They were accompanied by a clear stress on the cultivation and nurture of a sense of spiritual purpose and civic morality as the attributes not only of a Christian but also of an educated person.

The Holy Ghost mission school established at Bagamoyo in 1862 was unique in that it had an academic, an industrial and an agricultural/manual labour stream. The *academic* stream was for selected bright pupils who showed the potential for following more complex academic subjects such as Geography, Geometry, Trigonometry, Chemistry and Greek, over and above mere reading, writing and simple arithmetic, or the 3 Rs. This stream would spend the first five hours of the day on academic work and only half an hour on religious study. The *industrial* stream, for the less bright, concentrated on handiwork and technical trades such as carpentry, masonry, tinsmithing, carving and leather-work. Pupils in this stream spent ten hours of the day on these practical trades, one hour on the 3 Rs and half an hour on religious instruction. The *agricultural-cum-manual* labour stream, on the other hand, embraced pupils who were judged to be more dull. They were essentially part of the manual labour force used in opening up and tilling the mission's land tracts for agriculture and/or for constructing mission houses, school buildings and similar labour-intensive projects. They would spend nine and a half hours a day on such manual tasks, one hour on the 3 Rs and a full hour on Bible and general religious study.

When German rule was declared over Tanganyika, following the Berlin Conference of 1884/85 which partitioned Africa, it found already in place five such non-governmental organizations as well as a few educational institutions established under them that were actively working to 'modernize' the different indigenous communities in the territory.[1] The education offered by the missions in this early period was elementary. The major part of the curriculum was secular. The academic and scientific subjects taught had a direct relationship to skills needed in the formal sector within the mission or for the government. However, the religious context of the school environment predicated an initial catechetical instruction in satellite 'bush schools' and prescribed some time for Bible study. As can be gauged from a wide variety of literature (Lema, 1973; Gottneid, 1976; Kaara, 1977), the comprehensive curriculum at the mission schools aimed at achieving several distinct and highly valued objectives: character building; imparting of vocational skills for practical work and self-support; development of a sense of imagination, creativity and exemplary performance in everyday life; training in the moral values of civil obedience, humility and responsible citizenship; and, finally, enabling the individual to have closer contact with God's creation and to live in peaceful co-existence with his fellow men.

By contrast, the first state school, established at Tanga in 1892 by the German colonial administration (which ruled Tanganyika between 1885 and 1919), followed a syllabus dictated by the colonial state's urgent need for 'technical' hands in the administration of the colony, namely clerks, interpreters, tax collectors (*akida*) and customs officials. In the meantime government district officers were urged to begin building schools at their stations and to educate the sons of local rulers (headmen, or *Jumbe*) and their relatives so that they could be

---

[1] In addition to the Holy Ghost Fathers, these were the Universities Mission to Central Africa (UMCA), the Church Missionary Society (CMS), the White Fathers (WF) and the London Missionary Society (LMS). By the 1890s, the Holy Ghost Fathers (HGF) had moved further inland to establish a mission station and a school in Morogoro, the UMCA was operating in Zanzibar, Magila, Masasi and the Lake Nyasa areas of Likoma and Liuli, the CMS was working in Mpwapwa, while the White Fathers were operating in the Lake Victoria area of Bukumbi and the Lake Tanganyika areas of Ujiji and Karema, and the LMS was established in the Lake Tanganyika regions of Urambo and Ujiji.

sent to Tanga school for training in the various technical skills before returning for employment in their own local areas.

From this one state school in 1892, with a pupil enrolment of probably less than fifty, the public education system grew steadily to 20 establishments in 1903, 60 in 1914 and 84 in 1934, with a correspondingly expanding pupil enrolment. Table 9.1 shows the statistics in both the state and the non-governmental education sectors during these years.

Table 9.1 Trend of Primary School Establishment and Pupil Enrolment by Government and Christian Missions, 1862–1934

| Year | Government | | Christian Missions | |
|------|-----------------|-------------------|-----------------|-------------------|
|      | No. of Schools | Pupil Enrolment | No. of Schools | Pupil Enrolment |
| 1862 | 0 | 0 | 1 | n.a. |
| 1892 | 1 | <50 | 10+ | 500+ |
| 1903 | 20 | 1,550 | n.a. | 50,000 |
| 1914 | 70 | 6,200 | 875[a] | 110,000+ |
| 1934 | 84 | 7,979 | 2,668 | 157,069 |

Source: Calvert (1917); Tanganyika Territory (1934); Schlunk (1964); Thompson (1976: 17–24).
Notes: n.a. Records not available.        [a] 1911.

Secondary education, as we know it today, was first introduced and popularized in the country in the 1920s, thanks initially to the personal philanthropy of successful Indian businessmen: Jivanjee Karimjee in Tanga in 1923, and the Aga Khan, who opened a girls school in Dar es Salaam in 1928. More such schools followed, constructed out of personal philanthropy or by private community trusts. Only Galanos secondary school, set up by the Greek philanthropist, Christos Galanos, in Tanga in 1965, was from the outset open to pupils of all races. All the others were originally set up to meet the educational needs of children of the minority Indian resident community.[2]

The first government-sponsored and government-controlled secondary school was Tabora Boys, set up in 1925, a few years after the first initiatives by the voluntary sector. The school was initially intended for the sons of chiefs and the nobility within the indigenous system of African native authorities.

Missionary societies embarked on secondary school construction on a larger scale in the 1930s to promote wider opportunities for secondary education primarily for African children within the catchment areas of their denominational faiths. Eventually these mission schools began to admit a few pupils from other denominational and even other religious backgrounds (e.g. Muslims) in growing awareness of, and sympathy for, the educational and development

[2]  For example: the Indian Public School in Bukoba town (in 1939), which was renamed Grewal in 1961; Aga Khan Boys in Dar es Salaam (1955); Highland Secondary in Iringa (1965); Popatlal in Tanga (1966).

aspirations of Africans, especially in the first two decades preceding independence in 1961.

One generalization that can be made on the whole long period between 1862 and 1967 is that the relationship between the state and the various non-governmental organizations was a cordial one – governed by the principle of non-interference from the government and mutual consultation on matters of common interest. Public and non-government school systems co-existed, notwithstanding the sometimes open arguments and conflicts between missionaries and state officials over certain matters of principle or faith (Cameron and Dodd, 1970: Chs 4–7; Thompson, 1976: 34–99; Lawuo, 1984: Chs 4–6).

## Changing State–NGO Relations, 1967–80

A critical date in the history of Tanzania, 1967 marked not only a 'revolutionary' political turn-about which affected most spheres of national life, but also the beginning of a decline in many areas of education: a decline in the number and level of state–NGO partnerships; a decline in the stock of necessary material provisions and supplies for schools; and hence a decline in the quality of education across the nation. Following the Arusha Declaration in 1967 – the official declaration of a socialist policy – all major means of production in the economic sector were to be owned by the state. Moreover, in the education sector, schools and all major training institutions were to be taken over and managed by the state through the agency of the Ministry of Education. This aimed, among other things, to streamline and control the curriculum of the schools, to enhance ideological conformity, to eliminate denominational influences and to ensure equal ('mass') access to educational opportunities.

The actual nationalization of non-public secondary schools was carried out in 1971. It included all private trust-funded schools and all mission schools, apart from institutions specifically designated as seminaries. The schools were to be maintained by the state and were to conform with government regulations as regards accounting, reporting, financial and administrative procedures. The takeover embraced even changing the schools' names where, according to the authorities, they did not carry 'local', 'indigenous' or ideological' significance. The nationalization policy was further confirmed by the Education Act of 1978.

One of the immediate effects of this was a transfer of the burden of financing and resource mobilization for schools from 'private' but thus far 'co-operating' voluntary agencies to the shoulders of the state. Fairly soon this burden proved too heavy. The government proved unable to maintain the schools adequately, or to supply the equipment and the teaching materials needed. Another consequence was a demoralization on the part of the former school owners, whose experience with expropriation implanted a feeling of distrust about government intentions and promises with regard to future areas of co-operation (see Chapter 11 for a different view as far as the Catholic Church is concerned). A third but little publicized effect of the nationalization was the loss of actual financial and material assistance and the flight of potential capital destined for the now nationalized schools.[3] Moreover, a reduction in NGO interest and participation in educational expansion and development and a general desensitization, demotivation and/or lack of interest on the part of parents and the community in the everyday affairs of school progress followed the nationalization.

Only a few so-called 'private' schools emerged during this decade of estranged NGO–state estrangement. These were secondary school projects initiated, supported or partially financed by selected government institutions – particularly district and regional co-operative unions, and an organization affiliated to the ruling party, the Tanzania Parents Association (TAPA). And this seems to have been possible only because of the political influence of these institutions and because of the government's fear of a contradiction in an official rejection of their initiatives with its own official encouragement of the concept of 'self-reliance'. In this way some districts with strong co-operative movements and strong TAPA associations (such as those in Kilimanjaro and Kagera regions) managed to establish some 'private' secondary schools outside the regular public school system. The activities of this 'second' generation of organizations notwithstanding, the 1970s suffered an irreparable secondary education setback in school and enrolment expansion, which has continued to cause Tanzania to lag behind its neighbours (Ishumi, 1990: 34).

## The Emergence of Community Organizations in the 1980s

In the 1980s two major factors seem to have accounted for a change of course, leading to a 'third' generation of non-governmental organizations in Tanzania. The first was the conspicuous public frustration and disaffection caused by the severely limited number of secondary school places available for the many children leaving primary school. The bottleneck in the transition from primary to secondary education, against the background of a successful state-engineered universal primary education (UPE) programme, was too severe to be taken as a matter of course (Ishumi, 1985: 17–19). Table 9.2 illustrates the extent of the problem. It became apparent to parents and many local communities that the declared socialist ideal and the frequently avowed socialist strategies were no assurance of self-advancement. The 'anger of disillusionment' was eventually turned into resolute searches for self-help action, as explained below.

The second factor was the severe economic difficulties that hit Tanzania in the late 1970s and continued to worsen in the early 1980s. The mounting deficit in the country's internal and external economic balance, the curtailed purchasing power, the dire shortage of government funds to run the various national projects, the conditional withdrawal of aid from traditional and prospective foreign donors, and the heightened public demoralization and disaffection – all

---

[3] A well-known example was the case of Galanos Secondary School in Tanga, whose philanthropic creator, Christos Galanos, had set up a trust fund in Geneva in order to continue maintaining and expanding the school. No sooner had the government taken it over and changed the school's name to Nguvumali than the flow of funds from Europe stopped. It took some time and great efforts for the government to denationalize the school and legally restore the old name in order to get the flow of foreign funds resumed (when, unfortunately, the school was already in disrepair).

combined to force the government into radical reforms. Hence the introduction of the National Economic Survival Programme in 1981, the Structural Adjustment Programme in 1982 and the Economic Recovery Programme in June 1986. Among their aims were to restructure future economic activity through better incentive schemes and a less restricted market economy, and to reverse priorities in government spending in order to achieve a more sustainable internal and external balance and renewed economic growth. With respect to the education sector, the NESP and the SAP included measures to relax the hitherto rigid government control of the education system.

Table 9.2 Trend of Pupil Selection for State Secondary Education Against Primary School Output, 1961–83

| Year | Primary Std 7 | Secondary Form I | Number not placed | Percent not placed |
|---|---|---|---|---|
| 1961 | 11,732 | 4,196 | 7,536 | 64 |
| 1969 | 60,545 | 7,149 | 53,396 | 88 |
| 1981 | 212,446 | 8,907 | 203,539 | 96 |
| 1983 | 463,908 | 9,234 | 454,674 | 98 |

*Source:* Ministry of Education (various years) *Basic Education Statistics in Tanzania (BEST),* and various Ministry files and records.

These factors played a powerful role in the state's change of heart which led to a more tolerant attitude to private initiatives in educational development. This did not result in privatization in the orthodox sense. But the 1980s provided an environment in which community self-help in school construction and education provision became both an immediate point of focus in the sharing of the costs of national development and a rallying point for various communities in the competitive search for secondary education opportunities for their children leaving primary school. Locally based and locally oriented community development associations began to emerge.

These 'third'-generation associations range in size and focus from ward-level to district-level. They derive membership from one ethnic group within a whole district or from one or more sections or localities within it. Table 9.3 details a few of the pioneering associations and networks that trace their genesis to the events of the 1980s. These locally based movements towards the construction and running of private (non-government) secondary schools have grown stronger. Now, in the 1990s, they have spread to many other districts in the country.[4]

The growth of 'third'-generation associations also has political implications.

---

[4] These include Igunga District (in Tabora Region), Biharamulo, Karagwe and Ngara (Kagera Region), Kondoa and Mpwapwa (Dodoma Region), Ludewa (Iringa Region), Arumeru and Mbulu (Arusha Region), Iramba and Singida (Singida Region), Bariadi and Shinyanga (in Shinyanga Region).

The support given, or denied, to local political leaders and aspirants for political office, such as members of parliament and district councillors, now depends significantly on their ability to mobilize public and private resources towards the realization of self-help secondary schools. Moreover, the government has recently pledged assistance to one community school project in each of the 103 Districts in the country. This signifies a drastic change in policy compared with that established in 1984 which sought to restrict the number of such schools (Samoff, 1987). The Ministry of Education will now assist with roofing materials, some teaching–learning materials and teaching staff as long as a community, in collaboration with the district council, will undertake to construct school buildings or to renovate pre-existing buildings such as those formerly used by the now defunct middle schools.[5]

The Ministry's original objective was to have 8 day schools established every year, built by matching community and state resources, until all districts were covered. In practice, community responses, particularly in the wealthier districts, have been so positive and community pressure on government so great that the original plans have been surpassed. For instance, in 1989 alone, 28 community secondary school projects – pressing for the promised state assistance – were registered. The trend has accelerated since then.

The statistics in Table 9.4 illuminate the remarkably fast rate of secondary school construction and pupil enrolment in the private non-governmental sector compared with that in the state schools. Currently, NGO schools outstrip state schools by about 1.6 times in school establishments and 1.3 times in pupil enrolment.

## A Case Study of Community Self-Help Initiative

The 'third' generation of self-help NGOs – drawing from and in turn actively involving local communities in the design and provision of secondary education for their children – is epitomized by the Kanyigo Secondary School project, in the Kanyigo ward of Bukoba Rural District (North-western Tanzania). It is only one such story of local NGO dynamism and determination.

Kanyigo Development Association (KADEA) came into existence in 1984 basically as a result of the desperate situation in which the residents in Kanyigo ward found themselves, particularly with respect to educational chances for their children leaving primary school. The apparent success of the country's universal primary education (UPE) programme in increasing enrolment was eventually seen as deceptive and utterly frustrating when matched against the output from the primary into the secondary schools. In 1982, only one child out of a total of about 600 in the ward qualified to enter state secondary school. In 1983, only three children qualified. The rest had to return home to their parents – virtually unskilled and, at a tender leaving age of fourteen, quite unprepared for the adult

---

[5] The Ministry's advice to interested communities is to build day rather than boarding schools, on account of costs.

Table 9.3  Major Community Development Associations Since the 1980s[a]

| Name of Association | District | Formed | Area of Operation | Current Number of Sec. Schools Run | First School(s) Opened |
|---|---|---|---|---|---|
| Njombe District Development Trust[b] | Njombe | 1983 | District | 9 | 1983 |
| Mufindi Education Trust (MET)[c] | Mufindi | 1984 | District | 7 | 1984 |
| Kanyigo Development Association (KADEA)[b] | Bukoba Rural | 1984 | Single ward | 1 | 1985 |
| Buyango–Rusinga Development Association (BURUDEA)[b] | Bukoba Rural | 1984 | Two wards | 1 | 1985 |
| Tweyambe–Ishozi Development Society (TIDESO)[b] | Bukoba Rural | 1984 | Two wards | 1 | 1985 |
| Network of Madaba Villages (WILIMA)[c] | Songea | 1984 | Single-ward | 1 | 1986 |
| Bwanjai–Bukandika–Kitobo Development Society (BWABUKI)[b] | Bukoba Rural | 1985 | Three wards | 1 | 1986 |

[a] The only pre-1980 community development organization was the Kilimanjaro Education Fund (KEF) created in 1974 from the savings of the regional Kilimanjaro Native Co-operative Union (KNCU) and its subsidiaries just before a proposed government order to revoke farmers co-operatives. Today the KEF supports over 60 'private' self-help secondary schools across all the districts of Kilimanjaro Region and is helped financially by the local co-operatives, reinstated, along with others, since 1984.
[b] Provision of secondary education is one among several objectives.
[c] Only objective is to provide secondary education.

Table 9.4  Trends in Secondary School Establishment and Pupil Enrolment in Tanzania (Mainland) by Sector, 1980–90 (in '000s)

| Year | State Schools | | NGO Schools | | Total | |
|---|---|---|---|---|---|---|
| | No. of Schools | Pupil Enrolment | No. of Schools | Pupil Enrolment | No. of Schools | Pupil Enrolment |
| 1980 | 83 | 39 | 71 | 28 | 154 | 67 |
| 1983 | 85 | 40 | 84 | 32 | 169 | 71 |
| 1986 | 95 | 43 | 124 | 48 | 219 | 92 |
| 1989 | 124 | 57 | 195 | 75 | 319 | 133 |
| 1990 | 135 | 62 | 213 | 83 | 348 | 145 |

*Sources:* Ministry of Education (various years) and other Ministry records.

world of work in the village. Against this gloomy educational bottleneck, and in the face of a real prospect of unemployability, juvenile delinquency and crime, *something had to be done, and done quickly.*

A secondary school created by their own efforts, and based in their own ward, was the collective felt need at that moment. Indeed, the people of Kanyigo could have built the school 'at that very moment of anger and zeal', had it not been for the legalities and technicalities of the matter. It required well-guided preparation: a write-up justifying the project and seeking government permission, a skilled team to prepare it, a legally constituted body to own and manage the proposed school, and many other details requiring professional reflection and input. For these necessary preliminaries, ready and equally desirous partners were the many knowledgeable, determined and self-sacrificing Kanyigo-born professionals and individuals working in other regions and towns, especially those working in Dar es Salaam, the capital city of the country.

First, a legal body – a development association – had to be established. To be officially registered such associations must draw up a constitution with clear objectives and a known address. Within the year (1984) a voluntary development association of Kanyigo residents (workers, peasant farmers, professionals) was formed, with its headquarters in Kanyigo ward itself. The Kanyigo group also outlined a plan for resource mobilization. So, in a matter of a few weeks, a branch of the association was formed in Dar es Salaam, with most workers, professionals and businessmen of Kanyigo ethnic origin living there as members. In the following months the Dar es Salaam KADEA branch contacted Kanyigo ethnics in other towns and municipalities to urge them to form similar branches. These efforts had varying success in Arusha, Mwanza and Tanga towns. Now KADEA even has a few actively contributing members living outside Tanzania and even outside Africa.

With the formation of an Education Committee as one of the three sub-committees of the association's Executive Committee, preparations for the self-help community secondary school project also began in 1984. The programme of activities, drawn up early in March, is shown in Table 9.5. It represents almost exactly the course of events that led to the opening of the school in January 1985.

It is evident from this schedule that action towards establishment of the school was fast, for the committee members and others involved felt under pressure to meet the deadlines. There were slight bureaucratic delays in connection with official action on the different applications. They were, by regulation, supposed to be approved first by the regional officers after physical inspection of architectural drawings and the project location, and then by headquarters staff of the Ministry of Education in Dar es Salaam. Eventually, however, the school opened as scheduled.

It is also evident that, by 1985, in spite of the bureaucratic delays and technicalities involved, government attitudes towards 'private' educational initiatives had changed from simply ambivalent to positively accommodating and supportive. In the 1960s and 1970s, such non-government-initiated efforts were officially viewed negatively as 'exploitative' and 'anti-socialist'.

Table 9.5  Starting a Self-Help Community Secondary School: Course of Events

| | |
|---|---|
| 12 February– 12 March 1984 | Consult with Ministry of Education officials; secure application forms; and prepare school project write-up |
| By 15 March | Final version of project document |
| By 25 March | Present application forms to the Regional Education Office in Bukoba |
| | Form No. 6: Application by KADEA for ownership of the school |
| | Form No. 7: Application by KADEA to be manager of the school |
| | Form No. 8: Application to register the school as a private (non-government) school |
| April | Procuring syllabuses for all subjects |
| May–June | Order or secure materials (textbooks, maps, atlases, science/laboratory equipment, reference books, teachers' guides) |
| June | Look/advertise for teachers, including Headmaster |
| July–August | Teachers appointed |
| August–September | Arrival of ordered school materials |
| 16 October | Appointed Headmaster begins to prepare for the school start in January 1985 |
| 28–30 November | Hand-over meeting between KADEA Education Committee and the appointed teachers; contact to possible prospective donors |
| December | All teachers to have formally reported at the school |
| January 1985 | School opens |

Without rapid mobilization of financial resources, the speedy completion of the school would not have been possible. By March 1984, the registered KADEA membership in Kanyigo had reached 70 and cash contributions had reached T.Shs. 100,000. This is exclusive of the many more men and women – peasant farmers – who sooner or later became KADEA members by proxy, offering to have a certain percentage deducted from their coffee sales towards the school construction fund. (Subsequently, farmers in all the six villages agreed collectively to have 2% of the sales from all their coffee deducted for this purpose.) In the Dar es Salaam branch of KADEA, membership reached 52 in April 1984. The contribution pledges made averaged T.Shs. 3,000 per member. By July 1984 membership had reached 138, with pledges totalling T.Shs. 616,490 – a third of which had already been paid in full. These contributions in both Kanyigo and Dar es Salaam, and also those collected from branches in other towns, went directly into the purchase and transportation of building materials, into payment of construction labour costs as well as into the purchase of the necessary school equipment and materials.

Seven years later, in 1992, Kanyigo Secondary School was graduating a third annual batch of the secondary 'Ordinary-level' class of Form IV students and a second batch of the 'Advanced-level' Form VI class, both with encouraging national examination results (considering the nature and background of the school's pupil intake).

## The Issues of Quality and Sustainability

At this point, two issues might be raised: one concerns the quality of education provided in community-initiated secondary schools *vis-à-vis* that in state-maintained schools, the other the sustainability of community schools with respect to recurrent costs.

Quality of education depends on a number of factors, such as teacher supply and competence (as inferred from their academic and professional qualifications), the school buildings and the environment they create for learning, and the availability of teaching–learning materials and essential school equipment. Not all community schools in Tanzania are well endowed in these respects, according to formal school inspection reports and informal everyday experiences. This obviously affects the quality of education offered. To say this, however, does not rule out certain exceptions where quality has been surprisingly good, considering that community schools were allowed to admit rejected applicants after formal selection for government-maintained secondary schools. Moreover, a few community schools have been competitive in terms of buildings, teacher supply and qualifications, teaching–learning materials and/or school equipment, including a relatively functional library and science laboratory.[6]

As for sustainability, it is generally true that mobilization of community resources for capital costs (e.g. construction of buildings) has been relatively easier and faster than mobilization for recurrent costs. There tends to be a feeling among parents that, once a school building has been erected, everything else relating to the everyday running of the school follows quasi-automatically. In the past, there tended also to be a vague assumption that the state would eventually meet the running costs. This feeling has been discouraged over time, however, by a clear government policy which delinks it from any involvement in funding recurrent costs, apart from the special category of schools designated as government-assisted community secondary schools.

In the long run, those community schools without a clear long-term strategy for fund-raising and resource mobilization, and particularly those located in communities with a weaker economic base, a shorter tradition of an education culture, and a weaker organizational and management leadership, may face

[6] These include Mgololo in Iringa District, Makambako in Njombe District, Kanyigo in Bukoba District, and quite a few among the more than sixty community self-help secondary schools in Kilimanjaro Region.

extinction. In the meanwhile, however, no community-initiated school has so far been reported closed on account of problems of sustainability. Or, to put it differently, the potential crisis of sustainability has not yet come to the fore.

## Conclusion

Voluntary organizations have clearly made a considerable contribution to educational development in Tanzania (as in Kenya, Uganda and other African countries). Their enthusiasm has been fuelled by a driving motive among parents and pupils of finding work in the formal sector.

In the light of the change towards a negative state attitude *vis-à-vis* community-driven schools following the Arusha Declaration 1967, and of the vicissitudes of state–NGO relations since then, two lessons can be learned. One is that nationalization and monopolization by the state of social delivery systems can only serve to stifle the voluntary will and the creative energies of individuals and groups. Often they are able to deliver social services faster and more efficiently than the state on account of their specialized interest, their less constrained resource bases and/or their ability to respond to individual cases faster and relatively more appropriately. However, such initiatives will not succeed without close partnership and mutuality between the state and voluntary organizations, especially in the costly business of educational development.

The second lesson is that state dominance and pervasiveness (whether by design or by default, as typified by the decade of the 1970s) led to institutional lull and stagnancy, and to public apathy and disaffection. Both these elements are anomic and quite symptomatic of socio-political and intellectual degeneration. It is therefore necessary to nurture not only partnership but also a sense of competition among actual and potential providers of education. The net effect would be to promote vitality and competitiveness in teaching and learning performance not only among state schools or NGO schools alone, but also amicably between the state institutions and those in the voluntary sector.

The fact that the years since the mid-1980s have seen an upsurge of community self-help initiative and vitality requires a comprehensive study of the causes and particularly of the qualities of communities where this spirit may have revived and prevailed over the despair, resignation and sense of *fait accompli* that were so prevalent in the 1970s. Community studies that have so far been undertaken in East Africa (Mbithi and Rasmussen, 1977; Lillis, 1988: 85–93; Galabawa and Ishumi, 1990) seem to suggest at least three critical qualities or prerequisites with a strong correlation with a community's success in generating and managing self-help school projects: (i) a pre-existing education culture, that is, an inherent community awareness of and desire for education as an ingredient of progress; (ii) a strong economic base (without which the community cannot mobilize sufficient resources); and (iii) a community-based management and leadership capacity, augmented by external inputs from the state or donors and support from community-affiliated professionals and institutions.

# References

Calvert, A.F. (1917) *German East Africa*. London: T.W. Laurie Ltd.

Cameron, J. and Dodd, W.A. (1970) *Society, Schools and Progress in Tanzania*. Oxford: Pergamon Press.

Galabawa, J.C. and Ishumi, A.G.M. (1990) *Self-Help Secondary Schools: A Case Study of the Kanyigo Development Association (KADEA) Initiative*. Dar es Salaam: World Bank.

Gottneid, A.J. (ed.) (1976) *Church and Education in Tanzania*. Nairobi: East African Publishing House.

Ishumi, A.G.M. (1985) *Teach all Things to all Men?* Inaugural Lecture Series No. 37. Dar es Salaam: Dar es Salaam University Press.

Ishumi, A.G.M. (1990) *Educational Development in Eastern and Southern Africa: A Critical Review of Policy and Practice 1960s–80s*. Tokyo: Institute of Developing Economies.

Kaara, J. (1977) 'A Study of Attitudes of Teachers and Pupils Toward Agricultural Education: A Case Study of Nyeri District [Kenya]'. M.Ed. Thesis, University of Nairobi, Nairobi.

Lawuo, Z.E. (1984) *Education and Social Change in a Rural Community*. Dar es Salaam: Dar es Salaam University Press.

Lema, A.A. (1973) 'The Impact of the Leipzig Lutheran Mission on the People of Kilimanjaro, 1893–1920'. Ph.D. Thesis, University of Dar es Salaam, Dar es Salaam.

Lillis, K. (1988) 'Geographic and Social Inequalities' in M. Bray with K. Lillis (eds) *Community Financing of Education*. Oxford: Pergamon Press.

Mbithi, P. and Rasmussen, R. (1977) *Self-Reliance in Kenya: The Case of Harambee*. Uppsala: Scandinavian Institute of African Studies.

Ministry of Education (various years) *Basic Education Statistics in Tanzania (BEST)*. Dar es Salaam: Ministry of Education.

Samoff, J. (1987) 'School Expansion in Tanzania: Private Initiative and Public Policy', *Comparative Education Review* 31 (3): 333–60.

Schlunk, M. (1964) 'German Educational Policy: The School System in the German Colonies' in D.G. Scanlon (ed.) *Traditions of African Education*. New York: Teachers College Press.

Tanganyika Territory (1934) *Annual Report of the Department of Education*. Dar es Salaam: Government Printer.

Thompson, A.R. (1976) 'Historical Survey of the Role of the Churches in Education from Pre-colonial Days to Post-independence' in Gottneid.

# 10 JWANI T. MWAIKUSA
## Maintaining Law & Order in Tanzania

The Role of
*Sungusungu* Defence Groups

Some time in early 1992, the Prime Minister made a widely publicized tour of police stations in Dar es Salaam. The police reports presented to him during this tour showed an impressive decline in the rate of crime in the city, particularly robbery and related offences. A number of firearms and other weapons believed to have been used in various criminal acts were reported to have been seized during the previous year.

The reports were not merely police propaganda. Public opinion in Dar es Salaam tended to agree with them. The fall in the crime rate was attributed to one outstanding factor: the deployment of *sungusungu* in Dar es Salaam as well as other urban areas from late 1990.

*Sungusungu* are traditional defence groups. They are traditional in the sense that their formation, training, equipment and general performance have been initiated and organized in accordance with some traditional patterns of community life which present-day society often tends to ignore and discard. But more significant, perhaps, is the fact that *sungusungu* groups are also non-governmental; their initiation and organization have not relied on the facilities of the state. However, they perform a traditional government function: the arrest and punishment of offenders, and the general maintenance of law and order.

In the performance of that function the *sungusungu* groups have proved, at least statistically, to be quite efficient. As far back as 1983, the deployment of *sungusungu* was reported to be largely responsible for the falling crime rate in Geita District in Mwanza region (*Daily News*, 28 and 29 November, 5 December 1983).

Maintaining law and order is the oldest known function of the state. Indeed, Marxist theories attribute the very rise and existence of the state to the need for some kind of 'law and order' to save society from self-destruction as a result of heightened class contradictions and conflicts (Marx and Engels, 1969: 204). Law and order was not usually regarded as a 'service'. To regard the maintenance of 'law and order' as a 'function' of the state is a fairly recent development. This notion has tended to obliterate concepts and to neglect the fact that its maintenance constitutes a service as well (Friedman, 1972; Foulkes, 1990: 1).

In this chapter the maintenance of law and order is regarded mainly as a service to the community; it is indeed a traditional function of the state, but a function whose proper discharge serves the society in a particular way. For, without some kind of orderly arrangements enforced with the backing of law, society would easily plunge into chaos and render impracticable all currently imaginable schemes for the provision of other services. It is on this account that the maintenance of law and order should be regarded as a service. And, in its provision, the state in Tanzania today cannot claim exclusive monopoly and competence.

The present-day role of *sungusungu* has important historical roots, which are briefly described below. Then follows an analysis of the modern role of *sungusungu*, and of the problematic relations of *sungusungu* to the state and the law. Some speculations about the future are presented in conclusion.

## The Historical Roots of *Sungusungu*

*Sungusungu,* as a people's organization, originates from the traditional defence and self-help groups of the Sukuma young people of the Lake Victoria regions. Other ethnic communities in Tanzania may have had similar arrangements at one time or another but the Sukumaland *sungusungu* have a much more coherent history. They are also more directly linked with the modern *sungusungu,* which the government now seeks to deploy all over the country.

In Sukumaland *sungusungu* groups were initially conceived as self-help groups for the execution of tasks for the mutual benefit of their members and their communities (Kamara, 1991: chap. 1). Such self-help groups are a common feature in the communal life of traditional African societies. When a disaster hits an individual or a community, such groups are spontaneously formed and organized in order to alleviate hardship. They may, for example, congregate to erect new huts in a day to accommodate families who would otherwise have no accommodation for weeks or months. Later developments have extended *sungusungu* work beyond the spontaneous nature of disaster or rescue operations to include almost regular group work. A communal group, for example, assembled at a member's farm and got all the field work done in a day. On subsequent days they moved to other members' farms to do the same. They continued until every member's field work was completed for the season.

The integration of traditional societies into the wider system of international capital had a significant influence and ultimate impact upon the functions of these self-help groups.[1] The commoditization of labour disrupted many of the traditional patterns of communal life. Individuals were lured out of their

[1] For much of this and the following two paragraphs, the author is indebted to Kamara (1991).

communal groups to become wage labourers. The colonial state intensified this tendency by making the search for money an obligation, through the imposition of poll and hut taxes. Moreover, the destocking campaign launched in Sukumaland in the 1940s was not – as officially claimed – carried out for the sake of soil conservation and the maintenance of healthy herds of cattle, although these are an important source of nutrition as well as a measure of value and wealth among the Sukuma. The real motive was to compel the Sukuma to supply their cattle to meat plants set up by international capital first at Athi River in Kenya, and then at Dar es Salaam by the Tanganyika Packers Ltd.

These developments changed the scope and functions of self-help groups in two ways. On the one hand, the need for money to pay taxes meant that the groups extended their communal execution of tasks to include cultivation of farms other than those belonging to group members. This development gave them a more identifiable character; they would complete their own farm work and then continue working together to earn money as a group on farms whose owners hired them. Gradually the 'hiring' was opened up to extend to tasks beyond cultivation. On the other hand, the destocking campaign intensified the search for beasts to supply the meat plants at Dar es Salaam and in Kenya. Cattle for sale were sought vigorously by representatives of these companies, and this led to an increase in cattle raids and rustling, much to the chagrin of the affected Sukuma communities. The functions of the 'self-help' youth groups had to be extended in order to defend the interests of their respective communities. In this new task of 'defence' they were not being 'hired' as such, but they would readily respond and go in hot pursuit of cattle raided from anybody in their community and invariably retrieve them. These were the beginnings of the character of these groups as 'defence' groups, virtually defending their own interests as part of the communities whose cattle were raided.

Today the groups have the unmistakable characteristic of popular resistance groups (Campbell, 1989: 5). *Sungusungu* is now invariably referred to as an army. The members tend to organize themselves and to operate in a more or less military fashion led by 'commanders' of various ranks.

## The Modern Role of *Sungusungu*

Some decades ago the self-help groups functioned as 'defence' groups only very occasionally, depending on the frequency of cattle raids. But developments in the late 1970s and early 1980s led to some changes in this pattern. It was, in particular, the government's renewed efforts to destock in this period and its drive to promote cash crops, together with the increasing appearance of modern arms among cattle raiders, which contributed to shape the present role of the *sungusungu*.

Thus for a long time the policies of the government towards cattle-keeping in Tanzania have been in conflict with the interests of the cattle-owners themselves. The government, both colonial and post-colonial, has always insisted on destocking. When herders were not persuaded to sell their cattle for money to pay taxes and to buy the other attractions which go with a cash economy, the government consistently sought the support of arguments in favour of environmental sustainability: that without destocking the cattle population would soon lead to desertification.

At the same time, the government has pushed for the cultivation of a narrow range of export cash crops like cotton and tobacco on pastoral lands. Tragically, this has in itself proved to be very harmful to the environment.[2] Moreover, cash-crop farming has made no significant improvement to the health or wealth of the peasant population. Campbell (1989: 39) argues that the Sukuma peasants are paid such paltry sums for their cotton crop that they cannot afford to buy cloth made from the very cotton they produce. Many peasants, therefore, resist abandoning or reducing their herds of cattle in favour of cash-crop farming.

To this should be added the fact that cattle-raiding intensified in the 1970s and 1980s and raiders became better armed with modern weaponry like machine guns – the main source of which may well have been the army.

It is therefore not surprising that the Sukuma peasants and cattle-owners became suspicious of the government and its agencies, especially when their appeals to the government to act against the increasing wave of cattle raids appeared to fall on deaf ears. They finally lost confidence not only in the ability of the government but also in its commitment to deal with this particular crime. Naturally, they fell back on their own young people's 'self-help' groups, which now began specifically to operate for the purposes of defending their property, cattle, on a more or less regular basis.

In contrast to the failed attempts by the state to control cattle-raiding, the groups became quite successful. Such groups are now found to varying extents in most parts of Tanzania, and cattle raids have declined as a result. It should also be noted that this development seems to have occurred together with the practical demise of Tanganyika Packers Ltd, a parastatal company. Its plant in Dar es Salaam has virtually stopped operating and another one built in Shinyanga in 1980 has not been commissioned and possibly never will be.[3]

The Sukuma self-help groups have now acquired prominence; the name *sungusungu* is well-known to everybody. But, legally, they became an 'unlawful

---

2  Tobacco farming is particularly hostile to the environment. Moreover, the diminishing pasture lands are decreasingly able to sustain the remaining herds of cattle.
3  Although the link between cattle raids and parastatal economic interests has not been fully researched, additional evidence substantiates its existence. It concerns an incident in the now infamous campaign against economic sabotage launched in March 1983, under the retrospectively operational Economic Sabotage (Special Provisions) Act, 1983. The campaign was also aimed at cattle raiders. *Sungusungu* were actively involved, and made several spectacular arrests. One of the first people to be arrested on suspicion of having links with cattle raids was identified by the press as 'Pakasi Kengelemingi' – a nickname given to him after his own repeated reference to 'packers' – Tanganyika Packers Ltd – and its staff who made a lot of empty noise – '*kengele nyingi*' – each time he brought cattle to sell to them and would only take the cattle on credit. Thus while the herders were pleading with the government to stop the cattle raids, its parastatal may well have been getting supplies from those raids.

army, once they became more established and regular.[4] Nevertheless the state has not dared to condemn them. Instead, the formation of more *sungusungu* groups has been encouraged and they are now deployed in many parts of the country, including regions which did not have similarly elaborate traditional systems of self-help groups.

The present-day role of *sungusungu* was significantly boosted after the appointment of Augustine Lyatonga Mrema as the Minister for Home Affairs in November 1990. He encouraged the emergence of *sungusungu* or similar groups in the urban areas of the country, despite their rural origin. This development was generally welcomed, because in some places the groups were able to clamp down on the illegal possession of arms. But the Minister went considerably beyond merely encouraging *sungusungu*. In typical Tanzanian fashion, he ordered *sungusungu* work to be made regular and compulsory for every male adult. This brought a remarkable and immediate fall in incidents of robbery and burglary in the urban areas, thereby earning him much public approval and popularity.

With this regularization, *sungusungu* has now spread nation-wide together with the broadening of the categories of offences with which it is expected and encouraged to deal. Today, *sungusungu* may be heard of as having made arrests for all sorts of offences, from the most common such as theft, robbery or burglary to the more intricate like bribery and corruption. On the other hand, the regularization of *sungusungu*, and especially the attempts by the state to make it compulsory, has changed its relationship with the state and tends to erode its original character as a popular organization.

## *Sungusungu* and the State

The founding of the traditional self-help groups as briefly outlined above came about completely independently of the state and its institutions. They later developed into *sungusungu* groups because of dissatisfaction with the ineffectiveness of the state institutions in dealing with crime in society, particularly cattle rustling. But the argument can be taken further. The development of these 'defence groups' to attain identifiable characteristics as an 'army' was largely a reaction to certain impositions by the state and its policies aimed at serving the integration of rural peasant communities into the international economic system which, as Nyerere (1992) reiterated recently, is neither just nor democratic. In that system the interests of the peasant communities are not merely neglected but are aggressively subverted by international capital through the agency of national governments. The rise of *sungusungu* must therefore be seen as a form of popular resistance to the excessive commoditization of values in society (Campbell, 1989).

It is thus not surprising that people have been unable to comprehend the logic of the state laws against crime with their intricate procedures, as well as the

---

[4] Article 147 of the 1977 Constitution of the United Republic of Tanzania prohibits the formation of an army or military or quasi-military unit other than those established by the state.

remedies they provide. At the same time, there have been widespread allegations of corrupt practices in almost all state institutions. The result has been a growing loss of confidence in the government machinery, with many people feeling that the state has left them without protection. So they have adopted their own ways of ensuring their security, to defend peasant communities and to protect them from the lawlessness of the state. Present-day *sungusungu,* therefore, is born out of frustration with the state and its policies and practices.

Yet, far from being embarrassed, the government is apparently grateful for the emergence of the *sungusungu* armies. They are carrying out what is inherently the duty of the government, the suppression of crime, with a success not attained by the government itself and without costing the government a penny. The state has welcomed the *sungusungu* and called for their deployment country-wide, the illegality of their operations notwithstanding.

However, those groups that were established as a result of government orders died an early death, with many people refusing to comply, or group members lacking cohesion and quarrelling amongst themselves. Those that have continued to function meaningfully have done so entirely on a voluntary basis. It appears that, while *sungusungu* are willing to continue with their work, they wish to do so according to their own notions of peace and security, and not necessarily according to the standards set and required by the state. The people-based *sungusungu* seems determined to remain at arm's length from the state and has consistently refused to pay allegiance to it. The state, on the other hand, appears to want to enlist the *sungusungu* service of maintaining law and order according to state terms and criteria and, perhaps most importantly, to do so without incurring any cost. So state praise of *sungusungu* is always accompanied by directives, delivered in a patronizing tone, that remind them about how they should go about their work and that they should report to the police in accordance with state laws and regulations.

That such appeals are ignored is not surprising. *Sungusungu* signifies a deep mistrust of the state and its laws and institutions. There is plenty of evidence to support this claim. *Sungusungu* groups have, for example, often come into conflict with state agencies for law and order, notably the police and the courts. In some districts where *sungusungu* are active, they do not report a single case to the police or the courts, and arrested suspects are not always handed over to the police. The result is that many cases dealt with by *sungusungu* never reach the courts or the police or any other official records. Indeed, *sungusungu* do not always operate in conformity with state laws. *Sungusungu* investigate, arrest, detain, interrogate, conduct trials, pass judgment, and inflict punishment according to their own rules. There are frequent individual accounts of suspects being subjected to horrible ordeals of torture or exorbitant fines; there have even been reports of suspects dying in *sungusungu* lock-up cells.

The *sungusungu* initiation ceremony, called *kutemya,*[5] is itself quite significant

---

[5] This ceremony is mainly used in rural Sukumaland and the adjoining districts, and not by the other varieties of *sungusungu* groups, mainly government-inspired, that have mushroomed all over the country.

in so far as relations with the state are concerned (Kamara, 1991: chap. 3). It involves some training and simulated probation, and some ritual performances culminating in the taking of an oath of allegiance. Significantly, the entire process is conducted without any state involvement whatever. It is only on the final day of the initiation ceremony that a functionary of the ruling (and until 1992 the only) party (Chama Cha Mapinduzi) is sometimes invited, but even then the party functionaries are invited merely as guests. Most telling, perhaps, is the oath of allegiance which is taken on the final day; it makes no reference to the state or any of its institutions, even when some of those institutions have representatives at the ceremony. Instead, *sungusungu* units swear allegiance to their commanders and to *sungusungu* rules.

For its part, the government has always endeavoured to accommodate *sungusungu*. This attitude has perhaps been adopted by the government as a way out of its obvious dilemma. When in the early 1980s some members of the public voiced their complaints against *sungusungu* for not observing the law, it was announced that *sungusungu* would be integrated into the People's Militia (*Daily News*, 5 December 1983) – a move which would put an end to *sungusungu* as a people's organization. The People's Militia, although consisting of ordinary members of the public doing police and military work on a part-time basis, is a state institution. It was established in 1971 by a Resolution of the Party which, according to the one-party Constitution in force between 1965 and 1992, was a state organ.[6] Its members receive some training, usually under army or police personnel, are organized in ranks comparable to those in the police or the armed forces, and are subject to the orders of officers of the army and the police. In contrast, *sungusungu* have never wanted to be subjected to state control and have subtly resisted the proposed integration. They simply disregard police authority and get away with it.

Having failed to integrate *sungusungu* in the People's Militia, the government then went on to campaign for its accommodation. Certainly, it could not come out straight against *sungusungu*; such a move would render it extremely unpopular. Thus, when *sungusungu* units sometimes clash with the police – both of them claiming to be maintaining law and order – the government has invariably shown ostensible manifestations of siding with *sungusungu*. Over the years, for example, numerous *sungusungu* units have been arrested by the police for various offences committed in the performance of their work. But in 1989 the President announced a general amnesty to all such *sungusungu* units, both those convicted and those whose cases were still pending in the courts.

In another incident, in 1991, some *sungusungu* units in Sumbawanga District invaded a courtroom while the court was in session and pulled out the presiding magistrate, forcing the proceedings to a halt. Apparently, they had some allegations of corruption against him. They were immediately arrested by the

[6] The position of the ruling party, the CCM, has now changed with the introduction of multi-partyism under the Eighth Constitutional Amendment (by Act No. 4 of 1992) which came into force in July 1992. However, this amendment has not affected arrangements (like the People's Militia) lawfully made prior to the amendment.

police, who sought to charge them with assault and contempt of court, but the President quickly ordered that the charges should be dropped and the *sungusungu* units be set free at once. A more recent illustration was the announcement over the national radio on 11 June 1992 that some *sungusungu* units had been sentenced to five years imprisonment for having subjected suspects, four years earlier, on 17 July 1988, to *sungusungu* torture. A Presidential pardon was announced the next day (*Daily News* and *Uhuru*, 13 June 1992).[7]

State accommodation of this kind is not healthy. On the one hand, it encourages *sungusungu* to adopt an unjustifiable attitude of self-importance and to ignore the police. This is quite problematic, particularly in view of the fact that *sungusungu* are themselves ignorant of the intricate procedures under the law. On the other hand, some members of the police force become frustrated when the government and the President apparently support *sungusungu* in conflict with the police and the courts. This, in turn, has sometimes inspired the police deliberately to frustrate the efforts of *sungusungu* by simply ignoring cases reported by them and setting free the suspects handed over. There is a mutual contempt between the two, which sometimes erupts into open conflict. There have been occasional incidents of one arresting the other on unfounded allegations.

Although it is difficult to predict how this uneasy relationship may ultimately turn out, it would be a gross mistake to assume that the government has that much affection, or even respect, for *sungusungu*. It is an obvious cause of discomfort – a popular institution whose operations are a continuing reminder of the government's inability to use its institutions to maintain law and order and keep the peace, a primary duty of any government. This failure is probably the main reason why an outright ban on *sungusungu* has not been imposed. To attempt that would only add to the government's problems by provoking popular outrage and enhancing disorder. Moreover, there is always the likelihood that a ban would remove *sungusungu* operations from the surface, but not from beneath it. In fact, a cogent motive behind the government's attitude thus far towards *sungusungu*, a movement contrary to all its own laws, is to avoid driving it underground (Campbell, 1989: 19–20, 29–30).

## *Sungusungu* and the Law

Another problem area concerns *sungusungu* in relation to the formal law. The foundations of *sungusungu* and its operations are not based on law as an institution of the modern state, but on the moral values of rural communities which have not fully discarded their traditions. Thus *sungusungu* is essentially an institution of traditional communities which has been thrust up against the intricate demands of modern society with its institutions of state and law, without

---

[7] It is interesting to note that, in January 1977, President Ali Hassan Mwinyi, then Minister for Home Affairs, resigned on account of torture having been similarly applied to suspects, but at that time by state agents. At least two of the suspects died as a result and the state officers involved were subsequently charged and convicted of manslaughter; see: *Elias Kigadye and Others* v. *Republic*, in 1981 *Tanzania Law Reports*, 355.

having had the necessary orientation to meet those demands appropriately.

As an institution, *sungusungu* has no place under the law. As an army, which it actually now is, its existence, independent of the state, is contrary to the Constitution. The High Court of Tanzania has, at least once, declared it illegal.[8] Yet the institution has continued to survive and even to grow in importance. And *sungusungu* groups have power, even though they may not be armed. In fact, the law does not allow them to carry modern arms and this is meticulously enforced by the state. But the very fact that they have on occasion managed to contend with armed robbers and even to disarm them is in itself telling.

If *sungusungu* were only a popular civil organization, this would be no problem. But, by the very function it performs, it is not strictly civil. It does police work; it deals with criminal matters, which are always a primary concern of the state and its laws. The fact that *sungusungu* is also traditional, guided by native law and custom, contradicts the law, because customary criminal law was abolished by the Magistrates' Courts Act of 1963.

The disregard of state criminal law is what in most cases renders *sungusungu* activities unlawful. Practices like the forceful extraction of confessions from suspects by beating them up may well have had a place in customary notions of criminal justice where confessions, perhaps because of an implied repentance and a psychological reassurance of the community's own power to deal with evil, were valued more than proof of guilt. Similarly, the total divorce of all compulsory elements from criminal sanctions under state jurisprudence is not fully comprehensible under customary law. That is why the forceful seizure of property in retribution from a 'convicted' criminal is typical of the *sungusungu* administration of justice. But these customary legal notions are not acceptable under the criminal law of the modern state.

Thus, *sungusungu*, traditional and customary, and not owing its existence to any law, has been at variance with state law from the very beginning. The groups started organizing themselves and operating as an army without any legal sanction or recognition. The government, scared of banning the institution, encouraged its deployment by shouting from political platforms. When contradictions between the law and what *sungusungu* entails became too glaring, the government finally climbed down to insert the word *sungusungu,* for the first and so far only time, in the statute books with the People's Militia Laws (Miscellaneous Amendments) Act of 1989.

But that law does not say or do much. Its overall effect is to give *sungusungu* units powers of arrest comparable to those of a police constable. The problem is that *sungusungu* units do, or would like to do, a lot more against crime and criminal conduct than merely arresting suspects and handing them over to the police. They would like to do a lot more of not only what the police do, but also what the courts do. And, when they do so, they offend against the law. Apart from the atrocious excesses they commit, which could partly be attributed to ignorance regarding the legal limits of their powers, there is also the Public

---

[8]  *Charles Charari Maitari* v. *Matiko Chacha Cheti and Four Others,* High Court of Tanzania, Mwanza Registry, Civil Case No. 15 of 1987, unreported.

Order Ordinance prohibiting the usurpation of the functions of the police, not to mention the state Constitution prohibiting the formation of an army or military (or quasi-military) units other than those established by the state.

The problem, however, is wider than that. Present-day *sungusungu* are no longer spontaneous gatherings, dispersing after a particular task is accomplished. They are now more regular, thus giving rise to the need for remuneration. This is also a new thing, never envisaged in the traditional context of *sungusungu* origins.

In response to this need it appears that some *sungusungu* groups have turned their operations into a business. Some impose exorbitantly heavy fines in retribution, part of which they retain. This happens where the suspect has confessed and 'conviction' is entered. But others have designed a fee which they extract from anyone coming to seek their assistance or service. The fee is called *kiatu*, meaning 'shoe', i.e. that on which they walk in search of suspects (Kamara, 1991). None of these payments have the sanction of the law.

But the most disturbing aspect of all is that the government, while encouraging *sungusungu* to undertake police work, does hardly anything to help them learn even the rudiments of the law involved in such work.

## The Future of *Sungusungu*

The precarious position of *sungusungu* in relation to the state and the law makes their future very difficult. There appear to be three main possibilities: *sungusungu* could either be banned, or the government could try to bring it under much closer control. Alternatively, attempts could be made to strengthen *sungusungu* units as people's organizations that work within the law but with allegiances to the grassroots and not to the state. Each possibility is discussed in turn.

### Banning

So far, the spread of *sungusungu* operations has had the government's public approval, but it would be misleading to regard this as a sign of trust and confidence in *sungusungu*. Governments all over the world are known for their craving for a monopoly of power. Should the government find that *sungusungu*, as an institution, has managed to assert itself too independently of the state and its institutions, the drastic option would be effectively to ban it. But this would not be easy at present. The government approval that *sungusungu* has earned is mainly on account of its effectiveness in dealing with some of the most notorious crimes in Tanzanian society. This, along with the government's own miserable failure in dealing with these crimes, has so far been *sungusungu*'s trump card. However, this card is a tricky one. It could easily turn the tables against *sungusungu*, because of the latter's ignorance of and contempt for the law.

This may provide a perfect excuse for government action against *sungusungu*.

Given that the praise showered upon *sungusungu* has partly been responsible for the said groups' self-importance and glorification in their work, and that the government has condoned their illegalities to a surprising extent, the saying 'give a fool enough rope and he will hang himself' could easily come into play against them. An occasion may arise when *sungusungu* units will, in their zeal, seriously transgress the law and warrant government action. The government could, for example, pick on one or two incidents of the atrocious *sungusungu* ordeals of torture for 'interrogation' and orchestrate them for public support, following which *sungusungu* could be banned with some, even if not complete, public support. Such a move would put an end to an otherwise popular movement.

A ban is likely, however, to drive *sungusungu* underground. This would not only add to the problems of the government in dealing with law and order, but would also bring new ones for the public. If driven underground, *sungusungu* could very easily be hijacked and privatized, and then continue as a secret organization serving a clandestine group and not the interests of the poor peasants who gave birth to it in the first place.

## Controlling

A second possibility is for the government to try to bring it under closer control. In fact, the government has already tried to make *sungusungu* compulsory and regular in every locality. But this is proving unworkable. It also erodes the popular characteristics of the institution. Most of the people taking part in the government-created groups (which are also called *sungusungu*) are not doing so as willing members of their own institutions; they are pushed into it by the government.[9] And those who know that such *sungusungu* work under government compulsion is unlawful (which it is) simply refuse to take part in it. This is dangerous as it could undermine the efforts of genuine *sungusungu*.

Moreover, to make compulsory *sungusungu* workable, participants will have to be remunerated. Otherwise attendance would soon become very low. Remuneration, however, is not typical of *sungusungu,* the reason being quite simply that *sungusungu* work is not a profession like that of the police. Clearly the state has no money for this; after all, the government is happy with *sungusungu* precisely because it is doing police work at no cost. But, when *sungusungu* units increasingly carry out police work on a regular basis as encouraged by the government, which also encourages them to deal with an even wider category of criminal activities than the traditional concern of cattle raids, then some units feel justified in expecting and perhaps even demanding remuneration. This is likely to lead to conflicts with the government, thereby rendering the future of *sungusungu* even more precarious.

---

[9] Minister of Home Affairs Mrema has been particularly active in the drive to establish *sungusungu* everywhere, often disregarding the legal problems that this entails. He has also shown a penchant for administrative illegality and an acclaimed disregard of the rules in dealing with other issues (such as fights against crime through the police). Nevertheless, he has been the most popular government minister during the early 1990s.

## Adapting

The only possibility for the continued survival of *sungusungu* lies in their ability to change and adapt themselves to the demands of law and order in modern society while remaining a people's organization. To do this they need to know at least the basic law relating to the maintenance of law and order. At present they do not. In meeting this particular demand, it would be both unrealistic and unwise to expect the government to take the initiative and start teaching *sungusungu* the law they need to know. If that were to be done, it would threaten the non-governmental character of *sungusungu* just as much as the government tendency to make it both regular and compulsory.

The challenge should therefore be taken up by *sungusungu* and the communities from and for which they operate. Understanding the law would make *sungusungu* more secure as a people's institution, and the chances of government action against it for violation of state laws would be reduced. So, just as the establishment and continuing existence of *sungusungu* have come about independently of the state, its legitimization, in terms of state laws, will very much depend on how capable it is of acquiring some necessary practical knowledge of the law independently of the state.

In addition to this, the essential characteristics of *sungusungu* as an institution of the people have to be preserved. The possibility of the interests of the state being at variance with those of the people is quite usual. One clear example, of direct relevance here, relates to the problem of witchcraft murders. In many areas where the *sungusungu* operations originated and are well established and organized, there is also a high prevalence of murders of people believed to be practising witchcraft, most of the victims being elderly women living alone. It is generally believed that the murders are carried out by *sungusungu* units. The state has been trying, by political speeches, to persuade the *sungusungu* to put an end to the murders – but so far without success. For this problem will not be stopped by political speeches, and still less by encouraging *sungusungu* units to engage in fighting a wider category of criminal acts. The fact is that *sungusungu* is a part of communities whose traditional belief and fear of witchcraft lead them to condemn any person practising it to immediate death. *Sungusungu* cannot therefore be expected to prevent such killings. It is a popular institution conceived for the purposes of ridding society of all that is seen as the forces of evil. Witchcraft, because it is seen as a force of evil in traditional society, will continue to be the target of *sungusungu* attacks.

This does not imply that nothing should be done about such murders. Clearly, belief and fear of witchcraft intensify with poverty which is often manifested by poor health and a high degree of malnutrition. Observations by Oxfam, which runs a number of community projects in Shinyanga Region, indicate that, in areas with a high degree of malnutrition and infant mortality, the fear of witchcraft is immense and the killing of elderly women on allegations of practising witchcraft is frequent. Oxfam selected a few of these areas and encouraged the cultivation and use of nutritious food crops which are within the means of the peasants. Improved child health and reduced infant mortality resulted and this removed the fears and worries about witchcraft. The killings motivated by those fears came to an end.[10]

If some of the *sungusungu* energies were also harnessed towards such productive activities, which constitute the historical roots of *sungusungu* before it was turned into some kind of a regular army and enlisted to do regular police work, then *sungusungu* would strengthen its position in a positive way.

## Sungusungu *as POs*

The need for co-operation between the government and the people, which is certainly necessary for the maintenance of law and order, should not lead to the assumption that *sungusungu* or any other such popular organization can engage in maintaining law and order in the same manner and to the same extent as the police. Notwithstanding the impressive recent falls in crime rates and other claims in praise of *sungusungu*, it is only a people's self-help institution and should never be regarded as having the efficiency or the capacity to substitute for the police force.

In order to continue as part of their communities, *sungusungu* units should go on living like the other members of their communities, carrying on with the same subsistence and survival activities as everybody else. If they give in to the endeavours to have them engaged in police work on a regular basis, thus sacrificing their regular productive work, they will be seeking to elevate themselves above their own communities and to assume the status of state agents or institutions.

The emphasis should therefore be on two fronts, if *sungusungu* is to survive as a people's organization. One is that *sungusungu* units must know the basics of what the law requires or allows them to do; only in that way can there be genuine hope of avoiding collision with the government. Secondly, all defence and security work by *sungusungu* units should remain purely on a part-time and *ad hoc* basis; all attempts to make it regular must be discouraged. Only in that way can *sungusungu* hope to remain a people's organization, one on which the people can call as and when the need arises.

10  Based on discussions with Oxfam on observations made in Shinyanga Region following a tour of the region by the Legal Aid Committee in 1990.

# References

Campbell, H. (1989) 'Popular Resistance in Tanzania: Lessons from the Sungusungu', *Africa Development* 14 (4): 5–43.

Foulkes, D. (1990) *Administrative Law*. London: Butterworths.

Friedman, W. (1972) *Law in a Changing Society*, 2nd Edition. Harmondsworth: Penguin Books.

Kamara, M.A.J. (1991) 'Sungusungu and the Maintenance of Law and Order: a Case Study of Sungusungu Activities in Mwanza Region'. Unpublished LL.B. Dissertation, Faculty of Law, University of Dar es Salaam, Dar es Salaam.

Marx, K. and F. Engels (1969) *Selected Works III*. Moscow: Progress Publishers.

Nyerere, J.K. (1992) 'Who Shall Inherit the Earth?' *The Guardian* (London), 16 November.

# 11

## JOHN C. SIVALON
## The Catholic Church & the Tanzanian State
## in the Provision of Social Services

The churches have played an important role in the provision of social services in Tanzania since colonial times. How has this affected their relationship to the state? In answering this question, two types of conventional wisdom must be challenged. One is that in Tanzania NGOs, such as the churches, have been passive partners in the state–NGO relationship. A close scrutiny of the history of the contacts between the Catholic Church and the Tanzanian state shows that the Church does not simply react to initiatives made by the state, but seeks to shape its relationship with the state at any particular moment, in order to pursue its own interests.

The conventional wisdom also has it that relations between churches and the state became very tense when church-owned schools and hospitals were nationalized by the Tanzanian state following the Arusha Declaration in 1967. This is not borne out by historical evidence either. Some officials of the Catholic Church actually welcomed the move, because new activities to which it gave high priority could now be undertaken using resources released from the burden of providing social services.

Nevertheless, some tensions between the Catholic Church and the state did arise in the 1970s. They reflected the broader struggle evolving in Tanzania about its development strategy. The Catholic hierarchy were deeply worried about what they perceived as a move towards Marxism, by bringing radical elements more into control of the state. However, it is evidence of the generally good relations between state and church in Tanzania that such tensions did not affect the development activities of the Catholic Church.

There are signs that the churches will play a stronger role in service provision in the 1990s, for this is now backed by substantial funds from Western governments, and this involvement is supported by the Tanzanian state. On the other hand, the Muslim communities are increasingly concerned about the stronger Christian influence that they perceive will follow from this. Such tensions are likely to affect both state–church relations and relations in civil society between the various religious communities.

These conclusions will be reached through a closer study of the relationship between the Roman Catholic Church and the state in Tanzania. The study concentrates on the historical development of this relationship, which has developed in three distinct stages: the years of harmony (between 1953 and 1966); the tense years (1967–76); and – from then on – the years of the re-emergence of the church as a major service provider. The basic rhythm of the relationship can probably be generalized, although the Catholic Church in many respects differs from other NGOs. Chapter 9, for example, analyses the role of NGOs and POs in general in the provision of secondary education.

## The Years of Harmony: 1953–66

The extent of mission involvement in education in mainland Tanzania has been documented by a number of authors (Chapter 9 of this volume; Samoff, 1979; Mbilinyi, 1980). In brief, by 1900, education had become an integral part of the evangelization methods of most Christian missionaries. The White Fathers' founder, Cardinal Lavigerie,

> proposed that the White Fathers should establish understandings with strong rulers such as Mirambo or Rumanika and under their protection, Christianize their kingdoms. To begin with, some slave children were to be redeemed and educated in medicine and useful trades (Beetham, 1967: 9).

After the interruption of World War I, the Christian missions started to co-operate closely with the colonial government in formal education. However, literacy and education remained so tied up with Christianity in this period that

> 'Kusoma Christianity' is most characteristic of the period between 1920 and 1945. East African Christians commonly used to say they go to church 'kusoma' (to read), rather than 'kusali' (to pray), a reminder of the great literacy movements, which first appeared in Buganda in the 1890s and were repeated in so many other areas (Anderson, 1977: 111).

This involvement of Christian missions in education during the colonial period is clearly shown in Table 11.1.

Table 11.1 The African Educational System in 1945

|  | Government and Native Authority | Missions |
| --- | --- | --- |
| Primary Schools | 200 | 800[a] |
| Secondary Schools | 8 | 10 |
| Teacher Training Centres | 8 | 16 |
| University (Makerere) | 1 |  |

*Source:* Cameron and Dodd (1970: 71).
[a] Of which 300 were assisted by government.

Hence, Christian churches could claim to have been involved in educating, at one level or another, a large number of the political elite. A list of graduates for the years 1957 to 1958 of St Mary's Catholic Secondary School for boys in Tabora[1] indicated that 55% of the graduates were currently national-level officials in ministries, party departments, and international agencies or general managers of parastatals. From a random sample of former students of Marian College in Morogoro for the years 1961 to 1965, it was found that one-third are national-level officials in ministries, party departments or international agencies, and another one-fourth regional-level government officers.[2] In addition, one woman in the sample was a Central Committee member of the ruling party in 1992.

These schools provided the potential for special links to evolve between the church and many future leaders of Tanzania. This involved the development of social networks and personal relationships that continue to limit, shape and direct the worldview of the leaders. Two examples illustrate this.

The Catholic Old Boys Association (COBA) started prior to independence and continued up to at least 1963. It was an organization for graduates of St Mary's Secondary School mentioned above, at which Nyerere taught. Meetings consisted of debates and discussions centred around the social responsibility of Catholics and the social teachings of the church. For example:

> You may like to know that the COBA is now again flourishing amazingly well. I am President this year and although membership is not very big, the quality is excellent. . . . We meet every Friday to read and study the *Mater et Magistra*.[3]

The women graduates of Marian College claim to have what is called the 'Marian Spirit.' Although unable to define this precisely, interviewees[4] stressed that this 'spirit' seems to include the bonds that the women feel among themselves; the pride that they have in the many successful students; and a worldview shaped at Marian that contains a sense of service and duty, including the provision of social services.

This shared worldview concerning the provision of social services was explicated in the official teachings of the church in Tanzania at that time. In *Africans and the Christian Way of Life*, a major pastoral letter on social issues by the bishops of Tanzania, it is stressed that:

> All three agencies, the family, the State and the Church, have indispensable parts to play in education, the nature of which depends upon their respective responsibilities

---

[1] I was aided in the compiling of this list by a former headmaster, who in turn was helped by a former student.

[2] The list contained a total of 224 graduates for the years 1961–5. Although incomplete, the list did contain some women whose present profession was unknown, though none of these appeared in the random sample. It should be noted that the list may not be totally representative of all Marian graduates.

[3] Letter of 24 September 1963 from the Director of Information Services, Vice-President's Office, Ref. #5/9/9/173 to Fr. Walsh. File: Fr. Walsh. White Fathers Central Archives, Rome, Italy. *Mater et Magistra* is a Papal Encyclical that explains the social responsibility of the church.

[4] Four former teachers and four former students.

and rights. Their roles in this regard are, it is true, distinct but it is the intention of God that they should all cooperate in concord to develop the spiritual and physical faculties of people (Catholic Bishops of Tanganyika, 1954: 21).

In 1960 the bishops stated more clearly which distinct roles each institution was to play. They emphasized the fact:

[that] social services such as education, social security, medico-social assistance, community development and so forth, should not fall under the exclusive domain of the State is at once evident from the principles of the natural law. . . . The rights of the State over social institutions extends to the effective right of supervising, organizing and integrating the different social services according to the principles given above (Catholic Bishops of Tanganyika, 1960: 11–12).

This stress on protecting the role of the church in providing social services, especially education, had a broader context than just Tanzania. During this Cold War period, a central aim of the social apostolate (ministry)[5] of the Catholic Church was to combat what its leaders called 'atheistic communism'. The bishops of Tanzania implied this concern in the writing of *Africans and the Christian Way of Life*:

There are however certain Agencies which aim at the destruction of the heart of all human and divine values, the liberty of man, and may try to take advantage of the African people. For this reason the Archbishops and Bishops of Tanganyika are putting before you certain principles which should guide you in your task (Catholic Bishops of Tanganyika, 1954: 5).

One of those principles was that the church had a divine right and distinct role to play in providing social services. Any indication of the state obstructing this role was interpreted by Catholic Church officials as an indication that 'certain undesirable agencies' were gaining more control.

The ultimate evidence of how strongly this understanding influenced the bureaucratic class during this period are contained in the words of the then President Nyerere himself. Just after independence in 1961 he said in Parliament:

Does the Government help the voluntary agencies or do the voluntary agencies help the Government? Sixty-six percent of our children who are now in school are at the schools run by the voluntary agencies. They are teaching the children at half the cost which they would have required had they gone to a government school. I would have expected, Sir, that most of the speeches here referring to the voluntary agencies would be of gratitude and not of criticism (Sifuna, 1980: 211).

Even more dramatically President Nyerere wrote a memorandum in 1963 to the Roman Catholic bishops on the problem of education in the country. In this memorandum he officially requested the Catholic Church to provide education through 'true secular' schools for Muslims. He stressed how this would help to bridge the educational gap between Christians and Muslims

---

[5] While difficult to define in a precise manner, this ministry includes all those activities of the Church with explicit political, economic or social welfare aims. This is not to ignore the fact that most religious activities have indirect political and economic effects.

(Tanganyika Episcopal Conference, 25 January 1964). The bishops turned down this request. Also, even though they maintained a significant involvement in education up until 1969,[6] they began to rethink this commitment as early as 1963. They stated:

> For many years, education enjoyed top priority in the policy of Tanganyika's bishops. Recently that priority has been altered to a subordinate though important position in the total policy (Catholic Secretariat, 1963: 2).

This quote is important to remember. It helps support the view that the tension between the Catholic Church and the state which developed later, especially in 1969–70, had many causes other than simply the nationalization of church schools.

## The Tense Years: 1967–76

The years 1967 to 1976 were marked by the official promulgation of *ujamaa* through the Arusha Declaration in 1967. This was followed by a process of nationalization of industries, plantations, housing, and social services facilities; the publication of the *TANU Guidelines* in 1971 on workers' rights; and two years of villagization. Such events led the Catholic hierarchy to believe that more radical elements, as they perceived them, were gaining control over Tanzania's political development. This is the key to understanding the tension that developed between the Roman Catholic hierarchy and the Tanzanian bureaucratic class especially from 1969 to 1970. The nationalization of education was a concern to only some church officials.

President Nyerere reacted to the hierarchy's hesitancy towards Tanzania's new policies when he met the Secretary-General of the Tanzanian Episcopal Conference (TEC) and the Chargé d'Affaires of the Apostolic Nunciature in 1970.[7] In a government seminar for religious leaders in Tabora, which he attended personally, Nyerere complained that it was the Catholic priests who seemed the most worried about *ujamaa*. He also voiced his shock that the Catholic Church in Tanzania had just published a translation of the encyclical *Divini Redemptoris* entitled *Huu ndio Uhuru*,[8] and saw this as an attempt to undermine *ujamaa* by some Catholic officials. Nyerere was right. The translation is evidence that some bishops actually feared that Marxism was gaining ground. This conclusion is further supported by *Peace and Mutual Understanding* (Catholic Bishops of Tanzania, July 1972).

This pastoral letter contrasts significantly in tone and substance with that of 1968. It calls on religious leaders to refute the allegations that religion is an opium:

[6] The Five-year Development Plan for the Church's social services includes £1,899,400 for education and £3,702,861 for health.

[7] This information is taken from a copy of the interview between the above-mentioned parties. Archives of Tabora Archdiocese, file: Nyerere, 1970.

[8] Translated *Is This Freedom?* This encyclical was originally promulgated in 1937 by the Vatican against what it called atheistic Communism or Bolshevism. It describes the situation as a war between Christian civilization and communism 'concealed under the most seductive trappings'.

Religious leaders must strive to help people to overcome the widespread allegation that religion is 'The opium of the people.' Indeed, such intimidations do not flow from African philosophy. These are imported slogans that are liable to shock every serious thinking African. . . . It is obvious that such opinions are not Tanzanian, but come either from foreigners or from Africans used as stooges to spread atheism (Catholic Bishops of Tanzania, 1972: 8–11)

The pastoral letter reiterates the earlier contributions of Catholic officials in the fields of education, health, and agriculture. It then calls on these officials to continue to participate in the development of the nation and reminds the laity of their rightful role in society.

The letter ends with two warnings. The first concerns the relationship of the individual to the community. The bishops warn that the political leadership should not allow the party or its organizations to monopolize all responsibility. Instead, they should encourage personal initiative and personal responsibility. Secondly, the bishops warn against a perceived growth in animosity towards certain nations of the world and their populations. Such attitudes towards foreigners violate the African way of life and its revered custom of hospitality.

Compared with their earlier pastoral letter of 1968, the pastoral of 1972 reflects a dramatic shift. The bishops moved from a position of unquestioned support for 'our' Tanzanian socialism, which they said had nothing in common with those 'wrong kinds of socialism', to one in which they express their perception of 'widespread allegations' that 'religion is the opium of the people'. How can this shift be explained? Some claim the primary reason was the nationalization of schools in 1969.[9] However, the reaction to this policy by different church leaders was mixed. The executive secretary of the Tanzanian Episcopal Conference had actually indicated an openness to this type of move much earlier (Robinson, 1965). Other church officials stated that the nationalization was in fact a help to the church since the running of these educational institutions had become a tremendous drain on church resources. Nationalization assisted the church to concentrate its energies elsewhere (Catholic Secretariat, 1963). And, when the National Education Act was tabled in Parliament to enable the nationalization of schools to proceed, 'the Bill was passed in the National Assembly provoking little debate' (Sifuna, 1980: 218).

The shift does not appear therefore to be related to the nationalization as such. Rather, it was perceived by some of the hierarchy as another piece of evidence of Tanzania's rapid move towards a Marxist approach in its development strategy. This perception, however, was not related directly to the nationalization of social services. It was stimulated much more by a combination of other issues.

One of them was President Nyerere's call, in early 1970, for priests to live in villages. He did not simply challenge the priests to move physically into villages, but questioned the whole style of life and ministry that priests were following. He is quoted as saying:

[9] This was a major move which included primary, secondary and teacher training colleges. The size of the nationalization is shown by the difference in government expenditures from 1969 to 1970 on primary education. For 1968–9 it was T.Shs. 2,200,000. In 1969–70 it was T.Shs. 13,300,000 (Clark, 1978: 82).

I would like to make it clear that the *Arusha Declaration* says only children and old men can live on the sweat of others. We do not intend to add the word priest to that clause (*The Nationalist*, August 1970).

The first two meetings of the 'Baraza la Wazee'[10] in 1970 and 1971 clearly reflected the religious officials' concern with the government's criticism of their ministry. At the first meeting, Bishop Mihayo cautioned President Nyerere that the words he and other politicians used to refer to church leaders, such as exploiters (*wanyonyaji*) and parasites (*makupe*), were unwarranted. The contribution to development, education and health made by the various Christian denominations was proof of this, he argued. At the second meeting, the bishops were much more expressive of their fears of a shift in the definition of *ujamaa*.

> The bishops … met with the President and cautioned him about *ujamaa* remaining an African socialism which respects the individual and individual rights and is truly non-aligned. They expressed their sorrow at how some politicians were presenting Christianity as against development, *ujamaa*, revolution and African culture. Also, that church workers were being presented as exploiters and parasites. Finally, they went on to talk about the nationalization of houses and their fears about Church property.[11]

This feeling continued into the next meeting. By now the bishops were concerned about the implications of the *TANU Guidelines*, passed in 1971, for the churches. They disliked the right of the state to interfere in relations between the churches and their salaried workers, which the *Guidelines* made possible. In fact, the whole operational style of the church and its internal structure were challenged by a literal interpretation of the *Guidelines*. The bishops specifically reacted against the effects on the relationship between managers and workers; they argued that workers were out of control and endangered the security and tranquillity of society. They also feared a growing class consciousness and emphasis on class struggle in the transition to socialism and they disliked the atmosphere at the University of Dar es Salaam at the time. These elements taken together help clarify the tension that existed between the Catholic hierarchy and Tanzania's bureaucratic class during this period. The primary issue was clearly not the nationalization of schools.

In practice, the tensions had very little effect on the church's involvement in the provision of social services. The emphasis shifted from the formal national education sector to socio-economic development, rural health and non-formal education projects. It reflected a changing understanding both in the state and the church of their respective resources and their shifting development priorities. Many Catholic officials now saw activity in socio-economic development as an integral part of their mission. The resolution at the national meeting in 1969 of the *Seminar Study Year* dealing with *ujamaa* and development stated that:

[10]  A council made up usually of three Roman Catholic bishops, one Anglican archbishop, a Lutheran official and President Nyerere. It was a meeting where these Christian leaders could present their concerns privately to Nyerere.

[11]  'Mazungumzo ya Wazee wa Kanisa na Mtukufu Rais, Mwalimu Nyerere', at Msasani on 4 June 1971. Tabora Archdiocese Archives. The bishops present were Mihayo, Rugambwa, Sangu, Sepeku (Anglican) and Kisanji (Lutheran).

Church leaders are urged to take a more active interest in community development at the village level, using all means necessary to be well informed on government plans at the national and local levels, and – as a first step – to cooperate fully with whatever government machinery is already set up for development implementation. The Church was called to promote efforts to educate the people to a new outlook and understanding of the Christian principles of ujamaa upon which modern rural development is based (Murray, 1970: 5).

At first, individuals initiated and implemented this activity, but, gradually, diocesan programmes and even national development plans were devised. The extent of this activity is partially[12] shown by Table 11.2.

Table 11.2  CIDSEE Funds Approved for Tanzania from 1969 to 1977 (US$m)

| Period | Number of Projects | Funds |
|---|---|---|
| 1969–71 | 260 | 4.7 |
| 1972–74 | 259 | 4.3 |
| 1975–77 | 392 | 10.2 |

*Source:* CIDSEE (1979).

Although schools and hospitals may have been nationalized, the Catholic Church maintained a significant role in the provision of education and health care, as shown in Table 11.3.

Table 11.3  Projects Funded by CIDSEE, 1969–79

| Type of Project | Number of Projects |
|---|---|
| Health | 393 |
| Education | 220 |
| Agriculture | 116 |
| Economic | 81 |
| Social Welfare | 69 |
| Self-Help | 46 |
| Other | 20 |

*Source:* Ibid.

Some may question the appropriateness of this assistance and its effectiveness in bringing about development. Yet the Tanzanian bureaucracy saw it as a support and encouraged the Catholic hierarchy to continue. A high-ranking official stated in 1976:

12  CIDSEE (International Co-operation for Socio-economic Development) represented, at this time, only seven funding organizations in Europe. These figures do not therefore include funds from the religious institutions working in Tanzania. Also, they do not represent funds from non-CIDSEE, non-governmental agencies channelled through the Catholic institutions, or funds from organizations in North America. Therefore, even though the figures in the table are significant, they represent only a small portion of the assistance to development.

Your record speaks for itself; you contributed in the fields of promoting schools (primary, secondary and technical), Community Centres, Day-care Centres, Vocational Training Centres, Hospitals, Rural Health Centres, Dispensaries and water facilities. The Catholic Church has been involved in supporting major health, educational, agricultural, and water projects in virtually all regions. . . It is estimated that during the last five years you have invested in projects worth T.Shs. 200 million. . . My congratulations on behalf of our office (Neema, 1976).

He went on to call for this type of support to continue. These are hardly words that would support a conflictive understanding of state versus NGOs in the provision of social services.

## The Re-emergence of the Church as a Major Service Provider: 1977 and Beyond

The Tanzanian economy was weakened by crises in the 1980s, and gradually moved into a state of near collapse. In response, the social service provision of the Catholic Church changed to meet the many immediate needs facing the people at that time. With economic crisis, spells of drought, and the apparent failure of many socio-economic projects, Catholic social programmes moved away from an emphasis on development to relief assistance. A great deal of food relief, especially from Catholic Relief Services, was channelled through Catholic institutions. Donated clothing also started to be imported and distributed.

The importation of these relief goods spawned a growing dependence on the outside world by the Tanzanian Catholic Church. This dependence intensified when the government exempted religious and non-religious voluntary agencies from paying customs and sales taxes on their imported goods.[13] This shielded Catholic officials and their institutions from the effects of the economic crisis. It also helped to put them at the centre of the crisis with significant economic power.[14] While government dispensaries and hospitals lacked essential medicines and saw their services deteriorate significantly, Catholic dispensaries flourished. While materials for government educational institutions became scarce, Catholic seminaries continued to receive books and materials from outside Tanzania. This was part of a general trend as Fowler argues in Chapter 3 of this book.

A second shift in the approach of the Catholic hierarchy's social ministry was the development of the 'Justice and Peace' ministry.[15] It was stimulated by local abuses of the law like the illegal sale of land, and by external pressure from the world-wide church.[16] In 1982, the Religious Superiors Association of Tanzania sponsored a workshop aimed at increasing awareness not just of the 'Justice and

[13] The exemptions were announced officially in 1973 through Government Notices 175 and 176.

[14] For example, it was reported in an interview that one relatively small religious society received 62 containers of commodities a year in the late 1980s.

[15] This activity is a part of the overall social ministry of the Catholic Church. Its specific objective is to defend the basic rights of people and organize against the structural blockages to human development.

[16] The Spiritans, the Vatican, SECAM (the Secretariat of Episcopal Conferences of Africa and Madagascar) or AMECEA (the Association of Member Episcopal Conferences of East Africa).

Peace' ministry but also of specific issues flowing from a social analysis of Tanzania.

The bishops' reaction to this workshop and to justice and peace work in general provides some insight into the shift in the hierarchy's relationship to the bureaucratic class which characterized this period. One bishop said,

> In Tanzania the one thing we have is peace and tranquillity. We're not like Uganda where they're killing one another and being persecuted. This peace is a real value and we have to maintain it. We can't be endangering it for no reason.[17]

A lay leader also remarked that

> the leaders of our Church do not want it to appear that they are criticizing the government. But I don't know why. They just don't want to appear as if they are against the government. Also, if we take Nyerere himself, the older bishops look upon him as the intellectual among them. They also see him as a product of the Church and most importantly, not only the older bishops, but even the younger bishops see Nyerere as the one who can ensure the safety and tranquillity of the nation and at the same time the safety and security of the Church. There is no bishop who will belittle Nyerere on this point. They depend on Nyerere to care for the security of the Church.[18]

These quotes highlight the resistance of Catholic officials to any open criticism of the government or its policies during the time of near total economic collapse. The bishops were extremely aware of, and valued, the relative peace of Tanzania. The government, and President Nyerere in particular, were credited with this relative tranquillity which allowed the Catholic hierarchy to maintain its favourable position and to flourish in many respects.

During this period, then, Catholic Church officials for the most part may have been disgruntled and disheartened by the magnitude of the economic collapse in Tanzania, but they never officially criticized the government for its policies. In fact, the bishops came to enjoy even more favourable relations with the bureaucratic class and a significant amount of economic power, as the tax and custom exemptions illustrate.

It was also during this time that the Catholic Church embarked on a programme of internal renewal. This involved various campaigns to institute Small Christian Communities in all the diocese of Tanzania (AFER, October 1976). These small neighbourhood associations were geared towards reflection on the Bible in the light of the daily lives of the people. Renewed emphasis was placed on the church becoming self-supporting and self-governing.

But, as the economic crisis deepened and government services continued to deteriorate through the 1980s, the churches re-emerged as important actors in the social service sector. This is formally reflected in the Memorandum of Understanding between CCT/TEC[19] and the United Republic of Tanzania signed in February 1992. This agreed, first, that a Christian Social Services Commission with equal representation from TEC and CTT should be established to administer and monitor matters related to education and health. Second, a

---

[17]  Interview, June 1988.
[18]  Interview, July 1988.

Christian Social Services Trust Fund was to be established to serve as the recipient of all loans and grants and the depository of all moneys generated through the aforementioned services. Third, sub-commissions should be formed to oversee the two major sectors of health and education. Fourthly, the memorandum spells out the obligations of the government, which include providing spaces in its teacher training colleges for teachers to be placed in church-run schools; a commitment not to nationalize schools or hospitals in the future; and a willingness to endeavour to include financial assistance to church-run social services in its bilateral negotiations, particularly with the government of the Federal Republic of Germany (Mahalu, 1992).

While church and government officials stressed in the press the commitment not to nationalize church-run institutions, the major impetus for the memorandum was the bilateral aid negotiations. The German Government proposed that its aid, at least in the social service sector, should be channelled through a 'four-party co-operative' structure, the four parties being the governments of the donor and recipient countries and NGOs in both countries. This meant that the Federal Republic would grant through Misereor and EZE (the German Christian Aid agencies) a portion of its total aid package to the United Republic of Tanzania through the Christian churches of CCT/TEC. Initially, a donor contribution of DM15.8 million for social services (especially health and education) was planned.

This 'four-party co-operation' strategy is clearly a new chapter in NGO–state relationships in Tanzania, although it in no way indicates a major shift or break with the past history of church–state co-operation as illustrated earlier in this chapter. However, the memorandum caused some tension in the Muslim community. Thus, *An Nuur*, an Islamic newspaper, raised the alarm concerning the church–state agreement (*An Nuur*, March 1992: 1–3). It claimed that this was a major success for the Christian churches which would have a tremendous historical impact on Tanzania and negative consequences for the Islamic community. First, it would give the Christian churches a major voice in the education policies of the country. Secondly, the newspaper expressed fears that this was just a first step in a Christian conspiracy to build the 'Mtanzania Mpya' – a reference to the programme announced by Christian Professionals of Tanzania for building the 'New Tanzania' on Christian principles. This reaction reflects a widespread sentiment in the Muslim community. Closer state–church relations are seen as a threat to non-Christians. This adds a new and important dimension to service provision, and is likely to be an increasingly important political issue in the 1990s.

## Conclusion

The above analysis has shown that the relationship of the Roman Catholic hierarchy to the state in Tanzania in the provision of social services has almost

[19] TEC (Tanzanian Episcopal Conference) and CCT (Christian Council of Tanzania).

always been one of co-operation. There were moments of tension in the 1970s, but the major cause was not related to the nationalization of the social services infrastructure owned by the churches, although this is commonly believed. In fact, segments of the Catholic hierarchy had wanted the nationalization of schools because of the tremendous financial and personnel burden they imposed on the church. Rather, the tensions were caused by moves towards what the hierarchy perceived to be a more Marxist approach to socialist development.

Secondly, the shifting emphasis of the Catholic Church's provision of social services did not simply result from initiatives on the part of the state. On the contrary, it was caused by a number of factors of which the most important was the changing internal understanding of church personnel concerning the social ministry itself. In the 1960s tremendous emphasis was placed on rural and socio-economic development. Those involved in the social ministry of the church could not help but be affected by this emphasis and begin to rethink their priorities. Similarly, in the 1970s, there was another shift emphasizing a more critical stance towards structural obstacles to development. This led to initiatives geared towards the formation of the Justice and Peace Commission. Further-more, in the late 1970s and 1980s, the church was much more inward-looking as it strove to become self-supporting and self-governing.

These shifts had an effect on how the church responded to the call to provide social services. However, at no time did the church remove itself from the provision of social services. Nor was the church at any time completely replaced by the state in the provision of the traditional social services like health and education. Rather, the primary factor in the relationship of state and church in the provision of social services has been an attempt to co-operate. Thus, the 'four-party co-operative' strategy between the governments of Tanzania and Germany and Christian NGOs in the two countries that began in 1992 is not a qualitative break with the previous history of this relationship.

The analysis also challenges the notion that the increasing involvement of NGOs in the provision of social services like health and education is an a priori indication of a weakening of the bureaucratic class in Tanzania. Many of the same people are involved in both groups either personally, through familial ties or through other social relationships. Thus, the present increasing role of NGOs in Tanzania's social service sector is more an indication of a shift in strategy by the bureaucratic class to maintain its position within Tanzania's social structure than evidence of its weakening.

Yet it is a strategy which has heightened tensions in civil society between the Christian and Muslim communities. In the future this is an important factor to remember. It hints at how foreign sources of aid can affect the relationship among different organs of civil society and how, in turn, these will affect their relationship with the government. It is highly conceivable that alliances will be formed between particular political parties and organizations of civil society, with access to outside funding being the main bargaining counter.

# References

*AFER* (1976) Vol.18, No.5.

Anderson, W.B. (1977) *The Church in East Africa 1840–1974.* Mwanza: Central Tanganyika Press.

*An Nuur* (1992) 'Mkataba baina ya Kanisa na Serikali – Nini Tafsiri yake kwa Waislamu?' March.

Beetham, T.A. (1967) *Christianity and the New Africa.* New York: Frederick A. Praeger.

Cameron, J. and Dodd, A. (1970) *Society, Schools and Progress in Tanzania.* London: Oxford University Press.

Catholic Bishops of Tanganyika (1954) *Africans and the Christian Way of Life.* Tabora: Tanganyika Mission Press.

Catholic Bishops of Tanganyika (1960) *Unity and Freedom in the New Tanganyika.* Tabora: Tanganyika Mission Press.

Catholic Bishops of Tanzania (1972) *Peace and Mutual Understanding.* Tabora: Tanzania Mission Press.

Catholic Secretariat (1963) *Pastoral Information Newsletter* 7 (2): 2.

CIDSEE (1979) *Tanzania: Projects Approved from 1969 to 1979.* Brussels: International Cooperation for Socio-economic Development, Secretariat.

Clark, W.E. (1978) *Socialist Development and Public Investment in Tanzania.* Toronto: University of Toronto Press.

Mahalu, C.R. (1992) 'Memorandum of Understanding'. Christian Council of Tanzania, Tanzania Episcopal Conference and the United Republic of Tanzania. Signed 21 February.

Mbilinyi, M. (1980) 'African Education During the British Colonial Period' in M.H.Y. Kaniki (ed.) *Tanzania under Colonial Rule.* London: Longman.

Murray, F. (1970) 'SSY Report – The National Seminar: An Overview', *Service* 1: 1–11.

Neema, G.T. (1976) 'Tanzania Government Policies on Development'. Paper presented by the Principal Secretary in the Prime Minister's Office to the Bishops of Tanzania, November (unpublished).

Robinson, D. (1965) 'The Church, Schools and Religious Liberty', *AFER* 7 (1): 9–22.

Samoff, J. (1979) 'Education in Tanzania: Class Formation and Reproduction', *Journal of Modern African Studies* 17 (1): 47–69.

Sifuna, D.N. (1980) 'Church and State in the Control of Education in Africa: A Case Study of Tanzania and Kenya', *Présence Africaine* (1): 209–34.

Tanzania Episcopal Conference (1964) 'Minutes of the Administration Board Meeting' – January. Mbeya: Archives of the Diocese of Mbeya.

## 12

EMMANUEL NABUGUZI
Popular Initiatives in Service Provision
in Uganda

Uganda presents a dramatic example of the legacy of colonial rule and its effects on service provision. On the one hand, the country inherited one of the best health and education services in sub-Saharan Africa at independence in 1962, with law and order maintained by an authoritarian colonial state. On the other hand, the political inheritance soon helped to push the country into political, economic and social turmoil, from which it may only now be slowly recovering. The effects of this turmoil on service provision have been devastating. Today the access to and quality of services in Uganda are worse than in Kenya and Tanzania, although the situation – including that of security – is improving.

This overview presents an analysis of these developments. It is based on two basic propositions. One is that the intense post-colonial struggles for political power among various economic, ethnic and religious factions severely affected service provision. Moreover, partly as a result of this, service provision has, to a large extent, been left to popular initiatives. Without these, health and education services and the law and order situation would have been even worse than they are today.

The second proposition is that, in the post-colonial period, the role of the state in service provision – and the relations between the state and civil society – have changed significantly. It is possible to identify three fairly distinct phases, and these are reflected in the structure of this chapter. The first phase (1962–75) shows how, at independence, the state perceived itself as the motor of development and the provider of services. It therefore set out to centralize political and economic activity, secularize education and health institutions and disorganize non-state activity in general. In the second phase, covering the period 1976–86, the advent of Idi Amin eventually led to economic decline and anarchy. This, in turn, led to the collapse of state services. People's organizations (POs) and informal enterprises emerged to meet unsatisfied social needs. The NGOs were subjected to the vagaries of changing state policy and their organizational capacity in this period remained limited. In the last phase, dealing with the years since 1986, a Structural Adjustment Programme is being implemented. The state's institutions are being rehabilitated, and the emphasis has shifted from state provision of services to a market delivery system. The impact of this shift on access to services is discussed, as is the increased importance of donors and international NGO activity in Uganda's social sector. All this has led to a more complex articulation between the state, NGOs, POs, the private sector and donors in service provision. The voluntary sector has become more structured in this period. It has also become immersed in a mesh of political demands. However, it is argued that the state remains crucial to the equitable provision of services, even if its role and functions may be changing.

The overview focuses on the broad trends in health and education services. Chapter 13 deals in more detail with primary education, while Chapter 14 analyses the maintenance of law and order in rural Uganda.

## The Centralizing State (1962–75)

State attempts at centralizing political and administrative power have been one of the key features of the post-colonial era in Africa (Wunsch and Olowu, 1990). Uganda is no exception. Immediately after independence the political leaders began trying to concentrate political, administrative and economic resources under state control and to use them – among other things – to extend public services and fulfil independence aspirations. This was a significant trend not only during the Obote years up to 1971. It continued during the first part of Amin's military dictatorship, although in a more oppressive fashion, before the country eventually slid into chaos during the second half of the 1970s.

Struggles for political and administrative control of the state apparatus contributed to intense factional fighting under both Obote and Amin. Only four years after independence, the central state/local administration relationship that had prevailed in the colonial period collapsed (Wrigley, 1988). The precarious balance between the colonial order and the traditional governments was swept away, and with it the structures of service provision at the local level. This took place in a violent manner as the UPC (Uganda People's Party) government set about creating a republic in Uganda outside the existing institutional arena in response to challenges to its legitimacy (Mujaju, 1976). Thus the UPC Government overthrew the Buganda kingdom in 1966, dismantled all the traditional bases of authority, undermined the authority of chiefs, and abolished the local government system inherited at independence.

By the mid-1960s local government had become highly centralized under the Local Administrations Act of 1967 and the Urban Authorities Act of 1964. The powers of district administrations were circumscribed and concentrated in the central government. Eventually opposition parties were also banned and labour union activities curtailed. The overall aim was to cut down independent organization and limit pluralist and non-state activities.

The failure of the independence government to come to terms with the various fissures in Ugandan society (ethnic, regional, religious, economic disparities, etc.) led to its overthrow in 1971 by Idi Amin (Nabuguzi, 1994a). The Amin regime consolidated what had begun in the Obote period: the break-up of local administration related to the traditional ruling hierarchy. The administrative system was completely redesigned. The country was divided into ten semi-autonomous provinces and the existing sixteen districts were sub-divided into thirty-eight smaller units, the intention being to enhance the state presence in the rural areas and prevent the formation of strong regional or ethnic coalitions against the central government. It was also an attempt to stifle non-state organization.

Struggles for economic control were equally intense. Faced with popular resistance from Buganda, and with inter-personal conflicts within the army and the UPC, the Obote regime attempted to widen its support by an appeal to republican, nationalist and populist sentiments. The main vehicle was ideological appeals and attempts at constructing a new basis of legitimacy and authority which cut across ethnic identities. Between 1968 and 1970, Obote published a series of policy documents, *The Move to the Left*, accompanied by radical rhetoric, on both the national and the international scene. Following this, the state nationalized a large number of firms operating in Uganda and took control of all import and export business. It also greatly expanded the number of parastatals. By 1971, the state had either a majority or significant minority shares in such service enterprises as the airways, railways, telecommunications, electric and urban water supply and distribution. Thus state control increased in the service industry – co-operatives, banking, manufactures, including social services like health and education. There was a shift in the operation of utilities from private to public control.

Under Amin, moves to centralize economic power were continued. An economic war against the powerful Asian community was declared in 1972 and 50,000 Indians and Pakistanis were expelled. They dominated small-scale enterprise and the distribution sector and owned a large amount of urban property. Their expulsion contributed significantly to a worsening of economic mismanagement and the shrinkage of the official economy. On the other hand, this action considerably increased the resources available to the Amin regime to expand state activities and to buy political patronage. Many confiscated houses, shops, warehouses and factories were distributed to supporters of the regime. This move enabled the partial transfer of commercial networks and processing plants into the hands of African owners, thus modifying in a fundamental way the class structure inherited from the colonial period. But, far from consolidating the economic entrepreneurship of a new African middle class, the economic logic of the Aminist state gradually led to speculation and the growth of the informal sector. Shortages became chronic and incomes dropped, forcing the urban population to look to the parallel market for supplementary income and consumption goods. The effect of the disruption of the Asian commercial networks was therefore to draw economic activity away from the official realm into informal networks.

## State-Provided Services

What happened to state-provided services between 1962 and 1975? The answer is somewhat complex, for the statistical evidence is limited. But service provision was obviously affected by the combined effects of political, administrative and economic upheavals.

During the colonial period, the local administration had played a significant role in service provision. Primary schools and dispensaries were controlled by local authorities and religious missions, while secondary schools and hospitals were under the central government. After independence, the centralization of planning and provision was seen as crucial for efficient service supply. Obviously, this seriously affected the provision of services by the voluntary sector, as will be discussed later in this chapter. On the other hand, an impressive expansion in state-run educational and health facilities did indeed take place, as documented below. Economic growth, mainly based on coffee exports, provided the basis for this expansion.

Table 12.1  State and Non-State Medical Facilities in Uganda, 1970–88

| Facility | 1970 | 1975 | 1981 | 1986 | 1988 |
|---|---|---|---|---|---|
| State Hospitals | 36 | 43 | 44 | 46 | 48 |
| Non-State Hospitals | 29 | 26 | 31 | 33 | 33 |
| State Medical Centres | 210 | 311 | 365 | 745 | 763 |
| Non-state Medical Centres | 52 | 39 | 39 | 108 | 217 |

Source: Ministry of Planning and Economic Development (various years).

Table 12.2  Number of Educational Establishments in Uganda, 1970–89

| Establishment | 1970 | 1980 | 1986 | 1989 |
|---|---|---|---|---|
| Primary Schools | 2,755 | 4,276 | 7,350 | 8,041 |
| Middle and Higher Schools | 73 | 120 | 508 | 854 |
| Teacher Training Institutions | 26 | 31 | 73 | 68 |
| Vocational Schools | 21 | 15 | 56 | 52 |
| Colleges | – | 4 | 24 | 25 |
| Universities | 1 | 1 | 1 | 3 |

Source: Ibid.

Nevertheless, the intense power struggles during this period seriously changed the service provision 'game'. Political activity shifted from the local traditional arena to the district councils, where politicians vied with each other for the allocation of service infrastructure such as schools and health centres, and equipment such as tractors, etc. The basis of legitimacy for a local leader was his capacity to attract state resources to his village, clan or religious grouping. The patronage network set up by the ruling party led to the exacerbation of social inequalities as the 'big men' were variously successful in mobilizing state resources for their constituencies. Many of them were in fact often more interested in personal aggrandizement than in the welfare of their constituencies. Moreover, the nationalizations of voluntary sector service facilities and private enterprises were aimed primarily at political patronage and the building of political coalitions rather than the construction of new state forms of service provision.

It is part of the conventional wisdom that state-provided services collapsed as soon as Obote's regime was overthrown in 1971. The reality was much more complex. Riding on a populist tide, Amin's regime continued to expand state-controlled educational and health institutions. During the period 1970–75, state investments in health and educational facilities resulted in some growth (Tables 12.1 and 12.2). The number of state hospitals and medical centres grew by 3.6% and 8.2% per annum respectively. Growth in state health facilities was sufficient to compensate for the decline experienced in the voluntary sector. Performance in the expansion of educational facilities was equally impressive.

By 1975, the populist tide had started to subside. The 'economic war' declared by Amin in 1972 was beginning to take its toll, and organized opposition – especially from outside the country – was growing. The collapse of state-provided services accelerated from then on.

## Services Provided by Voluntary Agencies

The political struggles did not spare the voluntary agencies. The colonial legacy was a system in which primary education was provided by mission schools while higher education was provided by the government. Soon after independence the state moved to secularize the educational system and destroy the denominational character of the primary schools. The 1964 and 1970 Educational Acts were designed for this purpose: to reorganize the ownership and management of educational establishments. Unlike in Tanzania (see Chapter 11), this provoked resistance from the churches in Uganda, probably because the different denominations were closely associated with various political parties.

A similar policy was less successful in the health sector. Mission hospitals continued to function alongside the newly built state hospitals and dispensaries, but dependence on mission-based facilities in this period was, of course, reduced because of state expansion.

Parallel to the struggle between church and state for the control of educational facilities, community activities in education were widespread in the 1960s. Thus Uganda's Five Year Plan for 1966–71 noted that much of the capital investment in primary education is met by collective efforts of parents, who put up the schools themselves. The community efforts are supplemented by substantial contributions from the central government and local authorities. This matching of community and state resources was a prime mover in the rapid expansion of state-run services. Without community-based underpinning of these services, the expansion rates would have been much lower.

It is interesting to note that this matching was the basis for the expansion of state service provision both during Obote's regime and during the early populists years of Amin's rule. The disappearance of this populist support at the end of Amin's dictatorship did not seem to affect the expansion of state services. The explanations for this interesting phenomenon are given in the following section.

## Economic Collapse and the Illusion of Service Expansion (1975–86)

A few years into Amin's rule the economy collapsed. The coffee boom from 1975 to 1977 (when world prices increased by 350% because of frost in Brazil) gave only temporary respite to the downward spiral. Generally the external economic climate was harsh. In addition, the brutality of the Amin regime, its incompetence, the expulsion of large parts of the business community, and the flight of qualified manpower from the reign of terror all contributed to the economic collapse. The previous system of patronage employed by the UPC Government was replaced by a predatory system in which the military and local officials looted the rural areas with impunity. Insecurity of person and property became widespread. The rush for personal enrichment greatly weakened the state apparatus. The military men who were made provincial governors used their appointments to accumulate wealth, especially through participation in the sale of rural produce in *magendo* networks (Nabuguzi, 1992, 1993). The civil strife that followed Amin's fall destroyed the economic infrastructure even further. Factories and processing plants closed down. Prices of consumer goods multiplied, while the purchasing power of salaried workers plummeted. The political turmoil continued after Amin's downfall; between 1980 and 1986, five governments replaced each other in rapid succession.[1]

Quantitative evidence of the collapse shows that between 1970 and 1980, monetary GDP dropped by 25% – equivalent to a reduction of per capita GDP by about 42%. By 1980, imports and exports had fallen by two-thirds from their peak value of 1972, industrial production had dropped by 80%, the number of vehicles and electricity consumption had fallen to two-fifths of their 1970 value, and state revenues had plummeted. Prices of local manufactures skyrocketed. Inflation resulting from low supply was aggravated by the emission of currency as a means of financing budgetary deficits. The cost of living for low-income workers rose by more than 500% between 1971 and 1977, while the minimum wage rose by only 41% over the same period. Five years after Amin's fall from

---

[1] The UNLF (Uganda National Liberation Front), the Military Commission, UPC II under Obote, the Okello junta, and finally Museveni's National Resistance Movement.

power, in 1984, real wages were less than 10% of their value in 1971 (Ochieng, 1985; Jamal, 1988).

## State-Provided Services

With the rapid decline in the economy, increasing strife, and growing insecurity, it would have been logical to expect a similar collapse in state-provided services. In reality a more complicated situation emerged, which can be understood only by separating the trends in the physical expansion of service facilities from the actual service delivered. While a rapid physical expansion did take place between 1975 and 1986, the state was increasingly unable to run these services. Hence the actual service levels fell. From the users' point of view the expansion was illusory.

In other words, the dramatic increase in the number of state-owned health facilities, especially in the first half of the 1980s, was real enough, although the security situation must have prevented expansion in many areas and thereby left many communities unserved. But the expansion was not accompanied by a similar growth of operating and maintenance resources. In addition, the disruption of commercial networks destroyed the link between the pharmaceutical industry and the distribution of medical supplies. The resulting lack of medical equipment and drugs was combined with a dramatic drop in health personnel. Highly qualified staff (doctors in particular) fled the country. This brain drain started in the early 1970s. At that time there were 9,200 inhabitants per doctor; five years later the figure was 27,600. The expulsion of Asians and Amin's atrocities contributed significantly to this exodus. Similar or even worse declines occurred for nurses and auxiliaries (EEC, 1992: 45). By 1985 the state-run health services were seriously understaffed, underfinanced, and poorly equipped. The expansions from 1975 to 1986 therefore failed to result in improved services for the large majority of the population.

Educational services provided by the state followed a similar trend. Table 12.2 shows a rapid expansion in the number of state-owned schools from 1970, but especially in the early 1980s. In reality the educational services deteriorated, there was an exodus of expatriate teachers (which began in the early 1970s), standards dropped at all levels, and illiteracy receded only marginally. The drop in educational service levels started as soon as Amin came to power. His regime was suspicious of the intelligentsia and had several confrontations with secondary school and university students. But primary education standards also began to deteriorate, especially after the mid-1970s.

Educational statistics between 1970 and 1977, a critical period for changes in service provision in Uganda, indicate that overall there were slight increases in intake into government primary schools (from 46% to 58%). In post-primary education, however, intake dropped from 25% in 1972 to 23% in 1977. The pupil–teacher ratio in government schools increased from 33% in 1972 to 37% in 1978. Enrolment in government-aided primary schools increased from 719,000 in 1970 to 902,000 in 1974 but dropped in 1975 to 874,000. After

1976, public primary enrolments fluctuated, with increases of 10% in 1977, 6% in 1978, 1% in 1979, 5% in 1980, and 9% in 1981. By 1977, enrolments in government primary schools constituted 47% as compared with 20–25% for private schools (UNESCO, 1983).

However, a closer examination of the financial statistics shows that expenditures on education continued to drop in real terms until the mid-1980s. By 1984 they represented less than 20% of the level attained in the early 1970s (EEC, 1992). Payment of teachers' salaries absorbed most of the budget, with subsidies for scholastic materials, teaching aids and furniture dropping steadily.

In 1971, 29% of the school-going age group were in primary schools. By 1980 this figure was 56%. This increase occurred concurrently with a decrease in government expenditure on primary schools. Community and parental efforts maintained the educational system in this period. However, the absence of state resources gradually began to tell on the system. It is estimated that, by 1985, 40% of young people and adults of school-going age were illiterate. The drop-out rate also increased dramatically. As the 1980s approached, many parents were no longer able to afford school fees and some children preferred to engage in illegal transborder trade and hawking in urban areas in order to survive. Consequently drop-out rates at primary level and the number of repeaters increased. Up to 70-80% of primary school-leavers received no further education or training in the 1970s and 1980s.

Thus, although schools continued to function and even to increase in number and enrolment, there was a substantial drop in quality, as measured by material inputs, teacher qualifications, internal efficiency and performance in examinations. Administrative control and support services continued to deteriorate in the 1980s, while staff remained demoralized because of low pay. In addition, funds were routinely misappropriated through corruption both at the Ministry headquarters and at school level. Standards in schools deteriorated owing to lack of facilities, diminished teaching time, and lack of teachers. Subsidies to schools and universities were cut, provoking widespread resistance from students and teachers.

## Services Provided by Voluntary Agencies

The physical expansion of state facilities in the social services discussed above must have depended on a considerable mobilization of community resources. But for obvious reasons not much research on such issues was conducted from 1975 to 1986.

Nevertheless, it appears that the grass-roots demand for improved services was not much affected by the turmoil of the period – except, of course, in areas hit by outright war. Local resource mobilization must also have taken place on a large scale. State coercion of communities cannot have played a major role in this mobilization for the simple reason that the expansion of state-provided services could hardly have been a priority among the various factions fighting for power. On the other hand, communities and POs of various kinds were unable to build the physical infrastructure without matching resources from the state. These resources must therefore have been made available. Considering the widespread and increasing disintegration of the state in this period, POs may simply have converted state-owned buildings constructed for other purposes into health or education facilities and got them registered. Many local-level civil servants, working in disintegrating state bureaucracies on very low salaries, may have switched their loyalties away from the state towards the surrounding communities. They may therefore have helped the communities and POs to get hold of state-controlled resources to build the service facilities that were apparently so high on community priority lists. But, as noted earlier, this is to some extent speculation.

The situation looked different with respect to the running of facilities. Faced with collapsing services, POs and NGOs started organizing their own service provision or modified the way in which public facilities operated – especially from 1980 onwards. Alternative forms of private organization emerged based on local communities, individual entrepreneurs, NGOs or mission-based institutions.

Chapter 13 analyses in some detail how such organizations became active in primary education. In the health sector, private clinics, medical laboratories and pharmaceutical companies mushroomed all over the country. Many were owned by health personnel employed by the government. It was a privatization of sorts, but not as described in textbooks. Instead, state medical personnel used their official positions to gain access to official drugs and equipment, but sold them through private clinics. Private clinics reached the rural areas too. They were staffed by nurses and medical assistants on the government payroll. Rural shops started to sell pharmaceuticals. Some clinics shared personnel with government establishments, while others were independent. Yet others employed untrained personnel. There also seems to have been an increase in the number of patients attending traditional healers or doctors (see Chapter 1).

In addition to private services, health facilities run by NGOs and missions continued to provide medical services for which users paid a fee, but their operations were made increasingly difficult by the regime and the general unrest in the late 1970s. Muslim health institutions did, however, expand with state support from the Amin regime and with aid from Arab countries. All in all, the statistics in Table 12.1 show that the number of non-state hospitals and medical centres grew rapidly from 1975 to 1986. By the mid-1980s, a large proportion of the actual service delivery was provided by the voluntary sector, with the state playing an increasingly marginal role.

## The Slow Turn-around from 1987

Security and peace gradually returned to Uganda after 1986 following the military victory of the National Resistance Movement (NRM) under Museveni. For the first time for many years it was possible to consider how to rehabilitate the political, economic and social life of the country. It remains a considerable challenge.

The NRM Government introduced a unique brand of no-party democracy and attempted to come to terms with the complex political problems that had caused so much havoc in the past. Ethnic differences had been politicized and played out in political party affiliations. The NRM Government froze political parties for a period while it put in place a political structure embracing a broad political and ethnic base. A 'movement' non-party system (described below) evolved, largely hinged on popular local organization. The political debate in Uganda then focused on the justification for the freezing of party activity, the political system to be enshrined in a new constitution, and political demands from traditional monarchists and pseudo-monarchists. The old political parties (DP and UPC) challenged the NRM over the freeze of political party activities. The crucial issue was that of the distribution of power. The restoration of monarchies in 1993 which spurred a call for semi-autonomous entities threatened to be a strong point of contention between the central state and the powerful political lobbies.

The new non-party political–administrative framework referred to above is called the Resistance Council (RC) system. According to its opponents, the RC system is simply an attempt by the NRM to establish a political power base so as to undercut the support of the old political parties. But to the supporters of the RC system – many of whom do not necessarily belong to the NRM – it is an appropriate answer to the problems of promoting popular participation in development activities in a non-partisan way, and of dispersing power in society.

The RC system is elaborate. It links each small community into a hierarchy of committees that eventually reaches the national level. At the lowest level the basic RC cell is composed of at least ten households in a locality. These cells then expand into ever wider patterns (village, sub-county, county, district) with an RC council at each level, to form a pyramid-like hierarchy whose summit is the national parliament, composed of RC representatives at both county and district levels. Representatives are directly elected at the lowest level, but the higher the hierarchy the more indirect the representation becomes. Members of Parliament are, for example, elected by the RCs at county level, which are themselves indirectly elected by a college of RCs at the sub-county level.

The RCs are involved in a wide range of service provision at the local level. They are responsible for voluntary works, road maintenance, and the setting up of health units and schools. Moreover, they deal with domestic and land disputes and with law and order. Their role in this activity is analysed in detail in Chapter 14, which also provides more detailed accounts of the RC structure.

In addition to the non-party RC system, a decentralization of political and administrative power was initiated in 1990 (Uganda Government, 1993a, 1993b) at the instigation of the World Bank, but also in response to public demand. This aims to devolve some degree of autonomy in staff recruitment, preparation of development plans, financial control and service provision to the district level, where a revitalized local government machinery is being rebuilt.

The NRM is also trying to stem the tide of the past economic decline. A Structural Adjustment Programme (SAP) has been negotiated with the aid donors. Such programmes had already been tried in the early 1980s, but factional in-fighting and civil war then prevented their systematic implementation (Nabuguzi, 1994b). The SAP has since been more systematically implemented, although its political support within Uganda is uncertain. The conditionalities attached to the aid package are fairly standard. They involve:

- Budgetary and monetary reforms aimed at cutting down government spending by reductions of the labour force in the civil service, public enterprises and the military; removal of government subsidies on social services and consumer goods; and the privatization of parastatals.
- Fiscal reforms aimed at increasing state revenues through increased taxation of trade and incomes.
- Liberalization of the exchange regime and of internal and external trade.
- Poverty alleviation programmes aimed at assisting the 'new poor' who are hit by structural reform and the civil unrest of the past. This also involves assistance to local communities in constructing health and educational facilities (Uganda Government, 1989; Evans, 1994: 41).

The aim of the SAP in the services area is to pressure the state to increase its revenue-raising effort (through user fees) and to divest itself of much of the responsibility for service provision, including the removal of subsidies. This also entails a much larger role for the private for-profit sector and the voluntary agencies.

One of the basic assumptions of the SAP is that adjustment can only succeed if market discipline is imposed on the key producers of goods and services – including the state (Brett, 1991: 300). Consequently ways are sought to reduce the role of the state in the economy and to improve the accountability of the administrative and political elites. Liberalization and privatization are the key concepts behind the SAP.

All these policies have had direct consequences for service provision. Some effects are now emerging. The nearly 240,000-strong civil service has been substantially reduced, while a sizeable proportion of the military has been demobilized. Although inflation has been reduced, purchasing power for the majority of workers and peasants remains very low. It is difficult for people to make ends meet. Opposition to the structural adjustment measures has manifested itself through a number of strikes by urban workers and tax riots in the rural areas. Strikes to demand a 'living wage' are frequent in many government departments. Workers also strike in factories and parastatal firms but their position is weak because of deliberate attempts by the state to undermine the labour movement. To this should be added the fact that the structural transformations of the past decades have also made worker organization difficult. Workers have been forced to diversify their sources of income outside official or declared employment. This has reduced their capacity to exert collective pressure on government and employers.

From a macroeconomic perspective, however, some positive short-term results have emerged. The past decline in GDP has been halted and some positive growth has been recorded since 1987 (see Chapter 1). The improved security situation has undoubtedly played a major role in this. So has the inflow of concessionary aid, which now constitutes a significant proportion of government revenue, climbing up to nearly 60% of government expenditures in 1992. Public finance in Uganda in the 1990s can appropriately be defined as aid-driven.

The aid-financed SAP has an additional effect. Consistent with its privatization drive, donors are trying to switch some of their funds away from the state and towards the private and voluntary sector (see Chapter 3). This has encouraged the establishment of many new NGOs in Uganda, and has made it possible for international NGOs to expand their operations in the country. The details of this are discussed below.

## State-provided Services

The recent improvements in state allocation to the social services sector are not based on any significant improvements in Uganda's economic base. They are very dependent on donor assistance. This does not make them less important, but it does raise questions about their sustainability. The situation is, however, not the same in the health and education sectors.

The cornerstone of the liberal reform policy in the health sector is cost-sharing between the state and users. This, it is believed, will improve efficiency in production and use. It is also argued that, since the state has lost its capacity to provide free services, the solution is to institutionalize what *de facto* had become a payment for health services provided by the state.

However, a bill tabled in parliament in 1989 to implement cost-sharing was strongly opposed, despite the fact that Ugandans were already paying for their medication owing to the breakdown of government health services. This forced the government to shelve the scheme temporarily. Although cost-sharing continued to be practised on a local RC basis under some degree of decentralization, it remained a highly controversial subject. There remains substantial political resistance at the top, the President included, to implementing an overall cost-sharing strategy.

Why this resistance? Although state contributions to the health sector have receded considerably, there is still a high degree of interdependence between the informal health care system on which many people rely and the state health system – especially in terms of medical supply channels and equipment. Thus, reduction in state subsidies for public health would mean increased charges in both the formal and the informal health systems. Finally, it is argued that the national household budget survey conducted in 1989 indicates that the poor may not be able to pay even fairly low user charges (Uganda Government, 1991). This underscores the importance of a government presence in health service provision.

Decentralization of social services has also started. According to the New Health Plan drawn up by the NRM in 1989, for example, the district is expected to be the main implementation unit for health services. But the responsibilities of the district authorities, the Ministry of Local Government, the Ministry of Health, and the District Health Team will have to be streamlined. At the moment there is no clear accountability between these various actors. The district authorities have no direct control over the district hospitals which are under the Ministry of Health, and do not control NGO or private health services (Chapter 13 discusses the provision of primary education in the 1980s).

The new attempts to decentralize the political–administrative system that are now under way may result in more power – and resources – for the districts. The idea is to link the hierarchical system of political Resistance Councils with a parallel system of administrative units (World Bank, 1992a: iv). The objectives with respect to social services provision are to increase management efficiency and popular participation at the local level, and to improve financial performance through increased revenue generation[2] and rational expenditure decisions.

Implementation of the SAP has increased the state's capacity to finance basic services through increased donor support. But this is a short-term emergency measure. The ultimate aim of the SAP is that the health sector should be substantially privatized. It is, however, not yet clear how the income redistribution engineered by these programmes has affected access to health services by different social categories. The massive loss of income of urban workers and the new tax structures put in place may have created new vulnerable groups in addition to the rural poor who cannot afford market rates for health services. Furthermore, the short-term budgetary support of the SAP will not be able to tackle the structural problems that still bedevil the educational sector: the emphasis on higher rather than primary education, the drop in teacher performance, efficiency and quality, and the discrimination by gender, geographical location and family background.

## Services Provided by Voluntary Agencies

In the 1990s services provision by the voluntary sector must make a distinction between domestic NGOs and POs on the one hand, and international NGOs on the other. The latter have grown significantly in importance.

### NGOs and POs
The unprecedented economic crisis in Uganda has led to the emergence of vibrant local voluntary groups and community organizations. The introduction of Resistance Councils in the mid-1980s encouraged popular initiatives at local community level in service provision. They also became important channels for the moulding and recruitment of local leaderships. The results of mobilization and organization of local communities are visible in health, education, credit, environmental protection, law and order, etc.

In the health sector, mission hospitals regained their importance in service provision in the 1990s. The Catholic and Protestant churches owned and operated 42% of the country's hospitals. Non-state medical facilities contributed

---

[2] Local communities will be encouraged to support their health systems through user charges, voluntary contributions and retention of a large percentage of taxes collected at district level.

around 31% of total medical care. On the other hand, state channels of health service provision have in essence been 'privatized'. Although, in terms of ownership, the formal health system remained predominantly public in the 1980s, accounting for 86% of health facilities as compared with 14% by NGOs (Dodge, 1987: 106), in practice access to health services depended on ability to pay or on the private (informal) use of the existing state health delivery system by its staff. About 75% of expenditures on health were covered by out-of-pocket payments for services, whether the provider was government, private practitioners or NGOs. This was a popular manipulation of service provision to enhance access where formal channels had failed.

However, the state continues to play another important role *vis-à-vis* the non-state provision of health services. An increase in the training of nurses and medical assistants by the state-owned institutions has fed the informal health-care system with personnel, thus responding to the reduction in the number of doctors who had either fled the country or joined the private sector. The number of medical assistants doubled in the 1980s, while in the latter part of the decade the annual output of nurses increased by 21% (EEC, 1992). Since these categories of workers are in the lower echelons of the medical hierarchy and are therefore very poorly paid, they found ready employment in the private and informal markets.

While increasing privatization of the health delivery system may have improved allocative efficiency and cost-effectiveness, analysts are divided on the issue of accessibility. For example, Susan Whyte (1991: 147) argues that the state should encourage and guide local health-care initiatives rather than repress them. She recommends that such popular initiatives should be integrated into the local administrative control systems. On the other hand, Banugire (1987: 102) stresses the tendency for business clinics to maximize profits rather than render services. Issues of control, supervision and protection are crucial to the institutionalization of popular initiatives.

In the education sector, the main trend after 1987 has been a shift from public to 'private' education. Mission schools have regained importance, while the number of purely private schools increased. By 1992, purely private primary schools constituted 10% of the total number, while purely private secondary schools constituted 20% of the total (World Bank, 1992b). Mixed public–private schools also emerged. They are referred to as 'Tata' schools. The state provides the physical infrastructures but parents and communities shoulder the larger share of the costs of maintenance, salaries and educational materials. In these primary schools, by the end of the 1980s, parents contributed up to 90% of school requirements.[3] However, parents and communities have different capacities to pay for primary schooling. The system fosters inequalities in the provision of the education service. It is inherently discriminatory against pupils from poor families. Chapter 13 deals in more detail with these issues.

[3] More than 30% of the 'Tata' schools set up in the early 1980s had no permanent buildings, no proper laboratories, workshops or libraries. Generally the quality of education in Tata schools is poor.

*International NGOs*

International NGOs also proliferated and assumed an important role in service provision from the late 1980s. International aid agencies, whose presence in Uganda increased greatly after 1986, pointed to corruption, the lack of accountability, and the high degree of administrative control in state bureaucracies as justification for the preference for privatization and an increased interest in direct funding of NGOs. These NGOs operate in a wide range of activities: supply of medical equipment, family planning, water supply, construction, education, etc. They are a significant factor in health and educational services, although there are important variations between them in terms of quality and type of services provided.

By 1990, international NGOs were no longer marginal providers of social welfare but participated actively in the development process. While in the mid-1980s, local and international NGOs were in the range of 600 (de Coninck, 1992: 14), by 1992 the World Bank estimated their total number to range between 800 and 1,000 (World Bank, 1992c).

Their increased visibility threatens state legitimacy, which to a large extent is based on the provision of services in high demand. Therefore, as the Ugandan state rerooted itself after 1986, it also sought legal and administrative means to circumscribe and monitor NGO activities through the 1989 NGO Registration Act. The state even employed several government departments to attempt to make NGOs more accountable to the local authorities and provide a semblance of policy framework for them. These included a National Board of NGOs and an Aid Co-ordination Secretariat, as well as the Ministries of Finance and Economic Planning and Local Government. The multiplicity of intervening agencies, however, has made the aim of control futile and NGOs continue to operate with little government interference.

The issue of equity in service provision without proper co-ordination therefore arises. The role of NGOs as defenders of the poor has been challenged by some scholars. It is argued that NGO staff are emerging as a new privileged group surrounded by poverty, and that NGOs will tend to defend the interests of the relatively well-off in society; also that the middle classes will attempt to use NGOs as a launching pad into politics, and as a source of resources (Bratton, 1989a, 1989b; Clark, 1990; Fatton, 1992).

## Conclusion

There are many different actors engaged in service provision in Uganda today. They do not articulate with each other in a well-defined policy framework. People's organizations in health and education have largely perverted long-term state policies on equity and harmonization of service provision. Furthermore, they continue to manipulate state service provision by appropriating these services and using them to support their own initiatives. In addition, international aid agencies and NGOs use personnel from the state sector to provide social services, while foreign aid to the state sector for health and educational services provision is being rerouted to private provision.

POs and NGOs have developed their own dynamics within the economy. They have taken services to the rural areas which the state had not succeeded in doing. They are also allocating significant resources and employing personnel who have defected or been retrenched from a shrinking bureaucracy or have been demobilized from the military.

It is too early to discern the nature of the political relations NGOs and POs are forging with the state. However, their importance has been reflected in recent elections[4] during which choices between candidates in the rural areas were based on the perceived capacity of a candidate to provide local services through their connection to government or to an NGO, or through their individual wealth (Nabuguzi, 1994c).

An important lesson to be drawn from the Ugandan experience is the need for a strong state capable of maintaining law and order, fostering social justice, and setting the parameters for economic action and control of the bureaucracy and the army. NGOs were unable to thrive in Uganda during the period of state decay. Popular initiatives and community-based people's organizations also depend on the state for their services. Furthermore, only the state can tackle the systemic and structural causes of deficiencies in service provision.

Therefore, analysis of service trends should not introduce a false dichotomy of state/non-state. The nature of articulation between the two spheres is what determines the degree of access to these basic services. The definition of a new working environment for the various actors in the area of provision of social services is demanded of the Ugandan state.

---

[4]  For instance, the NRC elections for Parliament and the Constituent Assembly for the promulgation of a new Constitution.

# References

Banugire, F. (1987) 'The Impact of the Economic Crisis on Fixed Income Earners' in Wiebe and Dodge.

Bratton, M. (1989a) 'The Politics of Government–NGO Relations in Africa', *World Development* 17 (4): 569–87.

Bratton, M. (1989b) 'Beyond the State: Civil Society and Associational Life in Africa', *World Politics* 41 (3): 407–30.

Brett, E.A. (1991) 'Rebuilding Survival Structures for the Poor: Organizational Options for Reconstruction in the 1990s' in Hansen and Twaddle.

Clark, J. (1990) *Democratizing Development. The Role of Voluntary Organizations.* West Hartford, CT: Kumarian Press.

de Coninck, J. (1992) *Evaluating the Impact of NGOs in Rural Poverty Alleviation. Uganda Country Study.* ODI Working Paper No. 51. London: Overseas Development Institute.

Dodge, C.P. (1987) 'Rehabilitation or Redefinition of Health Services' in Wiebe and Dodge.

EEC (1992) *Country Profile. Uganda 1991*. Brussels: Eurostat.

Evans, A. (1994) 'Growth and Poverty Reduction in Uganda' in *Poverty Reduction and Development Cooperation*. CDR Working Paper No. 94.6. Copenhagen: Centre for Development Research, June.

Fatton, R. (1992) *Predatory Rule. State and Civil Society in Africa*. Boulder, CO and London: Lynne Rienner Publishers.

Hansen, H.B. and Twaddle, M. (eds) (1988) *Uganda Now, Between Decay and Development*. London: James Currey.

Hansen, H.B. and Twaddle, M. (eds) (1991) *Changing Uganda. Dilemmas of Structural Adjustment and Revolutionary Change*. London: James Currey.

Jamal, V. (1988) 'Coping Under Crisis in Uganda', *International Labour Review* 127 (6): 679–701.

Mujaju, A.B. (1976) 'The Role of the UPC as a Party in Government', *Canadian Journal of African Studies* 10 (3): 443–67.

Nabuguzi, E. (1992) 'Magendo, the State and Society in Uganda'. Ph.D. Thesis, Ecole des Hautes Etudes en Sciences Sociales de Paris, Paris.

Nabuguzi, E. (1993) 'Peasant Response to Economic Crisis in Uganda', *Review of African Political Economy* 56: 53–67.

Nabuguzi, E. (1994a) 'Ethnic Conflict and the Democratic Question in Uganda', *Journal of Behavioral and Social Sciences* 1994 (3): 111–30.

Nabuguzi, E. (1994b) *Structural Adjustment and the Informal Economy in Uganda*. CDR Working Paper No. 94.4. Copenhagen: Centre for Development Research, March.

Nabuguzi, E. (1994c) 'The Constitution Making Process and the Transition to Multi-party Democracy: Examples from Uganda' in Eastern and Southern Universities Research Programme, *The Cost of Peace*. Dar es Salaam: Tanzania Publishing House Ltd.

Ochieng, E.O. (1985) 'The Uganda Government Measures to Rehabilitate and Revive the Ugandan Economy' in P. Ndegwa, L.P. Mureithi and R.H. Green (eds) *Development Options for Africa in the 1980s and Beyond*. Nairobi: Oxford University Press.

Uganda Government (1989) *Programme for the Alleviation of Poverty and the Social Cost of Adjustment*. Entebbe: Government Printer.

Uganda Government (1991) *Report on the Uganda National Household Survey*. Kampala: Ministry of Planning and Economic Development.

Uganda Government (1993a) *Decentralization in Uganda. Popular Version of the Local Governments* (Resistance Councils.) Kampala: Decentralization Secretariat, February.

Uganda Government (1993b) *Decentralization in Uganda. The Policy and its Implications*. Kampala: Decentralization Secretariat, April.

UNESCO (1983) *Uganda. Educational Recovery and Reconstruction*. Paris: UNESCO, July.

Whyte, S.R. (1991) 'Medicines and Self-Help: The Privatization of Health Care in Eastern Uganda' in Hansen and Twaddle (1991).

Wiebe, P.D. and Dodge, C.P. (eds) (1987) *Beyond Crisis. Development Issues in Uganda*. Kampala: Makerere Institute of Social Research/Association of African Studies.

World Bank (1992a) *Uganda. District Management Study*. Washington, DC: World Bank, June.

World Bank (1992b) *Uganda. Growing Out of Poverty*. Washington, DC: World Bank.

World Bank (1992c) *Uganda. Social Sector Strategy*. Vol. I. Washington, DC: World Bank.

Wrigley, C.C. (1988) 'Four Steps towards Disaster' in Hansen and Twaddle.

Wunsch, J.S. and Olowu, D. (eds) (1990) *The Failure of the Centralized State: Institutions and Self-Governance in Africa*. Boulder, CO: Westview Press.

# 13

## FABIUS O. PASSI
## The Rise of People's Organizations
## in Primary Education in Uganda

Civil war and strife have affected all aspects of life in Uganda. Education in general and primary education in particular are good examples of this. What rightly used to be praised as one of the best educational systems in sub-Saharan Africa was wrecked in the 1970s and early 1980s. Nonetheless, the demand for education has remained high – even during periods of unrest and civil war. The provision of primary education has in large part been organized and financed at the community level with limited inputs from the state.

This chapter describes and analyses the upsurge in primary education over the last two decades. On the one hand, it shows the enormous potential and resilience of people's organizations, such as the Parent–Teacher Associations (PTAs) that now *de facto* run primary education on the ground. On the other hand, it also shows many of the serious problems of equity, quality and disintegration that result when the state is unable to provide basic services for its citizens. The first part of the chapter provides a short historical background to the present situation in primary education. Then comes a brief analysis of the rise of PTAs and their various roles in primary education in relation to School Management Committees (SMCs) and local government from independence on, followed by consideration of a number of issues arising from the prominent role of POs in primary education.

## Primary Education Before Independence

The early development of Uganda's education system was largely due to the pioneering work of voluntary agencies, mainly Christian missionaries, who eventually founded and ran schools in many parts of the country. Their initial aim was to raise the status of the indigenous people and convert them to Christianity. The early years of formal education were not therefore for the masses but for a small elite of chiefly and rich families.

In the following sub-sections, major changes in the financing and administration of primary education prior to independence are highlighted, because some of the features of the colonial system have survived in modified form until the present.

## Financing

The church, the colonial government, the community and the schoolchildren themselves were the important revenue sources. The financing of primary education was decentralized. Each church congregation set aside funds for education from the general revenue of the diocese. In this way, for example, the Mill Hill Fathers contributed up to £2,000 to Ugandan schools in 1910–12 and between 1909 and 1911 Anglican Church aid amounted to £4,151 (Colonial Office, 1911). The significance of missionary contributions continued until the late 1930s. From then on two factors affected the trend of financing education in Uganda. Christian missionary education concentrated on a few selected areas of the country, neglecting areas where Christianity had little impact. But the protectorate government was uncomfortable with the alienation of the non-Christian community. The 1942 Education Ordinance which devolved primary education to local governments aimed at redressing the situation. Moreover, World War II had adverse effects on missionary contributions as a result of economic measures introduced by their controlling bodies in Europe. By 1950 mission contributions amounted to only about one-fifth of recorded expenditure on education (Uganda Protectorate, 1950).

The second most important source of finance for education was the local communities, who contributed land on which schools were built, plus labour and other (in-kind) resources. On top of this, parents paid some school fees. The third source was made up of the direct contributions of the schoolchildren, who supplemented school resources by participating in self-help activities. For example, by 1912 schools under the White Fathers had planted 200,000 coffee and 80,000 rubber trees (Wandira, 1972: 218). Also the repair of school buildings was a normal activity for pupils. The older pupils provided the labour in a school system in which communal activities were a common feature. The importance of missionary and community contributions in the financing of education in Uganda was underscored by the Phelps–Stokes Commission:

> Practically every school in Uganda is a gift from the native community and education is being financed by the fees of the people and missionary financial sacrifice to a degree not visible anywhere else in Africa (Jones, 1925: 153).

Finally, the colonial government made some contribution. It started to give limited funds to schools from 1903. The initial state grant-in-aid to education was small (£10) (Wandira, 1972: 226), but the grant was consistently raised over the years. Ten years later half the school funds (£5,588) were provided by the colonial state (Colonial Office, various years).

In spite of the growing state support, financial requirements fell short of demand. Thus the Phelps–Stokes Commission recommended that the Protectorate Government should not only take over the direction of educational policies in the country but should also give adequate funds to the missionaries for running and building schools. The government responded by establishing the Department of Education in 1925 and setting aside 7% of its annual budget for education. This enabled the expenditure of £136,676 on primary education in 1939.

However, primary education faced a setback during World War II. The policy of self-sufficiency adopted by the colonial government resulted in strict economic measures that reduced expenditures on education. Thus the share of the total budget spent on education dropped from 8.1% in 1939 to 6.3% in 1942 (Uganda Protectorate, 1939, 1942). Improvements were registered after the war. Some 10% of government expenditure was allocated to education in 1950. Just before independence some 70% of the African pupils attending primary schools were enrolled in schools aided by the government.[1]

The Protectorate Government received minimum assistance from outside, although the budget deficits for education were occasionally balanced by the British Treasury. During the period 1940–60, financial contributions came from various development funds such as the Colonial Development Fund and the Colonial Development and Welfare Fund. Unfortunately, information on these funds is difficult to obtain.

## Administration

The evolution of organs for the administration, ownership and control of schools was closely associated with the development of the church machinery for consultation and decision-making. The close relationship between church and school was inevitable, because schools were established and developed as part and parcel of the work of churches. They continued for a long time to be regarded as belonging to the missionaries.

In 1904, the Board of Education was established to assist foundation bodies in managing schools; it was dominated by church dignitaries. Below the Board, the control of education followed the existing ecclesiastical system. For instance, from 1910 the Native Anglican Church became the legal owner of the various schools previously owned by the Anglican Church Missionary Society which started to set up schools in 1884.

The Education Ordinance of 1927, perhaps in response to the Phelps–Stokes Commission's recommendations, gave the Director of Education power to direct and control education policy. It recommended that the government and the missions should continue to work together, with the former providing policy guidelines and financial assistance while the missions continued to own and run the schools. The Director of Education could withhold aid for a school which did not meet specified education and bookkeeping standards.

---

[1] Asians had a few schools of their own. The only two European schools were established in the late 1950s. Europeans were sending their children to Nairobi and Dar es Salaam (Uganda Protectorate,, various years).

The 1927 Ordinance did not recommend government ownership of schools. Thus, government intervention in education did not lead to a concerted effort to build state schools. However, in 1942 primary education was delegated to local governments.[2] This was aimed partly at reducing the missions' influence in education and partly at committing the local authorities to raise funds for education. However, since many of them were poor, the Protectorate Government had to step up its financing of primary education by providing grants to local governments.

## Primary Education Since Independence

To many Africans independence meant not only 'freedom' but also 'free' provision of services (Chapter 1). As a result, the demand for education increased.

Although statistics on education should be treated with caution,[3] they do show a considerable, and at times extremely rapid, expansion of primary education, since independence. It is useful to analyse this expansion in relation to the three distinct periods into which Nabuguzi divides the post-colonial years in Chapter 12. He labels the period from independence to 1975 as the 'centralizing' period. He sees the period from 1975 to 1986 as a period of 'economic collapse and illusion of service expansion'. In contrast, he regards the years from 1987 onwards as a period of 'slow turn-around'.

Table 13.1 shows the quantitative growth in primary education since independence. The administrative and financial changes that took place in each period are analysed below. The changes in the general political–economic context are analysed by Nabuguzi.

Table 13.1  Uganda: Expansion in Primary Education Since Independence (Annual Growth Rates)

|            | 1963–74 | 1975–86 | 1987–91 |
|------------|---------|---------|---------|
| Schools    | 2[a]    | 8       | 4[b]    |
| Teachers   | 6       | 8       | 7       |
| Enrolment  | 5       | 8       | 6[b]    |

*Source:* Ministry of Education (1991) and World Bank (1991): Table 6.1.
[a] 1965–74.
[b] Includes some 950 private primary schools with approximately 10% of total enrolment.

[2] Starting in 1927 local government contributions had focused on building schools. However, local governments also instituted bursary and scholarship schemes to support needy students.
[3] There are several reasons for this: (i) the significant difference between sources; (ii) the tendency to over-reporting because the allocation of central government resources to districts depended on district-level reporting; (iii) classification problems.
   Some examples: 2,000 out of 9,000 schools recorded in 1991 are 'sub-standard' and offer less than the officially prescribed seven grades of instruction. The physical quality of some 'schools' hardly justifies the label. And it is not always clear how private primary schools are counted (in 1991 there were 950 such schools – mostly sub-standard – with about 10% of the primary enrolment). The figures used here are provided by the Ministry of Education and are similar to those used by the World Bank (1991).

*1963–74*

During the first decade after independence the number of schools, teachers and pupils grew fairly rapidly as indicated in Table 13.1. But underlying this trend was a deliberate attempt by the state to limit the influence of the churches on primary education. Thus in 1963 the government established its own administrative machinery to manage primary education. School Management Committees (SMC) were formed and Education Officers were appointed to replace missionary Boards of Education and School Supervisors, respectively. Although the ownership of schools was not affected, this reduced the influence of the missionaries (or owners) who reacted by reducing funding. This meant that the financing of primary education had to rely more on the central government, the community and parent participation. The latter gave birth to Parent–Teacher Associations (PTAs), more about which later.

The government financing of primary education since independence was the responsibility of the Ministries of Education and Local Government. The latter allocated three types of grants to the districts,[4] namely block, deficiency and capital grants. Block grants were given to cover expenditures on health, agriculture, water supplies, education, etc. Deficiency grants were sometimes given to local authorities that failed to balance their budgets. None of these grants were tied to any particular service and the distribution among sectors depended on the priorities of the local authorities. Finally, capital development grants covered the costs of erecting buildings, buying furniture and equipment. The Ministry of Education was allocated Development Teachers' Grants which covered the payment of teachers' salaries and Capital Grants earmarked for training purposes.

Community participation focusing on building schools was widespread. In the rural and urban areas people provided labour and cash, respectively, to match government inputs. Parents also paid nominal school fees as stipulated by government and were occasionally asked to contribute building funds depending on the specific investment project undertaken by individual schools.

It was the combined resources of the government, the communities and the parents that, in the first decade after independence, made expansion of primary education possible. And it was the government contributions which were the most important. This situation changed significantly during the following decade.

*1975–86*

As Table 13.1 indicates, this period was one of very rapid quantitative growth – faster than in both the preceding and the following decade. It was also a period of upheavals, civil war and widespread insecurity. That primary education expanded fast under these circumstances is generally not acknowledged, but it

---

[4] Local authorities could also raise their own resources (e.g. graduated tax) to supplement their income, but their capacity was very limited, even after the local government reform in 1967 which gave them more powers.

highlights the enormous resilience of parents and people's organizations and their strong demand for education, even under the direst of circumstances.

Amin's regime came to power in 1972. Soon thereafter the economy started to collapse (see Chapter 12). The effects on primary education of this and the liberation war that started at the end of the 1970s were enormous. They included the destruction of infrastructures and consumable goods; the collapse of the government machinery in many areas; the destruction of schools through burning, looting and vandalization; the killing and displacement of pupils, some dropping out of the school system and many joining the army; and the killing and displacement of the teachers, some retiring from the profession. Although the war damage inflicted on the educational system has not been evaluated, in momentary terms it is likely to amount to billions of shillings.

This is not reflected in the quantitative data presented in Table 13.1. They show a rapid expansion of primary education, but the figures hide a drastic fall in the overall standard of education (World Bank, 1993a: vol. II). Quantitative growth and qualitative decline went hand in hand. There are several reasons for this.

The ability of the state to run services declined rapidly as the economy collapsed. Nevertheless, the Amin regime – and later the second Obote regime – did allocate some funds for the expansion of the school system. In this way the regimes did respond to a popular demand for education, although the demand far surpassed the commitments of the government. Moreover, assistance from the Gulf States and the Islamic world grew during the Amin regime in the 1970s. Part of this aid went to education, especially Quranic schools. Reliable information is not available but these inflows are believed to have been substantial.

The expansion also depended on a considerable mobilization of community resources, but how this was done is not well researched, although Nabuguzi makes some interesting observations. It is, nevertheless, clear that, as the ability of the state to run the schools declined rapidly in the 1980s, new forms of organizations emerged – notably the PTAs. A more detailed analysis of these is presented in the next section.

By the mid-1980s more pupils than ever before were in primary school, but the quality of education was low compared with the past – especially in marginalized and war-torn areas. Illiteracy was increasing and drop-out rates were climbing.

## 1987 and Onwards

Nabuguzi marks 1987 as the start of slow turn-around. Although insurgency and rebel activities continued in eastern and northern Uganda up to 1989, civil strife climaxed in 1986 when the National Resistance Army took power. Gradually most parts of the country became peaceful.

In quantitative terms the expansion of primary education slowed down after 1986. Since then the thrust of government policy has been on the rehabilitation and development of the war-ravaged educational institutions (Ministry of Planning and Economic Development, 1991). Various projects, financed by the government and donors, are now under implementation.

The government, for example, spent U.Shs. 200 million on building materials supplied to schools in 19 districts.[5] The needy schools were selected on the basis of reports and recommendations made by the District Education Officers. The Ministry of Local Government and local authorities are the implementing agencies.

Moreover, a three-year programme, co-financed by the government and the World Bank, aims at expanding access to education by supporting community rehabilitation of the existing primary schools and the construction of additional classrooms. It is part of the Programme for the Alleviation of Poverty and Social Adjustment (PAPSCA) which was started in 1990. The estimated cost is US$1,265 m. Schools in 12 districts, selected on the basis of poverty, war damage and other needs by their District Education Officers, will be assisted under this scheme. It will cover 2,300 schools with some 750,000 students. The proposed Northern Uganda Reconstruction Programme, jointly funded by the government and the World Bank, is expected to supplement the already operating rehabilitation programmes, as discussed above.

The NGO projects aimed at primary education are operational in twelve districts.[6] The work of these organizations has simply begun and has not expanded because of the limited infrastructure in the areas of operation and the lack of an effective co-ordinating body for the NGOs.

As in the previous periods, people's organizations play a significant role, as explained in detail in the next section.

Regardless of all these initiatives, and the relative peace that Uganda now enjoys, primary education is still in a precarious state. Although by 1990 most children entered primary school, the drop-out rates are very high. In the last year of primary school (class VII), the gross enrolment ratio was only 48% for boys and 29% for girls.[7] Two explanations are generally believed to account for

---

[5]  Tororo, Palisa, Iganga, Kamuli, Jinja, Mukono, Mpigi, Luwero, Masindi, Kabarole, Hoima, Mbarara, Kabale, Kasese, Kisoro, Rukungiri and Kalangala.

[6]  The districts and NGOs involved are:

| | |
|---|---|
| Apac | – SCF (Save the Children Fund) |
| Arua | – LWF (Lutheran World Federation) |
| Gulu | – ACORD (Agency for Cooperation and Research in Development) |
| Kabarole | – PC (The Pentecostal Churches) |
| Kitgum | – Oxfam |
| Kumi | – Vision Terudo |
| Lira | – SCF |
| Moyo | – SCF/LWF |
| Mubende | – LWF |
| Nebbi | – ACFODE (Action for Development) |
| Soroti | – SCF |
| Kabale | – World Vision |

[7]  Figures are from World Bank (1993a, vol. I: 31–3). This source also notes that the enrolment figures by district are too unreliable to justify an assessment of geographical inequalities in primary education.

this situation. One is that the cost to parents of educating their children is too high for the poorer parents to afford (Ministry of Education, 1991). The other is that poor learning conditions discourage school attendance.

Central government financing of primary education is on the increase, reaching 1.3% of GDP in the 1992/93 budget and implying an average real growth rate of over 20% compared with 1989 (World Bank, 1993b: 110).[8] Yet it remains significantly lower than the levels in neighbouring Kenya, where central government recurrent expenditure on primary education is 4.9% of GDP. Local authority financing of education is non-existent in most localities (World Bank, 1993a). Donor funding of primary education, briefly touched upon above, is still modest – reaching only 4% of donor assistance in 1989/90 (Republic of Uganda, 1991a).

As in the civil war period, primary education would simply collapse without contributions from parents and communities. They contribute around 65–90% of the total funding required by the school (World Bank, 1993a, vol. I: 35). The rest of this chapter focuses on analysing this key feature of primary education.

# People's Organizations in the Provision of Primary Education

De facto Uganda now has a public primary school system which is largely under private management. This becomes apparent when the roles of the School Management Committee (SMC)[9] and the Parent–Teacher Association (PTA) are analysed.

The majority of primary schools (some 8,000 out of 9,000) are government-owned and aided. The SMCs manage the primary schools on behalf of the Ministry of Education and Sport. They are legally empowered to raise additional school funds and to supervise their utilization. The official sources of funds for the SMCs consist of school fees, bursaries and grants in respect of pupils; monies accruing from the sale of products; gifts, donations or endowments; and building funds, meal fees, etc.

However, as stated earlier, these funds and the grants from other official sources are insufficient. Additional money is needed to top up teachers' salaries, to buy textbooks and uniforms, and to pay for meals and transport. This is where the PTAs come in. Their growth rests on two factors. Firstly, communities, parents and pupils believe that the private benefits of education are high and direct. They are therefore prepared to shoulder a heavy burden to get access to education. Secondly, the official system has failed to deliver the goods.

[8] If teachers were to be paid a living wage, the resulting total cost of primary education is about 3.4% of GDP. It should also be added that it is not known how local authorities and central government actually spend grants earmarked for education.
[9] The SMC consists of representatives of parents (3), government (3), the PTA (1) and the foundation body (1).

*Organization and Financing*

The PTAs were originally started as school welfare associations in 1967 (Muwonge-Keweza, 1991: 71). They have no legal powers to own or manage government-aided schools. Every PTA has a constitution. These may vary from one school to another, but the basic components are similar; an example is shown in Appendix 1.

The general meeting is the ruling assembly for the PTA. The executive committee members are democratically elected during the annual general meeting and they serve a two-year term. This committee usually meets twice a term or six times a year to discuss school business. It is guided by the following general objectives: to bring together parents, teachers and pupils; to liaise with the School Management Committee; to promote and maintain the academic and moral standards of the school; and to cater for the welfare of students and teachers. Clearly these objectives do not provide scope for policy-making, decision-making or policy implementation, but this is consistent with the non-executive role of PTAs. They are in principle facilitators and their recommend-ations have to be approved by the SMC before they can be implemented.

Since the 1980s PTAs have become the major funding organs of primary education. They usually tap two main sources: first, PTA fees, which they have constantly raised. Table 13.2 provides data on PTA fees for a government-aided and a private primary school, which, in the absence of national-level data, can be used to illustrate the level of PTA contributions towards financing primary education. It should be noted that PTA charges vary from one school to another. The table shows that parents' contributions in 1992 ranged from U.Shs. 40,000 for government schools to U.Shs. 100,000 for private schools for P1–P4 (the first four grades), and U.Shs. 43,000 to U.Shs. 150,000 for the last two grades. It also shows the rapid growth in fees over the last decade. These fees to the PTAs should be compared with those that parents pay to the school through the SMC. Known as tuition fees, they amounted to U.Shs. 5,000 for P1–P4 and U.Shs. 8,000 for P5–P7 in 1991/92, of which the government pays

Table 13.2  PTA Charges in Sample Primary Schools, 1980–91 (in Uganda shillings per annum)

| Year | Grades I–IV | | Grades V–VII | |
|------|-------------|------------------|--------------|---------------|
|      | Public School[a] | Private School[b] | Public School | Private School |
| 1992 | 40,000 | 100,000 | 43,000 | 150,000 |
| 1990 | 15,000 | 45,000 | 20,000 | 100,000 |
| 1988 | 12,000 | 35,000 | 15,000 | 85,000 |
| 1980 | 6,000 | 25,000 | 10,000 | 40,000 |

*Source:* School Bursar Records.
[a] Kyambogo Government Primary School
[b] Kireka Private Primary School.

one half and parents the other. In other words, parents typically pay 15 to 40 times as much to the school through the PTA as they do through the SMC.

Secondly, PTAs raise funds from the community, private organizations, ministries and industrialists and from productive projects. Both domestic and external donors are solicited. PTAs with influential (rich, educated, retired, civil servants) executive members have managed to use their links successfully to mobilize substantial resources for their schools. Such funds may range from very low to substantial, depending on the school, its location and its connections and prestige.[10]

## Benefits and Costs

A definite benefit of the PTA system is that it has led to improvements in educational performance. Other things being equal, the absence of PTAs would imply less money for the construction of new schools, building repairs, purchase of school books and stationery, teachers' salaries, etc., and this would lead to a decline in the quantity and quality of education. For, although no empirical surveys have been made, there appears to be a positive relationship between costs per pupil and academic performance (*New Vision*, 3 February 1993). However, other factors may, of course, also be significant for academic performance (parents' background, etc.). And the PTA system is not free from problems of both operation and equity.

Operational problems relate to the working relationships between PTA executives and SMCs, as well as between PTA executives and PTA members. PTAs and SMCs keep and administer separate accounts. PTAs have a financial edge over SMCs and many have tended to use this advantage to take *de facto* control of their schools. PTA executives have tended to participate in a wide range of school activities such as guiding the academic programmes and extra-curricular activities, providing school menus, recruitment of teachers, and so on, areas in which they are not legally permitted to be involved. This has often brought them into conflict with the SMCs. In some cases, the executives of the management committee have worked hand in hand with the PTA executives. This has given PTAs a stronger grip over their schools. A number of schools, especially in Kampala and other urban areas, have been forced[11] to amalgamate PTA executive committees with the management committees or hold joint meetings in order to reduce conflicts.

The PTA executive committees also face problems in executing their duties because parents hold them responsible for what they often regard as exorbitant school charges. The financial burden has at times raised uneasiness among the

[10] Most of the donations are in the form of building materials such as roofing sheets, timber or cement. In a small survey of four Kampala schools by the author, these donations ranged from U.Shs. 0.8 m for one school to U.Shs. 10 m for another in 1990. The schools with richer parents also received most external support.

[11] Stipulated in a government directive to urban schools. If results are positive, the government intends either to abolish PTAs or to merge them with SMCs.

poorer members about their ability to participate effectively in school affairs. The poor and less educated parents tend to be dominated by the richer and more educated ones.

As noted earlier, the PTA rates are high, especially in private primary schools. PTAs compel parents to pay these higher fees, and promptly too, although they have no legal powers to do so. In fact, a 'privatization' of the power to tax has taken place. Parents who fail to pay have their children sent away from schools. This means that the schools are becoming increasingly discriminatory in favour of the rich parents, with PTAs gradually ceasing to be voluntary associations of parents and teachers. This has tended to reinforce inequalities between social groups. It is also obvious that schools located in better-off areas are able to charge higher fees than those in marginal areas. The link between the rich PTAs and external institutions (e.g. foreign and local donors), already noted earlier on, has tended to exacerbate this situation.

PTA activities have also led to unplanned expansions of school structures, which has put enormous pressures on the Ministry of Education which is responsible for supplying teachers. This matching of resources is essential to the operation of the school system. But, since school expansions are often made

Table 13.3 The Official Roles of the MOE, the MLG, the PTAs and the SMCs in the Provision of Primary Education Since the 1980s

| Task | Government-aided Schools | Private Schools |
| --- | --- | --- |
| Tuition Fee | MLG (50%)<br>Parents (50%)[a] | Parents (100%) |
| Investment | MLG<br>PTA & NGOs | Owner<br>PTA |
| Teachers' Incentives[b] | MOE<br>PTA | PTA |
| Teacher Training and Transfer | MOE<br>(PTA Influence) | MOE<br>Foundation Body[c]<br>SMC/PTA |
| Financial Management | SMC<br>Headteacher<br>PTA | Headteacher<br>Owner<br>PTA |
| Discipline/Expulsion | SMC<br>DEO<br>(PTA Influence) | Owner<br>PTA<br>Headteacher |
| Inspection | MOE | MOE |
| Exams | UNEB[d] | UNEB |
| Policy Matters | MOE<br>(PTA – No Influence) | MOE<br>(PTA – No Influence) |

[a] These tuition fees are controlled by the SMC.
[b] Monetary incentives to top up teachers' salaries.
[c] The founder of the school such as the church, the community or the government.
[d] Uganda National Examination Board which has the monopoly over school examinations and certification.

without involving the Ministry, lack of co-ordination has led to serious shortages of teachers, especially in the poorer schools and locations.

The official roles of the Ministry of Education, the Ministry of Local Government (MLG), the PTAs and the SMC in the provision of primary education are given in Table 13.3. The MOE is supposed to have considerable power over school affairs, especially in government-aided schools. In reality, the PTA often holds a dominant position based on the resources it controls. This is especially true for private schools in which the Ministry's only contributions are in teacher training, specification of the curriculum and the inspection and administration of public examinations.

The influence of PTAs has exceeded that allowed by law. The PTAs have in some cases been dictatorial in the transfer of headmasters and teachers; and they have strongly influenced matters regarding school discipline, 'coaching', extra-curricular activities and examination standards. They have especially strong influence on the items or services for which the PTA fees are directly charged.[12] However, they have done little to influence policy on school fees, syllabuses, the setting of examinations and the selection for secondary school, although in 1992 PTAs in Luwero District succeeded in getting the government to reverse the cancellation of the Primary Leaving Examinations of their schools by mounting protests and massive demonstrations in Kampala.

Suggestions to control PTAs have been, and continue to be, made. In 1989 the Ministry of Education recommended the introduction of uniform fees for all schools. This would redress inequalities inherent in the present PTA system. But the recommendation is difficult to implement unless the government is prepared to step up its contribution substantially or to accept a decline in the quantity and quality of education provision. Both options are hard to swallow. Furthermore, the government has expressed interest in formulating a unified constitution for PTAs, providing particular parameters for their functioning, streamlining their activities and harmonizing them with those of SMCs (Republic of Uganda, 1992). More specifically, it is intended that decisions made by PTAs on fund-raising should be brought under the scrutiny of SMCs before they become effective. This will be equally difficult to implement for the reasons already stated above.

## Conclusion

From 1975 for ten years Uganda was torn by civil war and suffered economic collapse. Yet primary education expanded faster in this decade than in both the preceding and the following years. This shows the enormous resilience of parents and POs at the grass-roots level who took over government schools and ran them during this period. Their initiatives and resources are still crucial to primary education in Uganda.

But the Uganda experience also shows the severe limitations of a public

---

12 Teachers' salary incentives; school buildings; coaching of pupils for examinations; welfare of pupils and teachers; provision of teaching material; school transport; etc.

school system which is *de facto* financed and managed by grass-roots organizations. The access to schooling for children from poorer families, and families in poorer districts, is much lower than in Kenya and Tanzania. Similarly the enrolment of girls is significantly lower in Uganda than in the two neighbouring countries.

The quality of education is generally also low with significant differences between schools. There seems to be a close relationship between the social and economic status of local communities and the quality of education provided in the local school.

Future improvements in primary education in Uganda will, therefore, depend on the willingness and capacity of the state to contribute significantly more to this sector than in the past. Such a change appears to be under way, if judged from a recent government policy statement. This states that the focus for the new decade and beyond will be primary education, in terms of both universal access and higher quality. It also acknowledges that this will entail shifting resources from secondary and tertiary institutions towards the primary level (Republic of Uganda, 1991a). Even if this does actually happen, it will take years before the quality of and access to education in Uganda are on a par with those of neighbouring countries.

# Appendix I: Excerpts from the Constitution of a Parent–Teacher Association

The following is taken from the constitutions of Wandegeya Primary School, Kampala.

Article 3: The aims shall be (a) to foster unity among its members, (b) to promote high academic and social standards among the pupils, (c) to encourage all worthy religious ideals and practices in the school and (d) to ensure that Islamic laws and principles are adhered to in the running of the school.

Article 4: Membership shall be open to (a) parents/guardians of bona fide pupils, (b) teachers of the school and (c) honorary members elected by the Executive Committee (such persons shall have no voting rights).

Article 5: Termination of membership shall apply when (a) a parent/guardian no longer has a child in the school and (b) a teacher ceases to be employed at the school.

Article 6: *Membership Fee* shall be U.Shs. 30 only, payable in respect of each parent. A parent shall also be required to pay the foundation fee, determinable by the Management Committee.

Article 7: The Executive Committee shall (a) run the affairs of the Association, (b) comprise the following: the Chairman; the Treasurer; the Secretary; the headmaster; 3 teachers elected by the teachers; and 3 parents elected by the Association at a General Meeting; and (c) be elected at an Annual General Meeting and shall serve for a period of two years.

Article 8: Elections of (a) the chairman, vice-chairman, secretary and treasurer shall be by secret ballot after nomination and seconding of candidates; (b) committee members shall be by show of hands after nomination and seconding; and (c) teacher members shall be by secret ballot by the teachers themselves.

Article 9: Meetings of (a) the General Assembly shall be held at least once a year ... A decision shall be carried by a simple majority of the members present and voting; and (b) the Executive Committee shall be held at least once a term ... Any Executive Committee member who fails, without good cause, to attend two consecutive meetings shall forfeit membership of the same, and members of the Executive Committee shall be eligible for re-election ... all matters at the meeting shall be recorded in a minute book ...

# References

Colonial Office (various years) *Annual Report on Education*. Entebbe: Government Printer.

Jones, J. (1925) *The Phelps–Stokes Commission Reports*. London: Thomas Nelson.

Low, D.A. and Pratt, R.C. (1960) *Buganda and British Overrule, 1900–1955: Two Studies*. London: Oxford University Press.

Ministry of Education (1989) 'Education for National Integration and Development'. Report of Education Policy Review Commission. Kampala: Ministry of Education.

Ministry of Education (1991) *Five Year Investment Program*. Kampala: Ministry of Education, June.

Ministry of Planning and Economic Development (1991) *Background to the Budget 1991–92*. Entebbe: Government Printers.

Muwonge-Kewaza, P.A. (1991) 'The Effect of Dual Control on the Management of Primary Education in Kampala District'. Unpublished M.Ed. Dissertation, Makerere University, School of Education, Kampala.

Republic of Uganda (various years) *Annual Report of Education Department*. Entebbe: Government Printer.

Republic of Uganda (1991a) *Five Year Sector Investment Programme. 1992/93 – 1996/97*. Vol. I. Kampala: Ministry of Finance and Economic Planning.

Republic of Uganda (1991b) *Background to the Budget 1991–92*. Kampala: Ministry of Finance and Economic Planning.

Republic of Uganda (1992) *Education for National Integration*. Government White Paper. Kampala: Ministry of Education, April.

Uganda Protectorate (various years) *Annual Report of the Education Department*. Entebbe: Government Printer.

Wandira, A. (1972) *Early Missionary Education in Uganda*. Kampala: Makerere University Press.

World Bank (1991) *Public Choices for Private Initiatives*. Vol. II. Washington, DC: World Bank, 12 February.

World Bank (1993a) *Uganda. Social Sector Strategy*. Vols I and II. Washington, DC: World Bank, 6 April.

World Bank (1993b) *Uganda. Growing Out of Poverty*. Washington, DC: World Bank, 31 March.

# 14

## PER TIDEMAND
## Popular versus State Provision
## of Local Justice

The Resistance Councils
in Uganda

Maintenance of law and order and security are the most essential functions of the state, according to the conventional wisdom. However, for most of the post-colonial period the Ugandan state has not even been able to maintain these minimal functions. During Amin's rule (1971–79) the state apparatus became renowned for its disregard of the rule of law and human rights. The situation worsened when Obote returned to power (1980–85). The central government lost control, notably of the security organs and the army. This soon resulted in a total breakdown of whatever law and order had existed before. The peasants in the southern part of the country especially suffered. State-inspired violence is estimated to have accounted for the death of up to half a million people in the period after Amin (Hooper and Pirouet, 1989).

The National Resistance Movement (NRM) that took over power in 1986 not only claimed to restore peace, justice, law and order, but also argued for greater popular control of these crucial functions. As Museveni (1992) put it:

> When we talk about the 'rule of law' we should always ask ourselves: whose law? Against whom are these laws and in whose interests do they operate? The laws we adopted at independence were colonial laws meant to serve the interests of the colonialists. We must revise these laws to suit our people and our present circumstances.

This chapter deals only briefly with the colonial period, but concentrates on the period from 1980 till today, during which a guerrilla war was fought from 1981 to 1986. Alternative forms of democracy and regulation of law and order and security were experimented with during this war, especially within the liberated areas of the Luwero Triangle in the southern part of the country. In these areas, elected committees, the 'Resistance Councils' (RC), became responsible for virtually all functions previously performed by the state. The NRM eventually won the war. Under Museveni the new regime seeks to institutionalize some of the war-time experiments. The most important political reform is the political–administrative institutionalization of the Resistance Councils.

This chapter deals with the question of popular versus state-controlled provision of justice in the rural areas of Uganda as implemented through these Councils. The study is based on field research carried out in Mukono and Luwero Districts of Central Uganda. As Uganda is a very heterogeneous society, this leads to limitations for some of the arguments, especially concerning the relationship between the present regime and the rural population in parts of rural Uganda where some rebel groups are still active. However, the main arguments relating to weak state penetration of the countryside and the consequently high degree of political space for the Resistance Councils, as well as the democratic character of Resistance Councils compared with previous local government institutions, are valid for the whole of Uganda.[1]

## State versus People, Order versus Disorder?

Issues of local justice in Uganda today cannot be understood without a historical perspective. Both colonial rule and post-colonial developments have an important influence on present events.

### The Colonial Administration of Law and Order and Security in Rural Uganda 1900–62

Throughout colonial times Uganda was ruled by a system of *chiefs* invented by the British rather than in any way 'traditional'. It was first established in the central part of the country – Buganda. For the purposes of this discussion it will suffice to note that a hierarchy of land-owning chiefs was created in Buganda, dependent on the British colonial power and thus subservient to colonial interests, but with wide-ranging authority *vis-à-vis* the Baganda peasantry. This system of 'indirect rule' was more or less duplicated all over Uganda, in some areas with the importation of Baganda chiefs. The administrative tasks of the chiefs were mainly to secure law and order (by administering justice through the Native Courts), to collect taxes, to ensure the maintenance of roads, to enforce the growing of specific crops, etc.

---

[1] Field work was carried out in two areas representing (i) the major opposition parties – the Democratic Party (DP) and the Uganda People's Congress (UPC); (ii) both former guerrilla-controlled and government-controlled areas during the 1981–85 war; and (iii) localities with both a majority of Baganda and a majority of people from the eastern part of the country. It thus captures the main political and ethnic dimensions in Uganda today.

This is important to bear in mind since observers categorically state: 'The National Resistance Movement (NRM) struggle did not involve a cross section of the people of Uganda, even though there was widespread sympathy with the cause for which it fought. It was in the main dominated by people from the western part of the country, and to a lesser extent, the Baganda from the South. The NRM did not have any roots in the northern or eastern parts of the country' (Oloka-Onyango, 1991: 324).

In addition to the field work described above, previous research on RCs in other parts of the country was analysed, as well as the extensive press coverage of events. Newspapers such as *The Citizen, The Exposure, Financial Gazette, Munno, New Vision, Ngabo, The People, Shariat,* and *Tarehe Sita* are a valuable source of information. At least 20 different newspapers are published in Uganda today. Competition is fierce and there is a high turnover. The press is very free. The UPC and the DP both run papers (*The People* and *The Citizen*) in spite of a general ban on 'party activities'. Each paper normally carries several articles every day relating to the RCs in one way or another. This is an abundant source of information.

During the later colonial period a number of laws were passed to give elected councils greater powers. However, powers of arrest and the authority to hear cases still rested with the chiefs, even in the areas where these councils were established – that is, mainly outside the kingdom areas. The power of the chiefs was *total*. The office of chief was not functionally specific and his powers were not checked by any other authority. As noted by the Commission of Inquiry into the Local Government System (Republic of Uganda, 1987: 13), power became 'fused and therefore personalized in the office of the incumbent'.

This system of administration and maintenance of law and order had replaced more decentralized 'segmentary' pre-colonial systems in the north and east of the country and more centralized and hierarchical systems as found in the southern and western areas such as those in Buganda and Bunyoro. However, even the centralized Baganda system had its own checks and balances of chiefly power before the colonial period, mainly exerted through clan heads, who had control over land. Because there was less pressure on land it was also easier for peasants to 'vote with their feet' by moving away from unpopular local rulers.

During the colonial era, only the colonial regime itself could curb the powers of the chiefs (Low and Pratt, 1960).[2] In the rural areas the chief remained in many ways the autocratic interpreter and enforcer of law and order and security. For instance, the chief would be in charge of tax assessment and collection, and arrest of defaulters. He would even be the judge of whether any injustice had occurred during his discharge of these powers.

## Post-colonial Developments

Independence in 1962 brought no major change in the system of government in the rural areas, although initially the African courts presided over by the chiefs were integrated with the formal courts. However, the 1967 Local Administration Act reinstated the chiefs to settle 'minor' civil cases. They also retained their powers over tax assessment and collection, enforcement of self-help labour and by-laws, etc. Although criminal cases like theft and murder remained under the authority of the Magistrates Court, chiefs were often the nearest to deal with the initial investigation and possible arrest of criminals due to the distances from police forces and Magistrates Courts. Thus in the rural areas, the chiefly system remained in undisputed charge of law and order for the first decade after independence.

The situation began to change in the 1970s. Between 1971 and 1986 large parts of Uganda experienced a serious and widespread breakdown of law and order, owing to disrespect for the law on the part of the supposed enforcers of law and order: the police, the army and the chiefs. A highy conceivable consequence of fusing many different functions in the office of the chief now came true:

> ... the post-independence period had drastically altered the basis and public regard for the institution of a chief. We have noted that the scope for extra-legal extortions, as well as its practice, has expanded enormously in the past two decades. This

---

[2] As happened by the passing of the Busulu and Envuju laws of 1928 that aimed to limit the amount of surplus value which chiefs could extract from the peasants.

tendency has gone hand in hand with marked deterioration in the quality of persons recruited to fill the position of chiefs ... wherever we went, we heard widespread complaints of how chiefs had abused the powers of their offices – ranging from extortion of money, to arbitrary arrests, to grabbing of land and property, to murders by proxy (Republic of Uganda, 1987: 15).

Without doubt there have been considerable local differences.[3] The political relationship between the central government and the particular locality varied considerably. The introduction of UPC chiefs in the southern DP-controlled areas would most probably be met with much greater resentment than in the UPC-dominated areas. It is also important to note that research into these developments has been even more scanty in the northern part of the country. Even the Commission of Inquiry into Local Government failed to collect information from a large part of northern Uganda.[4]

Nevertheless, two tendencies stand out clearly for the post-1970 period. One is that government civil servants – including chiefs, police and magistrates – experienced drastic declines in salary after the breakdown of the formal economy in 1973. A rough estimate shows that civil servants in 1980 were paid only around 10% of salary levels in 1970 in real terms![5] The other is that the chiefs became political appointees. Whenever the regime changed (in 1971, 1979 and 1985) the chiefs were changed as well, according to their relation to the new regime. People used the confusion to burn down the houses of the old chiefs, chase them away, or kill them. This happened especially in central Uganda.

The combination of extreme underpayment of civil servants and politically appointed chiefs with little legitimacy led to a highly inefficient, tyrannical and politicized administration of law and order.

## The Emergence of a New Order

A new basis for local justice slowly emerged during the guerrilla war from 1981 to 1986. It was linked to a new institutional framework at the local level – the Resistance Councils – and to a subsequent reform of state institutions dealing with the maintenance of law and order and security.

### War-time Establishment of Law and Order and Security

The overthrow of Amin in 1979 was followed by a number of very short-lived governments until a general election was held in 1980. The UPC was then declared the winner, and Obote became president for a second time. The elections were widely believed to have been rigged, and Museveni withdrew to

---

[3]  The above quotation notwithstanding, knowledge of the actual changes in the roles of chiefs and systems of law enforcement at the local level is very limited indeed – as noted in the most recent bibliography of Uganda: 'It is also essential to bear in mind the limitations of the empirical evidence on which much of the writing over the last twenty years has been based. ... This is especially the case at the local district level. ... (Gertzel, 1991: 20).

[4]  Gulu, Kitgum, Soroti, Moroto, Kotido, Lira, Apac and Moyo districts were not covered by the Commission (Republic of Uganda, 1987: 3).

[5]  The index of minimum wages in real terms fell from 111 in 1970 to 6 in 1980 (Jamal, 1991: 87; Chew, 1990).

the bush with a handful of men to start up a guerrilla war to overthrow Obote's regime. The main area of operations of the guerrilla army, the National Resistance Army (NRA), was the 'Luwero Triangle'[6] with its borders only some 20 km from the capital, Kampala. This proximity made it impossible for the central government to ignore the presence of the guerrilla forces, so the Obote II Government initiated violent counter-insurgency measures.

Museveni and the NRA began mobilization of the Baganda peasants in this area where the assaults of the Obote I regime against the Buganda nation were not forgotten.[7] Although support for the NRA in the beginning was limited, the undisciplined and cruel behaviour of Obote's army, the UNLA, soon totally alienated the peasants in Luwero from the regime and created conditions for supporting the NRA. For the peasants involved, the war was a 'liberation war'.[8] It was fought to liberate Uganda from Obote and the evils of state-inspired violence that he represented. The peasants in Luwero and the NRA had  common cause in this war: simply 'Eddembe lya Bantu', that is, 'freedom for the people'; a cessation of rape, murder and injustice; and peace within 'Eggwanga lyo'munto':

> It means the place where one resides. You cannot say that you are fighting for Kampala, yet you do not live in Kampala. When the (NRA) soldiers came, they told us you are fighting for your 'Ggwanga' (country). We knew that we were fighting for Kapeka – not any other place.[9]

When the NRA established local councils responsible for the maintenance of law and order at the local level and for communication between the people and the guerrillas, the idea was readily and eagerly accepted. However, the establishment of Resistance Councils was not initially part of the guerrilla strategy. As the First Deputy Prime Minister and National Political Commissioner, Eriya Kategaya, who fought in the bush, stated in an interview:

> These RCs were born out of necessity to survive during the struggle. When we started, we used to go and approach influential people in the village and convince them about our struggle, convince them of our strength and although the enemy looked very strong, we could transform that because of the correctness of our cause. This went on from 1981 to mid-1982, just contacting individuals. In the course of this, there was a problem that if you picked upon a wrong man in the village that would be the image of the Movement ... That is when we decided that the leadership in these villages should be elected. In any case, we were struggling for democracy ... The RCs are logical, natural. You cannot talk about people having power to decide their fate without constant [sic!] organizations (*New Vision*, 9 October 1991, p. 4).

Thus, for the NRA, the introduction of RCs was considered a necessity for

[6]  The area between the Hoima and Gulu roads in the districts of Mpigi, Luwero and Mubende.

[7]  In my interviews in the Luwero Triangle with peasant supporters of the guerrilla war, they repeatedly stressed the importance of the attack (led by Idi Amin) of Obote's forces on the Kabaka's palace, the subsequent exile of Sir Edward Mutesa in 1966, and the 'military occupation' of Buganda until Obote's overthrow in 1971 (so characterized by Mudoola, 1988: 284).

[8]  Writings on the guerrilla war are still scarce. Most are official accounts of the NRA's military strategy. For a fuller discussion, see Tidemand (1994) and Ddungu (1993).

[9]  Taped interview with a female peasant from Kapeka, translated from Luganda.

winning the guerrilla struggle. For the peasants involved, it was a new way of exercising democracy at the local level. It also represented a new and popularly controlled system of maintaining law and order. Furthermore, in a war-time situation where virtually all government agents (the soldiers, the police, the chiefs, etc.) were considered enemies by the civilians, the RCs were established to oppose ('resist') the state apparatus at large. They became a potential forum for popular control of all government institutions.

The development of the RCs was inhibited, however, by the character and scale of the government atrocities. Wholesale massacres were carried out repeatedly by the UNLA in the Luwero Triangle. Only in those parts of the Triangle that were fully 'liberated' by the NRA – and they were sometimes substantial – could the RCs operate in the open. Often the entire civilian population of large areas was forced to flee from the government army. For instance, the NRA was forced to evacuate large populations in 1983, when the UNLA advanced into the former liberated areas killing everyone in its path. Thus, the establishment of alternative forms of administration and popular control of law and order and security was allowed to develop only in selected areas – and only intermittently during the war period.

Nevertheless, the basic features of the RCs did evolve during the war. They functioned partly as support organizations for the NRA and partly as *the* government and administration of the liberated areas, as no government staff, chiefs or police were present to maintain law and order, settle disputes, collect taxes, etc.

## Post-war Developments: The Institutional Framework

In January 1986, the NRA captured control of Kampala and formed the NRM Government. Security was obviously an important issue. Peace and security could not be taken for granted at that time. Various bandits and dissident rebel groups roamed the countryside, especially in the northern and eastern areas. No proper police force functioned anywhere, and, as the NRA co-opted large numbers of ex-soldiers from the previous armies, it also became more difficult to maintain its hitherto acclaimed discipline.

The first major political reform was to extend the system of RCs to the whole country. Initially it was done without any legal basis. The RCs co-operated with the NRA in fighting the rebel groups, but also confronted undisciplined elements of the NRA itself. For more than a decade gun rule had been the order of the day in Uganda. Now the RCs would question orders from soldiers. They would report abuses of power to higher authorities or they would quite often simply disarm and arrest soldiers who misbehaved – something quite unheard of before. The RCs ensured civil control of the army. Their actions were backed by the NRA itself. Many Ugandans see this as the greatest achievement of the NRM.

Also the distribution of certain goods (especially sugar, but also soap, paraffin and salt) was initially left to the RCs. A review of the vernacular press of the period shows the concern people attached to this particular function. It went so far that the political cadres had to establish that 'RCs were not only elected to distribute sugar'.[10]

Linking sugar distribution to the RCs definitely led to their rapid spread throughout the country. But individual RCs also used the distribution of sugar as a disciplinary measure against villagers who refused to participate in meetings.[11] When they no longer controlled the distribution of sugar, RC members complained of lack of respect.[12] A cynical view of these early functions of the RCs might suggest that they were introduced in order to establish the system rapidly throughout the country. They were perhaps used as a compensation for the very limited capacity for mobilization by the NRM Government itself.

Conflicts over authority between the RCs and authorities like the court system, the chiefs, the district administration and the police were frequent immediately after 1986. Both the public and several of these authorities demanded that the rights and duties of the RCs should be more clearly spelt out. A number of laws were consequently passed in May 1987.[13] Technically, they constitute a local government reform outlining how popularly elected committees from village to district level should be established and describing their duties and functions.

Briefly the main features can be described as follows. The entire adult population of a village – in Uganda rarely more than a few hundred people, often less – constitutes the RC1 council.[14] This village council elects a nine-member committee: the RC1 committee. The gathering of all RC1 committee members within a parish makes up the parish council or RC2 council. This council also elects a nine-member committee, the RC2 committee. The assembly of all RC2 committee members from a sub-county comprises the next council in the hierarchy, the RC3 council, which also elects a nine-member committee; the RC3 committee. The next levels are the county, RC4 (which has only recently become functional) and the district or RC5 level. From 1989 the parliament – the National Resistance Council – has been partly elected via this system.

The district is a 'true' unit of local government; that is, it has its own staff and budget controlled by the elected district (RC5) councillors with the district government staff headed by the District Executive Secretary. Presidentially appointed District Administrators (DAs) are the political heads of the districts. They supervise, and occasionally interfere in, political developments and district council affairs.

Although the central government is thus directly represented at the district level, the lower levels of the RCs are far from powerless. All levels of the RC

10   The 'sugar issue' was extensively covered by the local press at the time. *Ngabo,* 15 August 1986: 'Resistance Committees were not elected to distribute sugar only'. See also *Weekly Topic,* week ending 23 July 1986, front page: 'Powers of RCs need clear definition'. *Ngabo,* 31 July 1986, and *Ngabo,* 4 July 1986.

11   See e.g. *Munno,* 28 May 1987, letter to editor: 'Please, attend the RC meetings'.

12   See, for instance, the article in *Munno,* 2 October 1989: 'Not getting allowances led the RCs to withhold the meeting'. Confirmed during field interviews in Mukono District.

13   The National Resistance Council passed the Resistance Councils and Committees Statutes in 1987 and the Resistance Committees Judicial Powers Statute in January 1988.

14   The average adult population of a rural RC1 in six south-eastern districts is between 186 and 672 depending on the district. However, the range is considerable, from 20 to 3,900 adults.

system can pass by-laws and the Resistance Committees at RC1, RC2 and RC3 levels function as courts with jurisdiction over civil cases and cases formerly defined within the sphere of customary law. It is these levels of the RC system that are especially important for the operationalization of local justice. They are supposed to deal with:

> Debts, contracts, assaults and/or battery, conversion and/or damage to property, trespass, land disputes relating to customary tenure, disputes concerning marital status of women, disputes concerning paternity of children, disputes concerning identity of customary heirs, impregnating of a girl under 18 years of age, elopement with a girl under 18 years of age, and customary bailment (Resistance Committees Judicial Powers Statute: Republic of Uganda, 1988: 14).

All cases are initially brought before the RC1 court, with rights of appeal to RC2 and RC3 level. If a case is not settled satisfactorily at the RC3 level it can, under certain circumstances, be brought to the Magistrates Court grade I.

## RCs: State or People's Organizations?

This is the formal set-up. But, before discussing how the RCs actually function as courts and enforcers of law and order, it is important to outline briefly how different groups within Uganda perceive the RC system. Ever since 1986 there has been lively debate in Uganda on the Resistance Councils. In 1988 Mamdani (1988: 1176) outlined three different characterizations of the RCs: 'bureaucratic, democratic or sectarian'. These views are still represented within the public debate on the RCs in Uganda.

### Three Views

The *sectarian* view holds that the RC system basically embodies the narrow interests of the present holders of power. It is widely expressed in connection with the current debate on multi-party democracy in the many 'opposition papers'.[15] One of these states, for instance, categorically:

> While Museveni has tried to implement some economic reforms he has done badly on the political reforms. He has continued to advocate no-party democracy which is a mockery of democracy ... also because the RC system does not give a voice to the people (*Shariat*, 5–11 November 1991).

Similarly, the front cover of *The Exposure* (No. 42, December 1991) shows an ordinary citizen strangled by a brute with the inscription 'Ban on Political Activities. RC System' written on his gigantic arm. In these papers the RCs are seen simply as tools of the NRM to suppress other channels of political expression.

Another criticism of the RCs is that they are basically *bureaucratic organs* imposed upon people in order to oversee government policy. They are compared with the former *Mayumba Kumi* (ten-cell system) under the transitional regime of 1979 (Ddungu, 1989). Oloka-Onyango (1989: 474) also compares the RCs with former security organs like *Mayumba Kumi*. He argues that the

---

15  These papers are, to a larger or lesser degree, in opposition to the NRM on the question of multi-party democracy. Among them are *Shariat, The Exposure, The Economy, Citizen, Star, Financial Gazette, Ngabo, Munno,* etc. The last two are examples of papers in the vernacular, which are especially abundant in Luganda.

RCs have been introduced country-wide in order to 'reinforce the NRM domination of political power in the country' and that power within the RC system is held by bureaucrats:

> Given that overall supervisory powers over RCs are vested in the Minister of Local Government, it is clear that the primary objective of the laws has been to bureaucratize rather than popularize the bodies (p. 472).

The third view is that the RCs are (or at least should be) *democratic* organs. It is, for instance, expressed by the Commission of Inquiry into Local Government, which also proposes that the name of the RCs be changed in order to underline their democratic features.

> ... To distance them from both the movement and the state and to underscore their popular democratic character, we recommend that councils at all levels be given an appellation which may accurately reflect the character of these institutions as organs of the people, for example Village Peoples Councils, or Village Popular Councils (Republic of Uganda, 1987: 28).

In the Ugandan press the 'sectarian view' is most prevalent. It views the RC system as important for power struggles at the national level, because it is regarded as an alternative arrangement to political parties in the election of members of parliament. It bypasses the political parties, thereby keeping the NRM in power.

From a local-level perspective, however, it is difficult to argue for the 'sectarian view'. First of all, lots of older UPC and DP politicians participated in the 1989 and 1992 RC elections. They were in many cases elected all the way up to the District Councils or the Parliament. Possible NRM control of the RCs also stops at the district level with the Presidentially appointed District Administrator; it does not reach the lower levels of the RC system. Moreover, the evidence of the real character of the lower-level RCs as people's organizations should be assessed on the basis of the practice of the RCs' administration. As discussed in the next section, such assessments show that the RCs at these levels are people's organizations. This is not the result of deliberate NRM policy. It is rather the consequence of the very limited capacity of the state apparatus and the NRM in the rural areas.[16]

## RCs in Practice

RC practice with respect to the administration of local justice is a good illustration of the argument. The government staffing in an average sub-county severely limits the capacity of state intervention in the rural areas. In a typical sub-county (RC3 level), with a population of some 35,000 people, there will normally be one magistrate and a police post with some 5 officers – but these are shared with some two or three other sub-counties. Each sub-county will always have a government-employed chief with a local defence force and a few assistants, plus chiefs at the parish level. The post of village chief has been abolished. One

---

[16] Anangwe (in Chapter 6), in his analysis of the maintenance of law and order in rural Kenya, uses a similar argument to characterize local KANU Youth Leagues.

NRM cadre is responsible for maybe ten sub-counties. The chiefs and the local government-employed police force are almost entirely preoccupied with tax assessments and collection and arrests of defaulters. Central government police posts mainly protect banks, etc. None of these staff have any means of transport, and their salaries are very low. A magistrate in charge of one or more sub-counties is paid a monthly salary of U. Shs. 15,000, equivalent to about US$12 – only enough to buy *matooke* for a family for 12 days.[17] All this obviously contributes to a village perception of these state institutions as being distant, and in a very real sense they are both remote and irrelevant. This has probably been accentuated by the post-independence wars in Uganda and the collapse of many state institutions and the formal economy during the Amin period. Furthermore, a number of studies indicate that formal institutions for the provision of law and order in the rural areas have been avoided by rural residents for decades.[18]

It is in this context that the attempts by the present government to introduce some state institutions for the maintenance of law and order in the rural areas should be seen. The objective was to increase the police force from the 6,000 in 1986 to 30,000 in 1994 and to 'decentralize' the police forces to the rural areas, possibly with up to 20 officers per sub-county (*New Vision*, 5 April 1989; 1 January; 16 January 1990; 14 October 1991). However, the policy has been severely constrained by the government's financial capacity. The police force currently constitutes some 16,000 people. It was supposed to increase by 1,000 in 1994, but the earlier established goal appears unrealistic and many officers live in grass huts owing to lack of housing (*New Vision*, 4 July 1993), just as the police force, even in Kampala, often fails to investigate crimes owing to lack of fuel for transport. At the same time, the quality of their services is constantly questioned by the public, the press and politicians (*New Vision*, 4 July 1994).

In short, the relative absence of state institutions providing for law and order in the rural areas not only has a very long history but also a bleak immediate future. To seek to institutionalize the RC courts is therefore not only an ideological but also a highly pragmatic move.[19]

## RCs as Administrators of Popular Justice

How then do the RCs administer local justice as people's organizations? And are they institutions of popular justice? The concept of popular justice as defined by Santos (1982) constitutes three elements:

> [1] It is class justice: that is, it appears as justice exercised by the popular classes parallel to, or in confrontation with, the state administration of justice ... [2] it requires that judges be democratically selected by the relevant communities ... [and 3] it operates at a minimum level of institutionalization.

[17] *Matooke* are green bananas, the staple food in southern Uganda. Prices fluctuate according to the season, but U. Shs. 4,000 per bunch was an average price in 1992. One bunch can support a family of 4 for approximately 4 days.

[18] See Heald (1982) on the problems of implementing Magistrates Courts in Bugisu in 1964.

[19] The NRM Government has a similar pragmatic argument for the introduction of the Local Defence Units (LDUs) – an informal police force selected, supervised and paid for by the RCs but trained by the army.

The two latter conditions, referring to the *form* of the institutions rather than the *content,* are obviously provided for in the formal establishment of the RC courts.[20] The courts are composed of elected members of the community, they are close to the people, their language is local, few if any technical terms are used, people bring their own case forward instead of using lawyers and, finally, the courts are inexpensive. The registration fee for an RC1 court case is U.Shs. 500 (50 US cents), U.Shs. 1,000 for an RC2 case and U.Shs. 2,000 for an RC3 court registration. Even these moderate fees, however, are not always paid as they can be beyond the means of some people.[21]

Technical rules of evidence are in general disregarded in favour of common sense. Elders are often co-opted in the court as 'advisers' and judgments are almost always based on consensus among the members of the courts. The penalties handed out are generally of a 'conciliatory nature'. As outlined in the Judicial Statute section 7, they encompass:

> reconciliation, declaration, restitution, costs, apology, attachment and sale ... and in case of infringement of bye-laws [the RC Court] may impose a fine or any other penalty authorized by the bye-laws.

Field interviews indicate that these features contribute to a general feeling among the majority of peasants that their cases are being dealt with in a fair and transparent way.

It is much more difficult to generalize about the content of the RC court proceedings. The legal framework defining the RC courts was passed two years after the country-wide establishment of the courts and some seven years after the first experiences gained during the guerrilla war in Luwero. However, compared with the Magistrates Courts the RCs seem to favour 'traditional' rather than 'modern' law, and tenants rather than landlords. They also favour popular rather than mob justice.

In the absence of reform of the existing laws, their enforcement, for example with respect to land, taxes and women's rights, would be instrumental in the general subordination of the peasantry, especially the poorer peasants and women.[22] Government officials have instead issued blanket permissions to the RCs, such as: 'you have the power', leaving the initiative to the RCs, especially the village councils, to dispense justice.

## Popular Justice

Analysis of a number of RC court proceedings shows that the RC courts emphasize popular concepts of justice rather than strict adherence to the letter of the law. Basaza (1989: 6–13) illustrates this by reference to divorce cases, where the RCs gave the right to custody of the children to the woman in spite of this being contrary to the Muslim law under which the couple were married. Turyahikayoo (1989: 70) quotes cases where RCs granted 'illegitimate' children

---

[20]  According to the Judicial Statute of 1988.
[21]  As recommended by the Director of Legal Affairs at the NRM Secretariat, quoted in Burkey (1991: 48).
[22]  New laws concerning land and women's rights are, however, expected.

the same rights to inherit their father's property as the children of the married wife. In the Luwero Triangle, an RC court granted a contract farmer the right to farm land he had hired from a landlord although he had actually neglected the contract.[23] Another RC prevented a land sale when parents complained that their son wanted to sell his land in order to get money for alcohol.[24] There are also instances of RCs forcing people to contribute to funeral expenses for fellow villagers. All such decisions are probably in line with those that the clan leaders or elders would previously have taken. Now they are co-opted into the RC committees. More important, all these cases would most probably otherwise have been decided upon otherwise by a Magistrates Court.

It is difficult to generalize about who benefits from this kind of court proceedings. However, it is clear that the RCs favour 'local interest' articulated by the 'village establishment'. This brings the RC courts into conflict with the magistrates and the system of Western administration of law that they represent and which is resented by the villagers. A magistrate expressed his feelings as follows:

> The ordinary people, when you stay near them, they are even jealous when we speak English. They say: 'You magistrates are the ones who went to school, but see, the powers have been given to us – the RCs. We can also judge cases! Why did you go to school? You used to be proud that you read law, but now?' – There is that tendency.[25]

The use of RCs to judge cases gives more legitimacy to the RCs and possibly to the whole NRM system. It is also part of a process whereby elected villagers gain more powers *vis-à-vis* state officials. From a pragmatic point of view it is probably also the only realistic, and definitely the least expensive, option for settling village disputes. The Magistrates Courts would simply be overburdened if they were to handle such cases.

Land disputes reveal a more clear-cut picture of (class) conflicts of interests in the way the RC courts operate than those discussed above. The present situation in Uganda is that land disputes can be settled by both RC courts and the Magistrates Courts, as most disputes would have elements of both customary land tenure claims and more formalized private property rights. The litigants are simply left free to choose which kind of court to use. Up to 50% of all cases dealt with by RCs and Magistrates Courts will in some areas be concerned with land disputes. The fighting that evicted many owners from their land and the 1975 Land Reform Decree (only partially implemented) have left many tenants and landowners with very insecure rights of tenure. A review of the cases brought forward to the RCs as well as the Magistrates Courts in Mukono and Luwero reveals a clear class preference in the choice of type of court: tenants prefer RCs, whereas landlords prefer the Magistrates Courts.

## Mob Justice

The dark side of popular justice is mob justice. Few authors have dealt with this

---

23  The case of plantation owner *Yosamu Sekabira Senkuzi* v. *Musa Begila* (a *waragi* brewer) finally decided upon by the RC3 court of Nakaseke Sub-county, Luwero District, on 20 February 1992.
24  Unrecorded case settled by Kamira RC1 in Mukono, August 1992.
25  Taped interview, conducted in English.

theme. Obbo (1988) gives some gruesome examples from villages in central Uganda, which show that a widespread culture of violence exists in the rural areas. The violence is primarily directed against successful economic competitors – especially 'foreigners' such as Banyarwanda or Banyankole. They risk being burned alive by villagers, accused of no more than delay in discovering the death of a neighbour (Obbo, 1988: 211–12).

The RC courts have not eradicated such cases of mob justice. But there is evidence from the field-work areas to show that cases, such as those on witch-craft, that often previously led to mob justice, are dealt with more humanely by the RC courts. Many thieves have also been rescued from mob justice by these courts.[26]

Even though the RC courts are not composed of people with law degrees, most evidence[27] points to their sincere attempts at exercising 'justice' – not the justice exercised by an angry crowd, but by trusted people deciding the case in proper meetings with all parties given the right to speak and with rights of appeal to higher RC courts.

## The Complementary Role of RCs

Villagers' concern and unease about such problems as mob justice and the loss of legal rights, and thus a certain arbitrariness in court decisions, lead them not only to accept but to request limits to the jurisdiction of the RC courts.[28] The RCs should not therefore be seen as fundamentally in conflict with state institutions – but rather as complementary and parallel. In this sense they also share features with many other institutions of popular justice elsewhere.[29]

Some shortcomings of the RCs are currently dealt with in the debate on revision of the Judicial Statute of the RCs. This includes the problems of separa-tion of powers, lack of education of the members, and the lack of payment for RCs which leads to the introduction of arbitrary fines. Unfortunately, the Ugandan Law Society and similar organizations occasionally indiscriminately import concepts and principles from British law, for instance on the separation of legislative, executive and legal powers. It is a sound principle, but neither

---

[26] See, for instance, an article in *Munno*, 19 September 1987 describing how a person who stole a pig where the 'mob was doing justice to him until he was handed over to the RCs...'.

[27] There are examples of RCs sentencing a man to death (Basaza, 1989: 7), although they have no such powers. Some RCs have also been involved in the unlawful eviction of people from their areas. See, for instance, the article in *Ngabo*, 2 July 1986: 'Resistance councils in villages have started exercising powers over people who misbehave.'

[28] This is reflected, for instance, in the popularity of the legal seminars held for RCs, where some RCs discover with considerable relief that they are not supposed to deal with every type of dispute and crime. The yearning for more and better state involvement in the maintenance of law and order is occasionally also reflected in sentimental accounts by elders – although committed to their villages – of how the *bazungu* (Europeans) in the 'good old' colonial days would investigate murders with all the resources of the colonial law-enforcement apparatus – and thus ensure justice. Villagers are also very much aware and critical of various instances of abuse of power exercised by their own RCs.

[29] The majority of community members interviewed about the people's courts working within workers hostels in Natal, South Africa, suggested limitations of the jurisdiction of their courts (Nina, 1993).

relevant nor easy to implement within a village with some 100 adults where most cases are matters of reconciliation. The existence and practice of RC courts can only be understood in this rural context.

## The Future of RCs

Uganda is currently in the process of debating a new constitution. The Constitutional Committee, in charge of drafting a first proposal, has received more than 20,000 memoranda from different groups and individuals. Initially the deadline for the committee to present a draft constitution was March 1992, but it has been postponed several times. The draft has therefore only recently been published. Some of the proposals presented to the committee aim to limit the jurisdiction of the RCs.[30]

Despite such opposition, the government position is clear: the RC system should be maintained and strengthened. Thus the government has already assigned the RC5 chairmen to be heads of districts in place of the Presidentially appointed District Administrators. This is part of a general move to decentralize decision-making and authority (Ministry of Local Government, 1993). Furthermore, at the end of January 1992 the National Resistance Council discussed an amendment to the judicial bill which basically proposed to abolish lower-level (Grade 2 and Grade 3) Magistrates Courts and transfer their jurisdiction to the RCs (*New Vision*, 22 January 1992: 16). Though the bill has not been finally approved (and some revision will certainly be made) it appears that the juridical powers of the Magistrates Courts will be further restricted. This is important because the significant positive experiences gained through the lower-level RCs' involvement in the provision of justice should not get lost in enthusiastic attempts to reintroduce British-style formalistic legal systems.

The limitations of such systems are also becoming clearer elsewhere. The Scandinavian countries, for instance, are currently trying to get dispute settlement out of the courts and into other forums for reconciliatory settlement. Such moves are even more appropriate in Uganda and many other African countries, given their particular situation. But it is important to stress that the dispensation of local justice through people's organizations such as the RCs should be seen as complementary to, and not in conflict with, the provision of justice through state institutions.

[30] See, for instance, the National Executive Committee of the Democratic Party (n.d.) Other critics are found, for instance in the Ugandan Law Society – see the article in *Munno*, 19 October 1991, where the head of the Uganda Law Society, Mr Remmy Kasule Kyonooneka, argues for a general abolition of the RC courts.

## References

Basaza, G.K. (1989) 'The Ideals and Set-backs of the RC Court System (based in Entebbe Municipality)'. Paper submitted in partial fulfilment of the requirement for the award of the degree of Bachelor of Laws in Makerere University, Kampala.

Burkey, I. (1991) 'People's Power in Theory and Practice: The Resistance Council

System in Uganda'. New Haven, CT: Yale University, 12 May (mimeo).

Chew, D.C.E. (1990) 'Internal Adjustment to Civil Service Salaries: Insights from Uganda', *World Development* 18 (7): 1003–14.

Ddungu, E. (1989) 'Popular Forms and the Question of Democracy: The Case of Resistance Councils in Uganda'. *CBR Publications* 4. Kampala: Centre For Basic Research.

Ddungu, E. (1993) 'On the Development of the NRM Struggle from 1981–85'. Working Paper. Kampala: Centre for Basic Research.

Gertzel, C. (1991) *Uganda: An Annotated Bibliography of Source Materials.* London: Hans Zell Publishers.

Hansen, H.B. and Twaddle, M. (eds) (1988) *Uganda Now. Between Decay and Development.* London: James Currey.

Hansen, H.B. and Twaddle, M. (eds) (1991) *Changing Uganda. Dilemmas of Structural Adjustment and Revolutionary Change.* London: James Currey.

Heald, S. (1982) 'Chiefs and Administrators in Bugisu' in A.F. Robertson (ed.) *Uganda's First Republic: Chiefs, Administrators and Politicians, 1967–71.* Cambridge African Monographs No. 1. Cambridge: Cambridge University Press.

Hooper E. and Pirouet, L. (1989) *Uganda.* The Minority Rights Group Report No. 66. London: The Minority Rights Group.

Jamal V. (1991) 'The Agrarian Context of the Ugandan Crisis' in Hansen and Twaddle.

Low, D.A. and Pratt, R.C. (1960) *Buganda and British Overrule – Two Studies.* Oxford: Oxford University Press.

Mamdani, M. (1988) 'Uganda in Transition: Two Years of the NRA/NRM', *Third World Quarterly* 10 (3): 1155–81.

Ministry of Local Government (1993) *Decentralization in Uganda – the Policy and its Implications.* Kampala: Ministry of Local Government.

Mudoola, D. (1988) 'Political Transitions since Idi Amin: a Study in Political Pathology' in Hansen and Twaddle.

Museveni, Y.K. (1992) *What is Africa's Problem? – Speeches and Writings on Africa,* Vol. I. Kampala: NRM Publications.

National Executive Committee of the Democratic Party (n.d.) *Proposal on the Future Constitution of the Republic of Uganda.* Kampala: Democratic Party.

Nina, I.O. (1993) 'Popular Justice and Civil Society in Transition: A Report from the "Front Line" – Natal', *Transformation,* 21.

Obbo, C. (1988) 'What Went Wrong in Uganda?' in Hansen and Twaddle.

Oloka-Onyango, J. (1989) 'Law, "Grassroots Democracy" and the National Resistance Movement in Uganda', *International Journal of the Sociology of Law* 17: 465–80.

Oloka-Onyango, J. (1991) 'Uganda' in Andreassen, B.A. and Swinehart, T. (eds) *Human Rights in Developing Countries 1991.* Oslo: Scandinavian University Press.

Republic of Uganda (1987) *Report of the Commission of Inquiry into the Local Government System.* Entebbe: Government Printer, June.

Republic of Uganda (1988) *Resistance Committees Judicial Powers.* Entebbe: Government Printers.

Santos, C. (1982) 'Law and Revolution in Portugal: The Experiences of Popular Justice after the 25th April 1974' in C. Abel (ed.) *The Politics of Informal Justice.* New York: Academic Press.

Tidemand, P. (1994) 'The Resistance Councils in Uganda. A Study of Popular Democracy and Rural Politics', Ph.D. Thesis, International Development Studies, Roskilde University, Roskilde.

Turyahikayoo, R.E. (1989) 'The Effectiveness of Resistance Councils and Committees in Uganda (A Case Study in Kamuganguzi Subcounty Kabale District)'. Paper submitted in partial fulfilment of the requirement for the award of the degree of Bachelor of Laws, Makerere University, Kampala.

# Index